ALL YOU CAN BUILD IN THE GARDEN

Marshall Cavendish

Edited by Leo Zanelli

Published by Marshall Cavendish Books Limited
58 Old Compton Street
London W1V 5PA

© Marshall Cavendish Limited 1972 — 1984

First Printing 1974
This printing 1984

Printed in Yugoslavia

ISBN 0 85685 048 9

About this book.....

Do you ever dream of your own private swimming pool? A greenhouse? A garden pond? A glamorous patio and barbecue for entertaining your friends? But how could you possibly afford them? Here is the answer—with this book you can build them yourself at a fraction of the professional cost. Clear, concise and accurate instructions will make the most inexperienced amateur into a competent handyman, capable of tackling the most exciting outdoor projects.

You can increase the value of your property enormously. You can become the envy of your neighbours. Even the most modest garden can become the focal point of a superb living environment. A garden seat would give you somewhere to relax on a warm summer day. A planter would show off your delicate blooms to their best advantage. A shed would provide storage space for your garden and household tools. And you can go further with this book. A tree house for the children, or a climbing frame, could be easily within your range. And how about that greenhouse, a carport or even a swimming pool?

All you can build in the garden is a project handbook, full of ideas that are within the scope of your technical skill – and your pocket. If you want to make the best of your home, this is the book for you.

Contents

Free standing swimming pools

A swimming pool gives a new dimension to your life. It greatly increases your recreational facilities and adds value to your home. And with the development of free standing pools, you can give a touch of luxury to your home for a fraction of the cost of conventional pools.

Free standing swimming pools have many advantages over conventional, sunken, pools. They are portable, attractively finished and strong but fairly light. They are very much cheaper than ordinary pools—sometimes as little as a quarter of the cost. In addition, free standing pools usually stand above ground which is a lot safer if there are toddlers around.

The installation of free standing swimming pools is straightforward, requiring no major excavation or plumbing. They take up less space than conventional pools and are ideal for smaller gardens.

Planning the pool

To make a real success of your pool you must plan the project thoroughly. The positioning of the pool is very important here, as a badly placed pool will soon fall into disuse, especially if it is simply tacked on at the bottom of the garden.

The best place for a pool is an open sunny spot that is sheltered from the breeze and yet is

Below. *A pool in the medium price range. It can be put up in a few days, with a capacity of around 11,000 gallons. A boardwalk is a very suitable addition for children, as then steps are not the sole point of easy entry.*

CRANLEIGH POOLS LTD., CALCOT, READING

relatively accessible. Trees make ideal wind breaks but don't put the pool near an overhanging tree as the leaf fall will cause unnecessary cleaning work. Alternatives to trees as wind breaks are lattice style screen walling or birch lap fencing.

To find the best site, make a scaled plan of your garden. Take the measurements and mark the positions of the main features—the house, trees, paths, fences, walls and steps. Also mark on it the estimated position of septic tanks or underground sewerage or drainage pipes. You must, of course, avoid putting the pool over these. Then make a cardboard or paper cutout of the pool and try it in different positions on the garden plan. When you have decided on a site, study it for a few days to see where the house and tree shade falls. One point to remember though—small children need supervision and putting the pool within sight of the house is a valuable safety factor.

Your swimming pool will need a hard surround at least 2ft (610mm) and a sunbathing area—a level, well trimmed lawn or patio nearby. You can landscape the pool with a combination of screen walling, low growing coniferous shrubs or thicket plants, or a rockery, to help give the pool a luxurious setting.

Don't put sweet smelling plants close to the pool as these attract bees and wasps. Prickly or thorny bushes or trees with surface roots too near the pool will soon cause inconvenience.

Types of pool available

There are many different types of free standing pools on the market. Trade associations of pool manufacturers can provide details of these. There are, however, three main types of pool.

The temporary, or Splasher, pool is erected and filled when you want to use it. Usually, they do not have a filtration system and have to be emptied to clean. They do, however, require chlorination (see below) since, even though they may not be up for long at any one time, bacteria collect and can make the water unsafe.

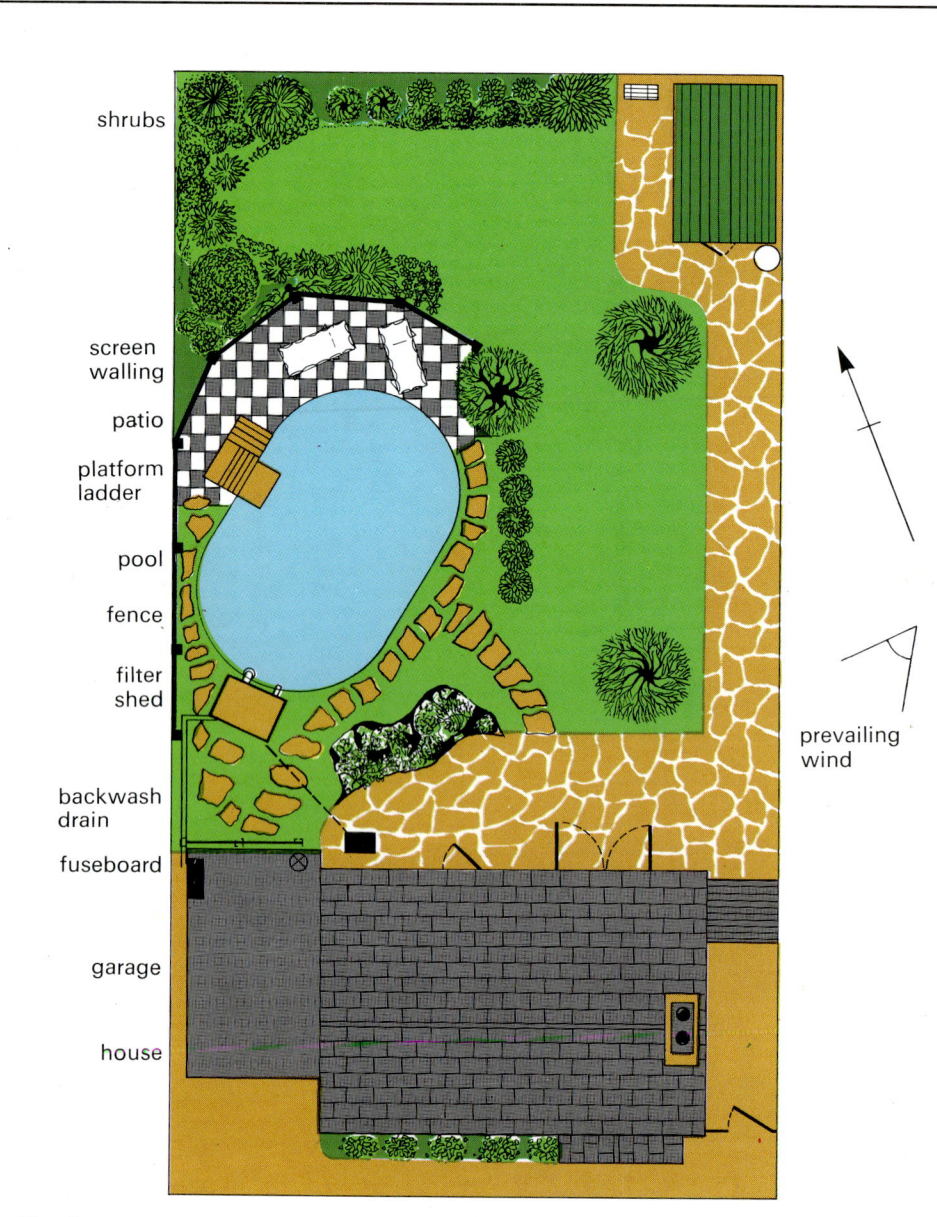

board and spirit level

levelling pegs to check ground level

string for level guide

Fig. 2

shrubs

screen walling

patio

platform ladder

pool

fence

filter shed

backwash drain

fuseboard

garage

house

prevailing wind

Fig. 1

TRI-ART

Fig.1. A garden layout showing many of the best design features. The pool is sheltered from the wind by a fence, trees are sited so that leaf fall will be carried away from the pool, there is a paved patio for sunbathing and the pool is close enough to the house to allow you to keep an eye on the children. When you are planning a pool draw a garden map like this —it will solve many of the design problems.

Fig.2. The ground under the pool must be perfectly level—if it slopes the weight of the water will put a great strain on one of the pool walls. Prepare the site using a spirit level to check that the ground is level.

The lightweight portable pool has a flexible steel side wall and a supporting structure that can be erected once the ground has been prepared. These pools take a day or two to fill and then a few more days for the water to warm up.

Sometimes mains water is cloudy and it helps to pre-clean it by filling the pool through a porous bag containing some diatomaceous earth. This is a fine powder composed of tiny sea plants and consisting of silica or opal that filters bacteria from water.

The larger pools of this type have a capacity of between 10,000 and 12,000 gallons or 45,500-54,500 litres. You need some sort of filtration system with this type of pool and the water should be chlorinated.

The heavy duty portable pool has interlocking prefabricated plywood wall panels, or concrete sections with a maximum weight of 2cwt (102kg). These are supported by steel stan-

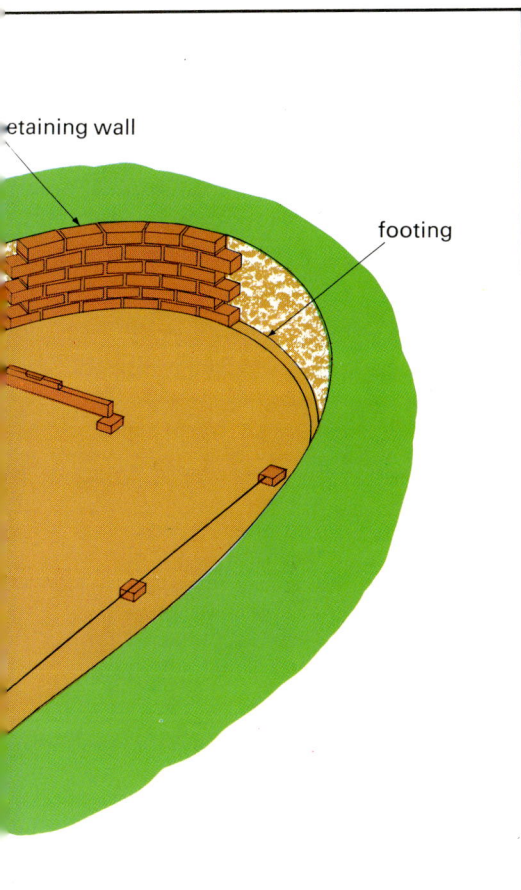

retaining wall

footing

TRI-ART

Right. An oval pool, formed by joining two halves of a circular pool at either end of a rectangular pool. Notice here the concrete edging running all the way round, the fence and trees at the back serving as a windbreak, and the very practical horizontal railing.

chions to form a box beam structure, with buttresses to prevent the sides spreading.

These pools are designed for school as well as for family use, so the filter system and equipment is stronger than for other types of free standing pools. The pools are modular in design so they can be extended up to a maximum residential size of 45ft (13.7m) with a capacity of 20,000 gallons (90900 l).

Equipment

Essential equipment, such as the filtration system and pool liner, must be hard wearing and resistant to the corrosive action of water. The filtration system should be able to cope with the full amount of water and the pool liner should resist ultra-violet rays—most suppliers now give a ten year guarantee on this point. There should not be any sharp edges or bolts in the pool.

Probably the most useful accessory for a free standing pool is a heater. This adds about six weeks to the swimming season in the spring and autumn but you will need a pool cover to reduce heat loss from the pool surface. Pool decking and ladders are useful, particularly for the less agile. A skimmer, to collect surface debris and leaves from the filtration system, and an underwater vacuum cleaner will help keep the pool clean and tidy.

Preparation

You do not have to get planning permission for free standing pools but, as with any structure you build, you should check what the by-laws stipulate in your area. In the case of swimming pools you should inform the water authority of your plans—they may wish to install a meter.

When the pool kit is delivered, check all the items and read the manufacturer's directions carefully. These give full instructions on the erection and maintenance of the pool.

There are, however, several points that you should be particularly careful about:
—make sure that there are water and electrical services near the planned position of the pool. The filter will have to be backwashed, that is, the flow of the filter reversed to clear waste material from the mechanism, and if you cannot use the drains to get rid of this matter, then a small backwash soakaway can be built. An ideal size for this is 2ft x 2ft x 2ft (610mm x 610mm x 610mm).

—pool liners should not be set directly into gravel, asphalt or tar, or on ground recently treated with weedkiller.

—if the pool is to be set into a slope, surface drainage water should be channelled around, and not into, the pool.

—clear all weeds and stones from the area in which the pool is to be set. A concrete base for the pool is not essential, a loamy soil being ideal provided it is tamped down.

—the bottom of the pool area must be level. This is a very important job since a tilting swimming pool will throw considerable weight onto one side. This could cause it to fail.

—if you want your pool to be set into a slope you must dig out the slope. Do not create a slope by making up ground. Water weighs ¾ tons (762kg) per cu yd and it will cause the pool to sink.

—if any of the banks around the pool are more than 1ft (305mm) high, build retaining walls to stop soil washing down into the pool.

—the base rails of some makes of pool have to

be set on concrete blocks. Sets of blocks should be parallel and you can check this by measuring the diagonals. If the soil is wet or loamy, set the blocks in a concrete mix.

If your pool is of the type that is set partially in the ground the following points are important:
—reinforced concrete should be used in retaining walls.
—you must provide adequate drainage to carry away surface water.
—high water tables present considerable problems but ways of overcoming these are discussed in PROJECT 8.
—the Splasher pool and the lightweight portable must not be set into the ground.

Erecting the pool

Again, you should follow the manufacturer's instructions closely when putting your swimming pool kit together and in place.

Erect the pool around the required amount of soft sand for the floor—the required depth is **usually 2in (50mm). 1 cu yd of sand covers 18 sq yds or 16 sq m.**

Set the perimeter rails absolutely level, fit the stanchions and corner posts and install the side panels or uncoil the sheeting. Secure the sides to the framework. Cover the area with fine, damp sifted soil for the floor covering and then spread and tamp down the soil underlay.

A sunny day is ideal for lining the pool as vinyl sheeting will soften in the warmth and become more pliable. Wear soft soled shoes also, to guard against tearing the pool lining.

With adhesive tape, stick the liner edges to the pool wall, lining up the inlet/outlet holes in the liner with those in the pool walls. Cover the floor with 1in. (25mm) of water and smooth out any wall creases. Continue to fill the pool, smoothing out creases after every 12in. (305mm) of water. Roll the liner edges over the top of the pool and double the edges over before fixing the top rail coping. If your particular make of pool requires it, use non-corrosive nails or staples to fix the lining at the top.

If your ground work was accurate and level, the full pool should show a level water line. The pool liner is now protected by the water which cushions it against sharp objects. If a tear develops later, though, it can be easily repaired

Right. *A standard circular pool, which has been imaginatively landscaped into the side of a grassed slope. Allowance has been made for a foot bath, to wash off any loose dirt before it is carried into the water.*

with a piece of vinyl and the manufacturer's recommended adhesive.

Filtration systems

A filter system is essential if your pool's capacity is more than 2,000 gallons (9090 l). Splasher pools, which don't have a filter, need to be emptied about once a month and filtered pools should be cleaned thoroughly once a year. A filter is a mechanical cleaner which removes dust, dirt and dead algae—the water in unfiltered pools soon becomes cloudy and unwholesome. Even if you have a filter you must still treat the water chemically to kill bacteria and insects (see below).

Some manufacturers specify that their filter systems should run continuously—they should certainly operate for at least 12 hours at any one time.

The length of time it takes to filter a pool depends upon the rate at which the water flows through the filter. This period, known as the turnover, takes between 8 and 16 hours depending on the rating the manufacturer gives to his make of filter. The first period of turnover, however, does not filter all the water. The first turnover cleans $\frac{2}{3}$ of the water, the second and each subsequent one cleans $\frac{2}{3}$ of the remainder until the seventh turnover when 99.9% of the water has been filtered. Fig.5 shows the continuous circulation system and the main components. The equipment should be set on a dry concrete slab and protected from the weather.

There are two main types of filter available and these are discussed more fully in PROJECT 8. The diatomaceous earth type, mentioned above, filters through a candle/plate or cartridge membrane, or septum, at a minimum flow of 2 gallons (9.09 l) per minute per sq ft. This type of filter thoroughly cleanses the water but it needs re-charging after every backwash (see below). The pressure sand filter is perhaps less efficient, but it filters water at a high speed through a sand bed at about 16 gallons (72.7 l) per minute per sq ft. The sand bed does not need re-charging.

When the filter gets dirty, pressure builds up inside it. You should then reverse the flow of the filter and this carries out the waste in 2 to 3 minutes. This process, called backwashing, should be done about once a week.

Both the filter systems mentioned above, though, are fitted with a strainer to catch large debris before it reaches the filter.

When you install a heater, it must be fitted after the water has been filtered, and parallel to the flow, as in Fig. 3. PROJECT 8 gives more information on heaters.

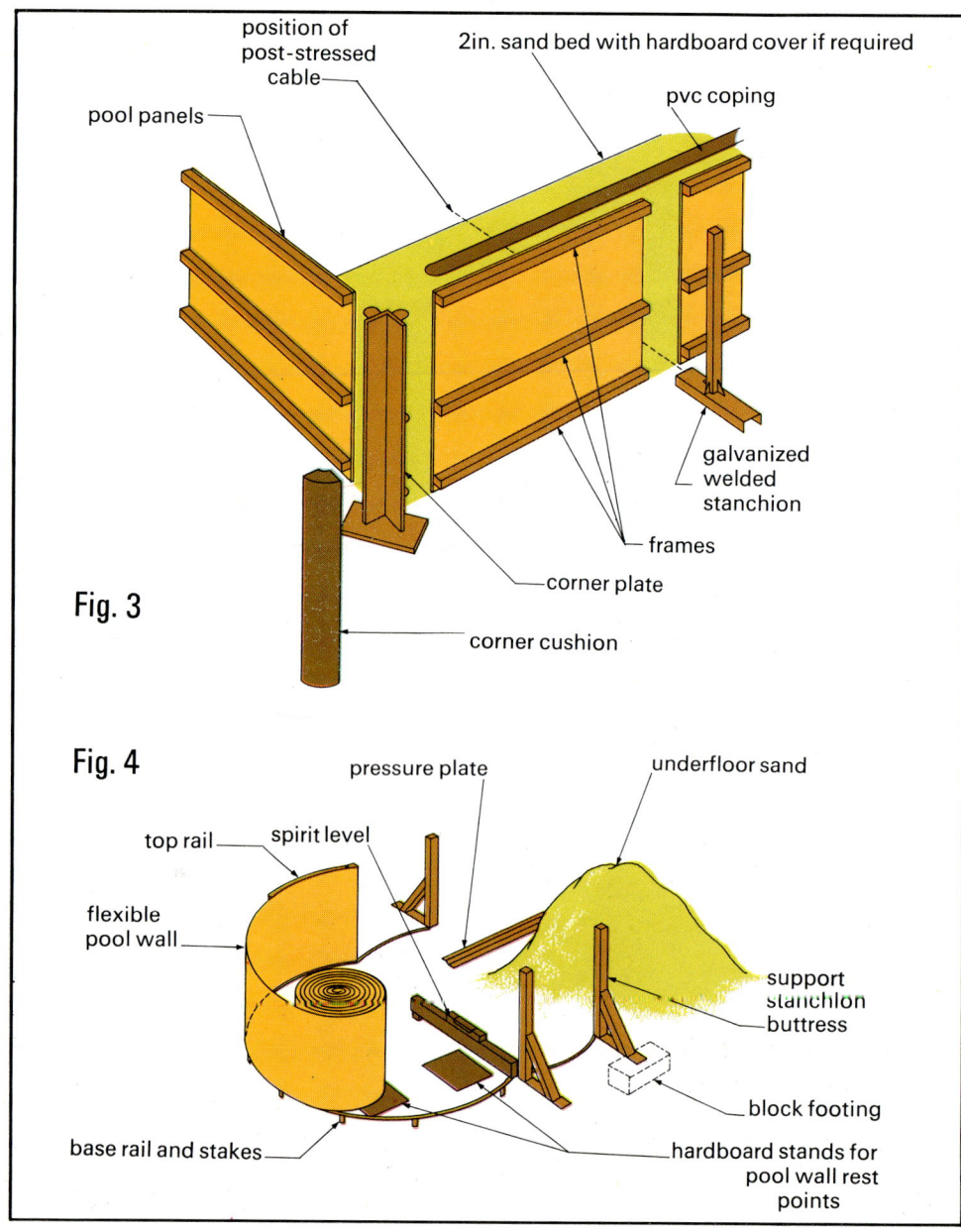

Fig. 3 (top left). *An exploded view of the assembly of a standard type of pool, showing major constructional components.*
Fig.4 (bottom left). *Detail of the building of a pool using flexible walling. It is vital to ensure the base is level, as the pressure of water can cause serious stresses later.*

Fig. 3

position of post-stressed cable
2in. sand bed with hardboard cover if required
pool panels
pvc coping
galvanized welded stanchion
frames
corner plate
corner cushion

Fig. 4

pressure plate
underfloor sand
top rail
spirit level
flexible pool wall
support stanchion
buttress
block footing
base rail and stakes
hardboard stands for pool wall rest points

TRI-ART

CRANLEIGH POOLS LTD., CALCOT, READING

Chemical treatment of pools

All pools have to be treated with certain chemicals for reasons of hygiene. Most manufacturers supply materials and information about the treatment of pool water. It is useful to know what the various chemicals are for.

Chlorine is the chemical most used to kill bacteria. You should use enough chlorine—the pool manufacturer will tell you how much you need—to have some left over in the water. There should be a chlorine residual of 0.3 to 0.5 parts per million. It is this residual that goes on killing bacteria that enter the pool after the initial treatment with chlorine. This action causes a process of oxidation to occur—which uses up the chlorine, so it should be replaced regularly.

The water has to be neutralized as it may be acidic or alkaline, hard or soft. The chlorine raises the alkaline level so a control chemical (acid) is added to adjust the acid/alkaline level. This makes the chlorine more effective and prevents the water causing eye irritation. The acid/alkaline content is measured as the pH value and pool water should be alkaline to a pH value of 7.2 to 7.6, 7.0 being neutral.

An algaecide should be added to the pool regularly to control algae such as black spots and green slime. This does not replace chlorination.

A simple water test set is used to measure the chlorine level and the pH adjustments, and the results of the test are compared with standard colour codes supplied by the pool manufacturers. Further details of the chemical treatment of pools are in PROJECT 8.

Fig.5 (below). A typical circulation system, showing the main components:
1. Skimmer and strainer fitting.
2. Overwall outlet/hair and lint strainer.
3. Pump and base.
4. Motor with overload protection and stainless steel shaft.
5. Switch and control valve.
6. PVC pipe with drain cock.
7. Filter tank, media, and base.
8. Pressure gauge.
9. Air relief valve.
10. Filter lid.
11. Backwash pipe to waste.
12. Heater, with shut-off valves shown. The heater can be by-passed using these.
13. In-wall inlet.
14. Pool wall.

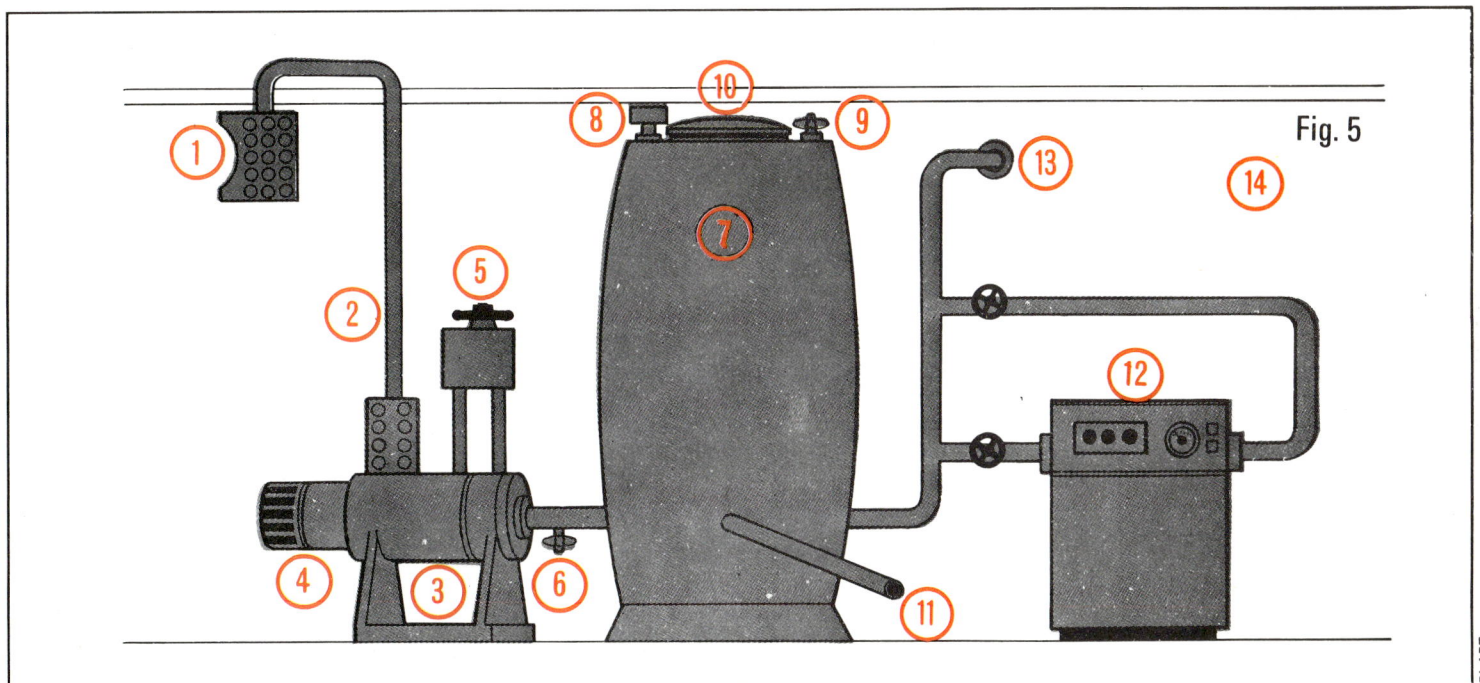

Fig. 5

TRI-ART

Build an outdoor dining room—1

A patio built from brick and paving is one of the most attractive of outdoor home-improvement features. It can add greatly to the value of your home and embellish a very small garden. There are probably few things more pleasant than to sit outdoors on a fine day or evening. Moreover, meals in the open air, in a congenial setting, can add greatly to your enjoyment. This patio incorporates five built-in plant tubs, bench seating for eight people and a barbecue section for cooking outdoors.

The patio may be built to the 12ft 6in. size illustrated, or readily scaled up or down to suit a different location. It is partially walled, giving a degree of privacy, and incorporates five built-in plant tubs. Four of the tubs are slightly higher than the basic 3ft (910mm), to add interest to the wall line. Built-in seats provide comfortable seating for six people. A barbecue grill is incorporated, and a built-in charcoal store could be added.

A single-skin wall is used on one side of the structure. An open double wall is used on the other. This can be covered, fully or partially, with loose-laid patio slabs, to provide a serving area for the barbecue, or left uncovered as a shrub or flower planter. Offset openings provide a walk-through to the garden.

The patio was designed to suit the standard 9in. (450mm) bricks or blocks available anywhere, and was built in Redland 'Kentstone' walling in a random pattern of lilac, sandstone and slate-blue shades to give a rural, textured effect. The paving is Redland 'Polygon' in lilac and sandstone shades.

Choosing the site

When choosing the site, remember that the patio floor needs to slope about 3in. overall so that it will not collect rainwater. Even more important, your patio walls must not touch the house wall above the line of the dampcourse, or damp from the patio masonry may penetrate the house. Even if you take the paving slabs up to the house as part of your scheme, ensure that the top of the slab is at least 6in. below the house dampcourse.

On a flat plot of land, the easiest solution is to leave the width of a path between house and patio, and slope the patio floor away from the house.

If the ground slopes towards the house, you will need to excavate so that the patio site itself slopes away from the house, and leave some drainage holes in the brickwork. In areas where rainfall is average, as in Britain,

these holes plus the gaps between the paving slabs will allow the water to seep away. In areas subject to heavy rain, you may need a land-drain from the rear of the site to a point well clear of the house.

If the ground slopes away from the house, there may be height enough to butt the patio walls against the house below the dampcourse—provided, that is, that the steps from house to patio do not intrude too far on to the patio floor. In this instance, of course, you slope the patio floor away from the house.

On a steeply sloping plot, you may need to excavate for part of the patio site and raise the ground level for the rest. In such a case, always excavate for at least two-thirds of the total area. This is because much of what you dig out will be useless as 'fill', and replacement material may be expensive. Any 'fill' will, in any event, need laborious tamping down to provide a stable base for the floor.

Clearing the site

First, equip yourself with a dozen pegs of 2in. x 2in. or 50mm x 50mm timber about 1ft long, sharpened at one end—these will be used at several stages of the job—a spade, a hammer and a steel tape.

Using the steel tape to measure both the distance from the house and the dimensions of your patio, drive four pegs into the ground, one at each corner of your proposed site. Now mark out with the spade an area about 3ft bigger all round than that enclosed by the pegs. Clear off all the grass and stack the turves well out of the way; you will need some of them later. Clear away all loamy topsoil and remove any tree roots since, if left, they might eventually dislodge the paving or crack the foundations.

Remove the four marker pegs and store them for later use.

Levelling the site

An apparently flat piece of land can often conceal, over a distance of just a few yards, a difference in levels of a foot or more. So the next stage is to get the site truly level—except, of course, for the 3in. slope for rainwater drainage. For this you will need some of your pegs; a builder's level either 3ft or 1 metre long; some

Plants in the built-in tubs add a gay splash of colour to the brick-and-paving patio. The use of block and random colour in the brick and paving adds texture and interest. The optional screen walls give privacy and enhance the overall appearance. A charcoal store can be built under the barbecue slab.

NELSON HARGREAVES

blocks of wood 3in. and 1½in. thick; and a straight-edge about 8ft (2.40m) long.

Mark your pegs with a thick pencil line right round them 2in. (50.8mm) from the top. This line represents ground level. Now drive three pegs into the ground at intervals along one side of your patio site (Fig.1)—one at what is to be the highest point when you have excavated; one in the middle; and one at what is to be the lowest point. Put a 1½in. block on the middle peg and a 3in. block on the peg at the proposed lowest point; these will compensate for the fall you want on the ground.

Use your straight-edge and builder's level over the three pegs to see how far 'out' the ground is. Where the ground is too high, pare it away with the spade until you can see, by driving the pegs in a bit more, that the levels are correct.

Next, work sideways across the site, using more of your pegs as you go; and then check the diagonals. Finally, use your straight-edge on the ground while you pare away any intermediate 'bumps'.

Setting out the site

Setting out foundation and wall positions is a job that needs some care. Should the layout go 'out of square' it will probably not be noticed immediately, but will show up badly when the paving stones fail to fit. (In house building, similarly, the error usually goes unnoticed until the roof turns out to have a 'ragged' bottom edge.)

For this job you will need profile boards and a home-made timber try-square. This latter is based on the principle that any triangle whose sides are in the ratio 3:4:5 *must* have a right angle in one corner. In practice, perhaps the handiest tool is a timber triangle whose outside edges measure 4½ft, 6ft and 7½ft respectively; it is big enough to check the 'square' of rooms (when laying floor tiles, for example) but small enough to store upright in the garage (see inset, Fig.2).

The profile board (Fig.2) consists of two crossbars of planed timber, each about 4ft 6in. or 1.5m long, mounted at right angles to each other on three pegs of 2in. x 2in. timber. For this project, a simple rectangle, you will need four sets.

Before you make up your profiles, you must first establish your 'building line'—the main line from which all other dimensions are measured. Measure the desired distance from the house at one corner of the patio site, and drive in a peg. Measure out the width of the patio, check that the distance from the house is the same as before, and drive in another peg. A line between the two is the building line.

To set up the profiles, a single stake is first driven into the ground about 2ft (610mm) diagonally outside the actual foundation area. This is called the 'datum' peg. As all other references—vertical and horizontal checks in laying foundations and in building walls—are

This plan view of the patio shows the arrangement of plant tubs and barbecue. The slabs on the wall alongside provide a serving facility, but are loose laid and some or all could be removed for planting shrubs and flowers.

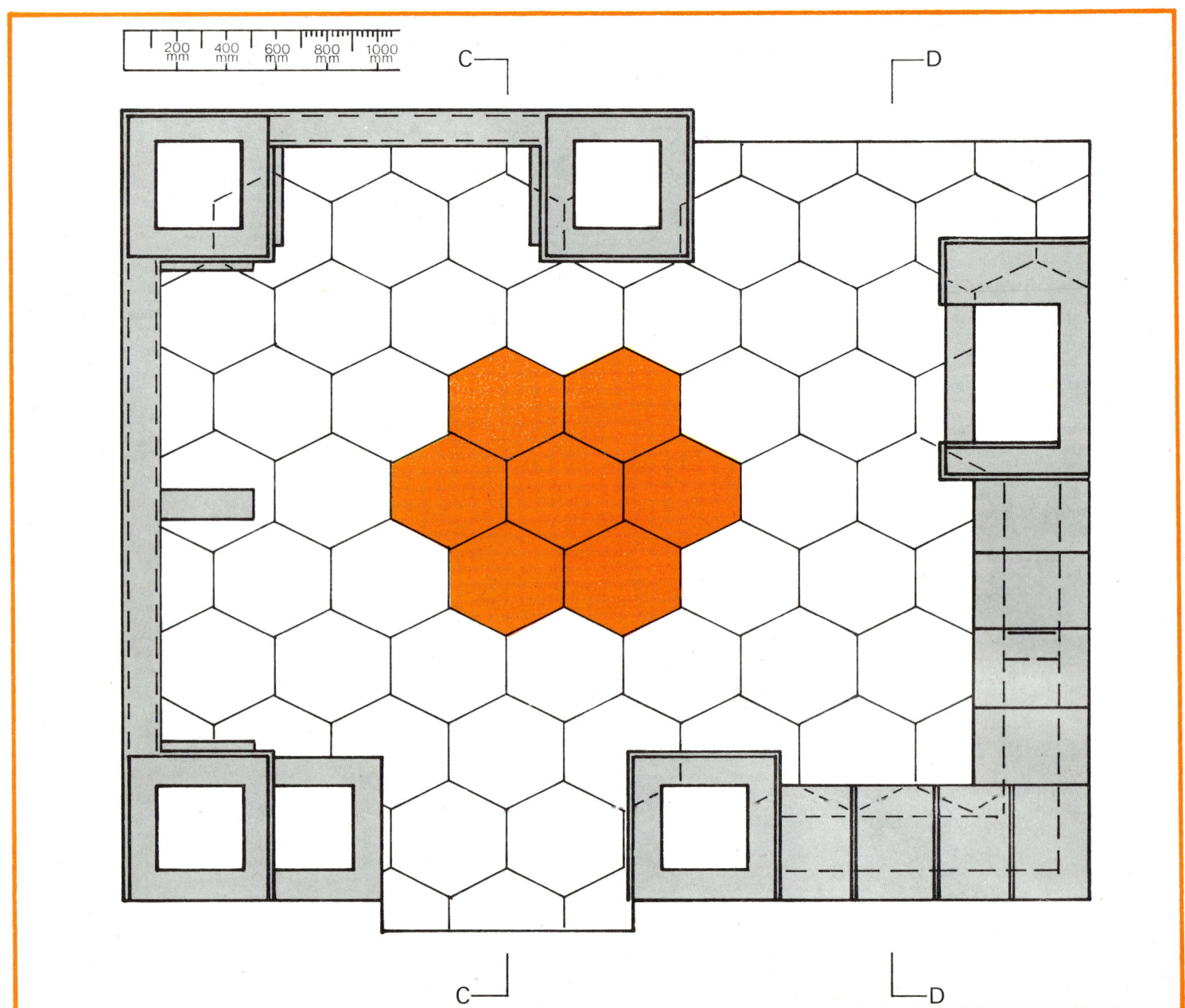

taken from this peg, it should never be disturbed. Ideally, it should be set in concrete and uprooted only when the job is over.

Next, pegs are driven in at right angles on either side of the datum peg (Fig.2) and the first profile boards are nailed to these. Each board must be exactly level along its own length, and the pair must be level with each other; use the builder's level to make sure.

Similar sets of profiles are built outside each of the other three corners. No matter how much the ground slopes, all four sets must be exactly level with one another. You can check this by using the straight-edge and builder's level; where the span is too great for the straight-edge, temporary pegs can be driven in as intermediate supports. (Since a length of timber is almost never exactly straight, even a so-called straight edge will produce some inaccuracies. To correct this, each span should be checked first with one edge up and then with the opposite edge up, and the builder's level should always be placed in the middle of the board.)

Once the profile boards have been levelled, the next job is to stretch lines across them to mark exactly where the outside edges of the brickwork will be. For this, nylon fishing line is better than string, which sags as the humidity varies.

Sight the first nylon line (marked a-b in Fig.2) across the profiles and directly above the two pegs that marked your original 'building line'; make a tiny saw cut in each profile board; and draw the line tightly between the notches, securing it with a knot at each end. Repeat the procedure for the two lines running off at right angles (a-c and b-d in the diagram), using the large wooden try-square to see that the corners are square. (You will need some help at this stage.) Again using the try-square, site the line c-d, at the opposite end.

Now check that the dimensions are correct at both ends and on both sides. Check that your levels are accurate—and not, for example, 'high' at one corner—by lying down and sighting across the lines at opposite ends. Finally, measure the diagonals a-d and b-c with a steel tape; unless the diagonals are exactly the same you are 'out of square' and must make some adjustments. When you are satisfied that your lines are true, rule vertical pencil lines down the inside of the profiles so that, after you have moved the nylon lines later, you can replace them in the correct notches.

The other line positions can now be marked quickly, and by measurement only. The outer edge of the foundations, or 'footings', should be 4½in. (112mm) wider than the walls. Working from your existing nylon lines, measure outwards for 4½in. all round, cut a new series of notches, and again rule vertical lines down the insides of the profiles.

This project, to save having a complicated series of footings, uses a wide 'slab' footing to run the full width of its planters and seats. The third series of lines on Fig.2 is to line up the brickwork on the inside of the planters and so on. The correct dimensions (shown in the plan, on page 12) should also be measured from your first set of nylon lines, the profile boards notched and the usual vertical lines ruled.

Digging the footings

Trenches for the footings should be dug to a depth of about 9in. (222mm) so that neither footings nor bedding mortar will show above ground level. Although the patio floor is intended to slope, the walls (and hence the foundations under them) should be level. So you will need to dig deeper than 9in. as you work up the slope.

While you are digging, use only the inner and outer profile lines as a guide—any other lines will only get in the way.

Once dug, the trenches can be checked for width and alignment by using the builder's level, this time held upright against the profile lines (Fig.3). To establish the correct depth of concrete and an accurate level on which to begin bricklaying, next drive in a series of pegs so that their tops will be level with the top of the concrete; this should be about 4in. (102mm) thick. Since these pegs will finish up jammed in the concrete, use pieces of boxwood or other scrap material. Use the straight-edge and builder's level to see that the tops of the pegs are, in fact, level (Fig.4).

If the site slopes steeply, you may have to 'step' the footings to keep them out of sight below ground level. Make each step the same depth as one brick and its mortar joint, or two bricks and two joints. This is so you can begin your bricklaying on the lowest step, bringing other courses into line as you work upwards.

Pouring the concrete

A mixture of one part (by volume) of Portland cement, 2½ parts of sand and four parts of coarse aggregate is a suitable composition for the concrete. It should be mixed fairly dry and, once poured in, well tamped to remove air pockets, mix in the water and 'hydrate' the cement. In hot weather, the mix should be covered with sacking or old cement bags and kept moist. Although concrete takes about 21 days to cure, the foundations should be firm enough for bricklaying in about a week. Avoid laying concrete in icy weather, since frost can damage it.

Now you are ready to begin bricklaying.

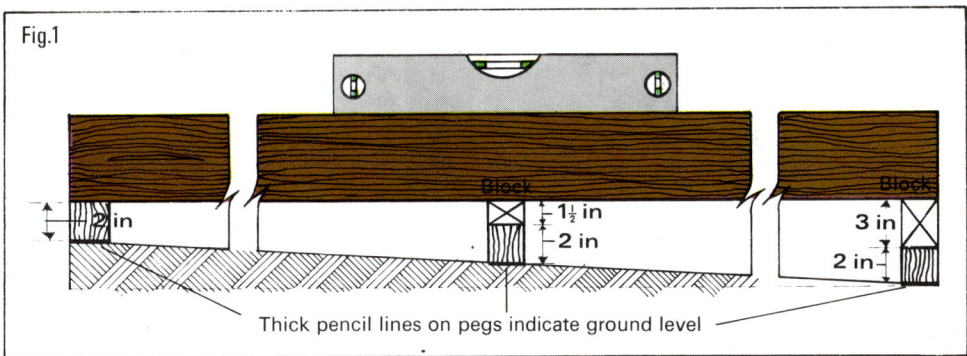

Fig.1
2in   1½ in   2 in   3 in   2 in   Block   Block

Thick pencil lines on pegs indicate ground level

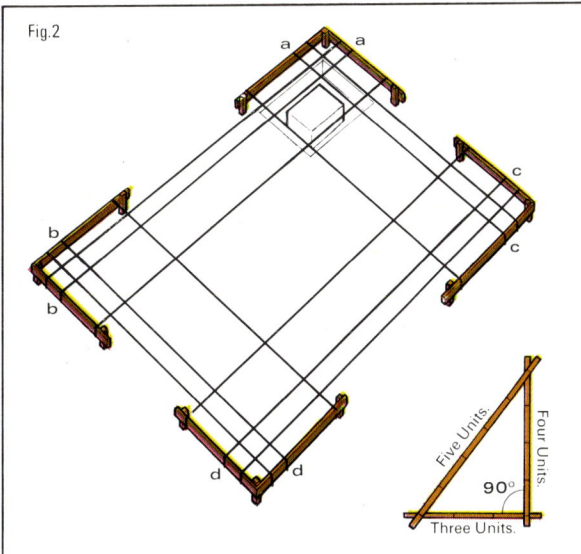

Fig.2
a   a   c   c   b   b   d   d

Five Units   Four Units   90°   Three Units

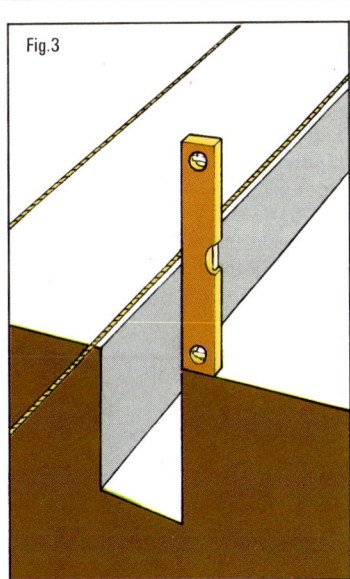

Fig.3

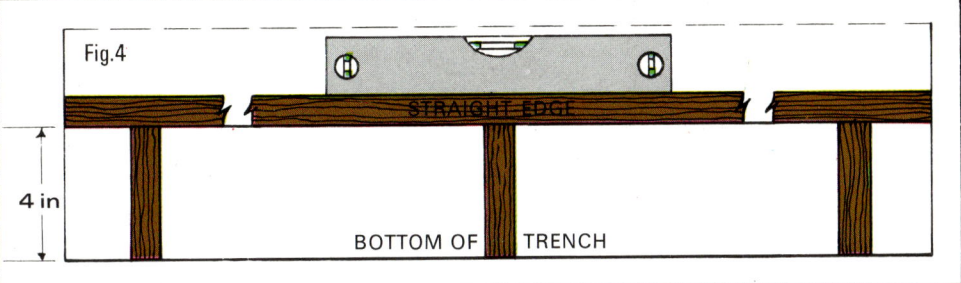

Fig.4
STRAIGHT EDGE
4 in
BOTTOM OF TRENCH

Build an outdoor dining room—2

A well-designed patio is a valuable addition to the home and also a social asset, a place to invite people to meet and to enjoy themselves.

Top right : *A barbecue is an open fire, consisting of a simple grill with a tray of burning charcoal beneath it. All manner of foods can be prepared on this out-of-doors 'kitchen range'.*

Bottom right : *This shows the layout of the seating between flower tubs. The central area enables a table as well as extra seating to be introduced.*

A patio is very much a room outdoors, an extension to the home which is best enjoyed in fine weather. It is an ideal place on which to throw a party and to serve food cooked over the barbecue grill. As a prelude to that party, this chapter shows how to complete the job and add that extra vista to your home.

Preparing for bricklaying

Once the foundations for your patio have been laid, you can set out the site ready for bricklaying.

First, you want one set of your profile strings lined up with the outside edge of the brickwork. Move them to the appropriate notches on the profile boards. At intervals of about 6ft (or 2 metres), space out 'spot' boards about 2ft (or 600mm) square, made from scrap wood, to hold supplies of mortar. Stack your bricks neatly between them. You need about 25 bricks for each square yard covered.

The tools you will need are the spirit level ; the straight-edge ; a 10in. or 11in. (254mm or 279mm) bricklayer's trowel ; a small pointing trowel called a *dotter* ; a club hammer ; a wire brush ; a bolster or cold chisel, for cutting bricks and paving slabs ; a shovel for mixing the mortar ; and a pair of bricklayer's pins with a few yards of cord.

Bricklaying mortar mix consists of one part (by volume) of cement to eight parts of sand, with one part of lime or its equivalent in proprietary plasticizer (see the instructions on the tin) to make the mixture 'fatty' and more easily workable. In cold weather, slightly less sand should be used.

Before laying the first course of bricks, spread a *bedding* course of mortar screed about 1in. (25mm) thick along the foundations. Before this has set, draw on it the 'course line' to which you lay your bricks. You do this by holding the builder's level upright, resting on the mortar and with its edge against the profile line, and scratching a trowel mark on the mortar. Do this every few feet, and then join up the marks. When you come to lay the bricks, lay them to this line, but be careful not to cover it.

Laying the bricks

Bricks can be laid either longways or endways, to give a variety of brick styles or bonds. The one used here is a *stretcher bond* ; all the bricks are laid lengthwise.

In bricklaying, the ends of a wall are always built up first. Then a cord is stretched from one end to the other while the intermediate bricks are laid. This keeps each successive course level, and ensures that the top of the wall is straight.

Begin by building up your first two *quoins* (corners) at opposite ends of the patio. Form the corners by laying bricks alternately on each other at right angles. Build up to the full height by *racking back*—laying one brick less in each successive course. Remember to allow for drainage holes, where these are needed. Use the builder's level as you go to check that the bricks are level, plumb and flush. Any adjustments to the levels of the bricks are made by tapping down the bricks with the handle of the trowel, and striking off with the trowel edge any excess mortar that is squeezed out.

With the first pair of quoins built up, use a cord stretched between two bricklayer's pins to help level the intermediate bricks as you lay them. The pins are tucked into the mortar joints around each corner of the wall, with the line snagged over the top edges of a quoin brick at each end. Take up any slack in the line by winding it over the spade-shaped part of the bricklayer's pins.

Laying out a few bricks 'dry' will help you to ensure that you are spacing them correctly. Minor adjustments can be made by varying the thickness of mortar in the vertical joists. If some cutting is needed, use the bolster and club hammer, and work right round the brick with even blows. The professional will cut a brick with the edge of his bricklaying trowel, but this is a practised art.

Before you build any of the interior walls, note that the barbecue pit requires some steel insets in the brickwork, and that built-in seating, should you desire it, requires coping stone insets as supports. So check the instructions for both barbecue and seating before proceeding too far.

Pointing and coping

As each wall is built, the joints must be *pointed*, or finished, while the mortar is still fairly soft. The flush joint illustrated here is achieved by scraping horizontal joints with the edge of the bricklayer's trowel, and vertical joints with the 'dotter' trowel.

After the mortar is surface-dry (usually overnight), any surface blemishes on the bricks are removed by a light wire brushing.

Once the walls are built, the *coping* (capping) pieces are mortared in, using the same technique as for bricklaying.

NELSON HARGREAVES

Paving the patio

When buying patio slabs, allow about 5 per cent extra for breakages; however careful you are in cutting, a few will always break in the wrong place.

Paving slabs need a firm base. If the ground is soft, it is advisable to provide a foundation of well-consolidated hardcore. Where this is done, use the straight-edge, level and pegs again to see that the base is even, with the correct 'fall' for rainwater drainage.

Paving slabs should always be laid with the textured, non-slip surface upwards. Before laying begins, a few slabs should be set out, 'dry', to see where cutting will be needed. You do not want to finish with three-quarters of a slab on one side of an opening and only a quarter of a slab on the other. A nylon line stretched across the ground will help you align your first row.

The actual laying technique will vary according to the density of the sub-soil, the local weather, the amount of 'traffic' you expect on the patio, and your personal taste:

1, Where some slight settlement of the surface can be accepted, or where rainfall is sparse, a layer of finely sifted soil or sand can be spread over the area and the slabs laid, carefully but firmly, on this.

2, Where you want greater surface stability, spread sifted soil or sand as before, and lay the slabs with a trowel-full of mortar under each. Larger slabs—18in. or 457mm each, say—should have a spot of mortar under each corner. Leave the paving to set for two or three days.

3, Where the surface is to be subjected to heavy wear, and especially in sub-tropical areas subject to heavy rain, prepare a fairly stiff 1:5 cement mortar mix and spread it evenly over the surface, covering just enough ground for one slab at a time.

Slabs should not be 'pummelled' into place to correct unevenness, but tapped gently with the base of the club hammer. Use a straight-edge as you go, to check that adjoining slabs are flush.

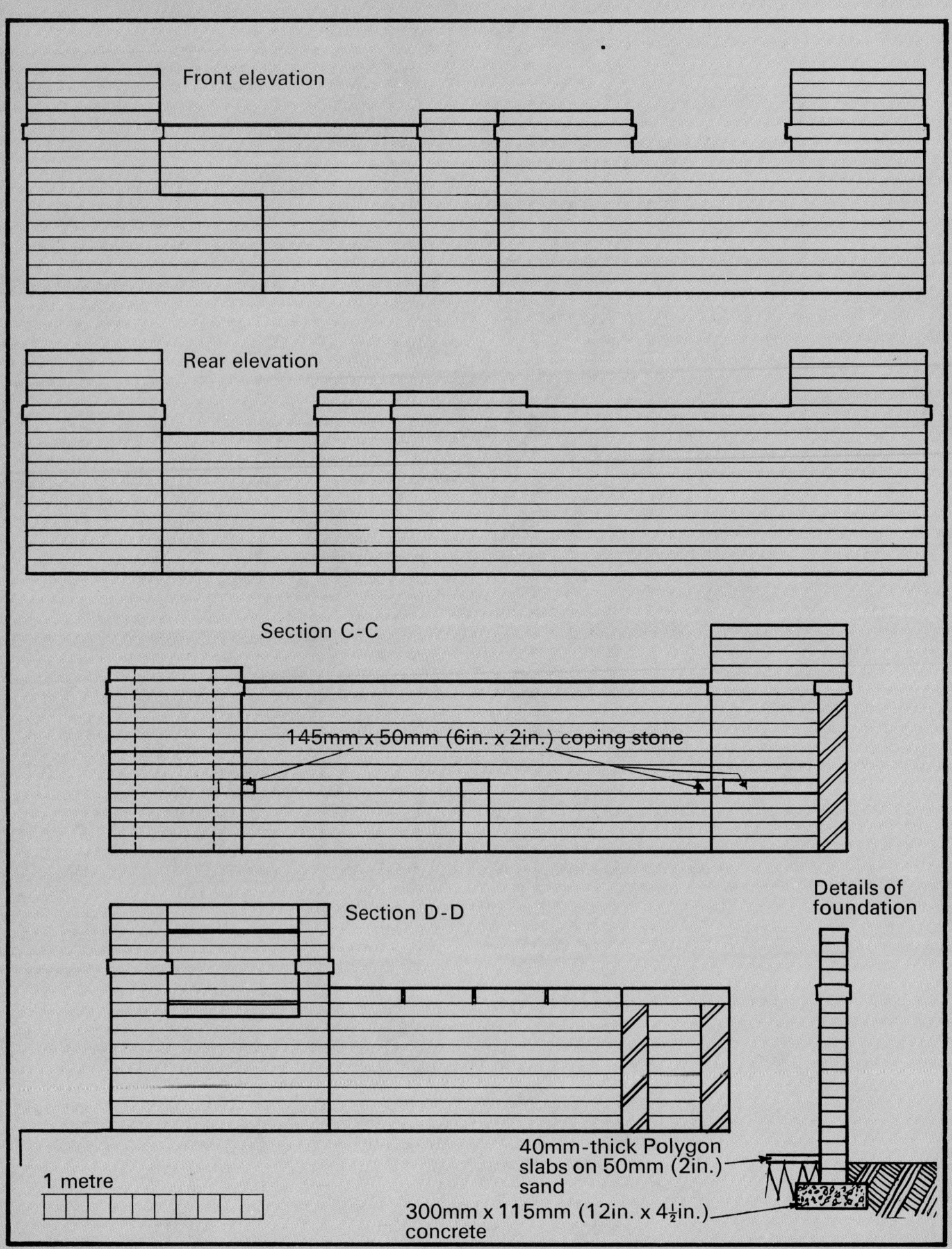

Front elevation

Rear elevation

Section C-C

145mm x 50mm (6in. x 2in.) coping stone

Section D-D

Details of foundation

40mm-thick Polygon slabs on 50mm (2in.) sand

300mm x 115mm (12in. x 4½in.) concrete

1 metre

When you need to cut a slab, first mark the cutting line with pencil and straight-edge. Now tap gently with the hammer and bolster or cold chisel to cut a shallow scratch across the face of the slab. Do the same on the back, and join the scratch lines at the edges.

Deepen the scratches by working progressively round the slab. After a while, the ringing note of the blows will deaden, indicating that the slab is cracking apart. A few more taps will make it break neatly along the line; minor irregularities can be carefully chipped off.

Once the paving has set, a dry mortar mix can be brushed into the joints. This is known as *grouting*. Be sure you leave none on the surface of the slabs; what you cannot brush away, a damp cloth will pick up.

Alternatively, the joints can be filled with finely sifted soil (you will have to keep 'topping it up' for a few weeks) and tiny plants allowed to grow.

Fitting the barbecue

The barbecue consists of an adjustable grill made of mild-steel rods and a metal tray for holding charcoal. These are mounted on angle-iron runners.

The supports for the brazier tray are made of two pieces of 2in. x 1½in. (50mm x 38mm) angle-iron. These should be 17in. (426mm) long and set 1½in. (38mm) into the mortar above the fifth brick course.

The brazier tray is made from a sheet of 22-gauge mild steel 22in. (560mm) wide—or slightly narrower if required to fit between the brickwork on either side—and 19in. (492mm) long. The front and back are bent upwards (for about 2in., and at about 45°) to retain the charcoal. Holes, 1in. (25mm) in diameter and about 4in. apart, are drilled in the bottom to provide a draught.

You need six pieces of the same size angle-iron for the grill supports. The first pair is set above the eighth course of bricks, the second above the ninth, and the third pair above the tenth course. These positions allow the grill to be set at three levels to provide different cooking temperatures for various types of food.

Ten pieces of ⅜in. (9.5mm) mild-steel rod, each one 22¼in. (565mm) long, are used for the grill surface. These are welded to a U-shaped rod of the same thickness. The grill should be made so that the ends of the rods rest on the angle-iron supports, and the U-shaped rod fits between. If you do not have a welding kit, a smith or garage can do this for you.

The arrangement of the walls beside the barbecue allows for a charcoal store to be incorporated if desired. In this case, a sheet of polythene should be introduced beneath the coping slab. A door can be set in, using a simple frame work attached to the brickwork with masonry nails.

Seating

The type of seating used is optional. Deck chairs or garden loungers, park-bench type seating or metal garden seats can be used. If built-in wooden seating is required, support it by building paving slabs into the appropriate walls, at the points shown in section CC so they project about 2in. (or 50mm). Intermediate supports in brickwork are shown in the same diagram. Before cutting and fitting the seats— they are made up as complete frames—lay a dampcourse of bituminous felt between masonry and woodwork. Ensure that nails and screws used in making the framework are of the non-rusting type.

NELSON HARGREAVES

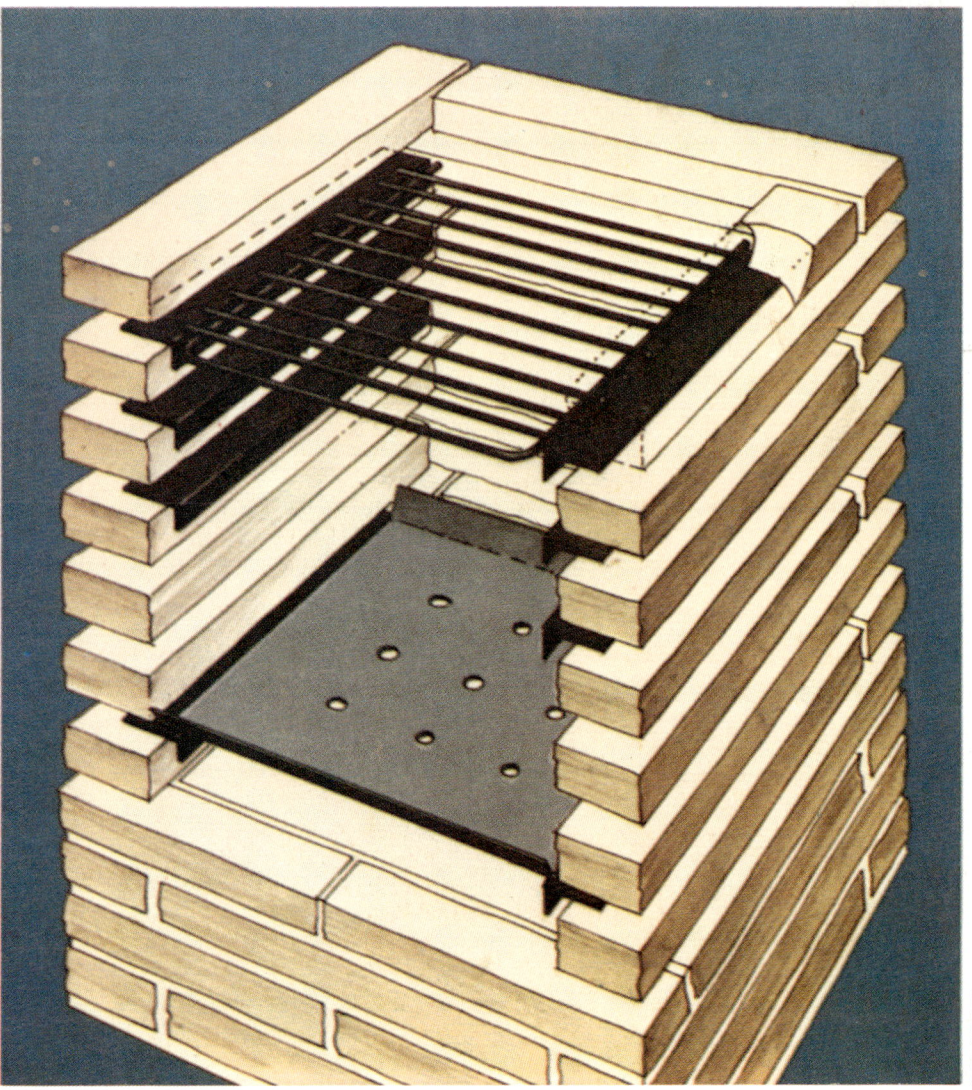

DON KIDMAN

Fig. 1 (left). The elevations show where coping stones have to be set in to provide support for permanent wooden seating.

Top right. The serving area alongside the barbecue is an optional feature. As an alternative, the top slabs could be left off and this area used for planters.

Fig. 2 (right) The grill, made from ⅜ in. rods, can be set at three different levels to adjust the cooking temperature. The tray is of mild steel sheet.

How to put up a carport

In many situations a carport is much better value than a garage. A garage costs more and takes longer to build, but a carport performs much the same function and can be just as attractive. If you want to provide cover for your car, a carport could be the answer.

A carport is not necessarily a cheap, unsatisfactory structure—in fact it has certain advantages over a garage. It could be constructed with the idea of providing a garage in the future; for instance you can lay a good solid foundation under a simple superstructure that can be replaced by solid walls and a door at a later date.

What is a carport?

There is no single definition of what constitutes a carport, but broadly speaking, it is a shelter that protects the car from vertical rain, but not necessarily angled rain or snow driven in by the wind. At its most elaborate, a carport could have a roof and side walls, but no doors at the front or back (see Fig.1). The simplest type would be a relatively light roof supported with struts or columns (see Fig.3).

It is important that you get a clear idea of what a carport is for the purpose of obtaining planning or building permission. The trouble is that various local authorities have slightly different opinions about the definition of a carport, so it is best to contact your own local authority before you start to draw plans. Some councils will allow carports but not garages; some rule the other way round!

Why build a carport?

Some of the reasons for building a carport —time, cost, or using it as one stage towards eventually building a garage—have been given above, but there are many more. For instance the space you have available might be wide enough to take a car, but too narrow to enable the car doors to be opened if a wall were on each side. This would make the construction of a garage impossible, but a simple carport consisting of corner columns or struts could

Left. This structure is a composite of some of the carports described here. In this case it serves as an extended porch and carport, with room for three cars. The main supports are of timber; on one side the supports are filled in between with brickwork which has four-course slots left in, mainly as a decorative feature. The opposite side has a brick plinth wall that also acts as a fence—a useful item, bearing in mind the drop below!

DOUGLAS BAGLIN

well provide your car with some form of cover while still enabling you to open the doors.

Another point is—how often do you actually garage your car? Many people park their cars in the drive most of the time, and only garage it in the fiercest winter weather. And when you consider that a warm damp garage actually accelerates rust corrosion, such cars would actually be better off in a carport, protected from rain yet never becoming warm.

If you already have a garage that is set well back (in many cases the drive runs along the side of the house and the garage is located in or about the rear garden) then a carport built on to the side of your house would provide additional protected parking, either for a second car or when you are using the garage for other purposes, such as a workshop. And it will normally be closer to the front door—an added convenience in wet weather.

Types of carport

As mentioned, carports can range in structure from the very simple to the fairly complicated. There are also carport kits available in most countries. These are usually well worth considering, although you have not got the same flexibility that you have when doing the whole job yourself; for instance sometimes you are limited to specific dimensions.

The most simple carport is a light roof supported by metal or timber struts, as shown in Figs.2 and 3. The roof is a timber frame covered with corrugated plastic sheet or timber panelling and roofing felt. Its vertical supports are metal struts in either mild steel rod or aluminium tubing as shown in Fig.3, or sturdy timber members as in Fig.2. If the base is suitable to park a car on, you only need to dig a small hole immediately under each of the supports in the way of foundation work.

More complex carports are shown in Figs.1 and 4. The one in Fig.4 has a roof supported on one side along the house wall, and on the other side by three brick piers. The spaces between the piers at the sides can be left open or filled with plain or stone-faced ornamental bricks. The port in Fig.1 is built on the same principle, but here the piers consist of special screen walling pier blocks. The base has a brick plinth wall, and the spaces between the piers are filled with screen walling. For both these types you must have a strip foundation running underneath the walling and piers.

If your house is of timber construction, or perhaps faced with timber, you might consider a carport constructed entirely in wood. This is a much more complex stucture, however, and is outside the scope of this project.

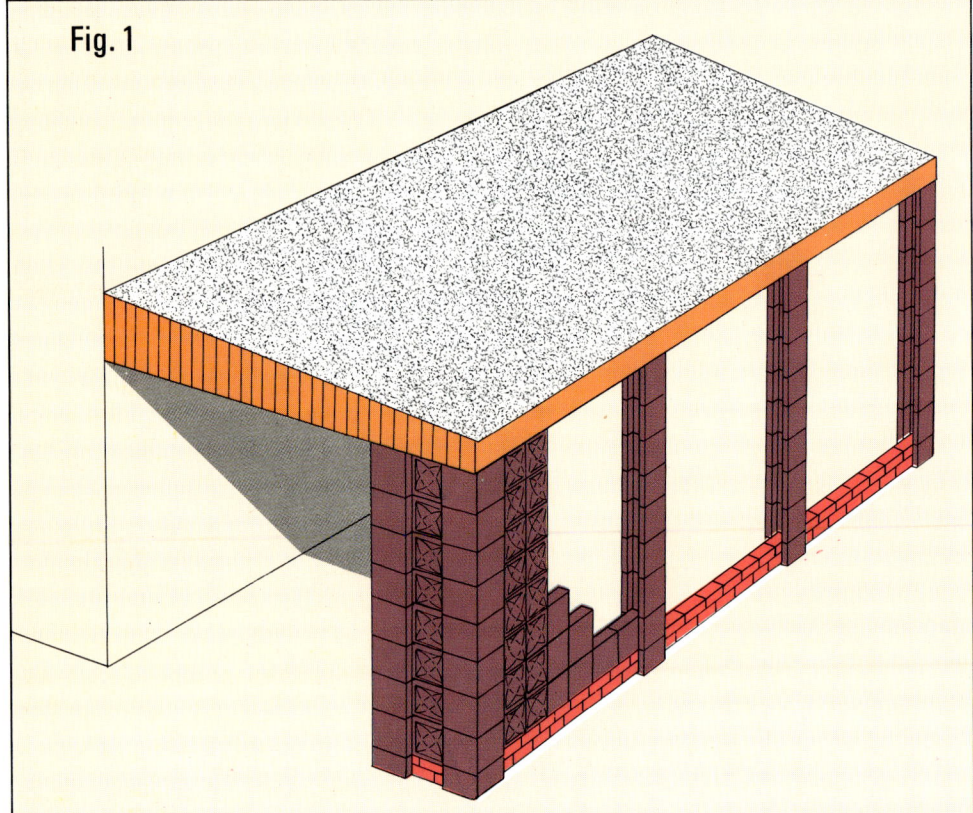

Planning and design

A carport is a relatively light form of construction, so planning or building permission is usually easily obtained for one. However this does not mean that you do not have to seek approval, because in most countries permission must be obtained for any external work that involves an extension of some sort. So submit building plans to your local authority, to make sure you are not contravening any local bye-laws, before you start.

When planning the actual design of the carport, bear in mind that it should harmonize with your house in design (sketches on paper will help you here), and that the materials and colours should also match. If you put up any old carport just for convenience or cheapness, the house and carport might make an ugly combination. For instance a carport with a roof of corrugated plastic, supported by chromium plated steel rods, would look unsightly against a Victorian house.

The base, where the car will be parked, is the first stage in planning. It may be that you only require a lightweight carport such as those shown in Figs.2 and 3, in which case the surface already in existence will probably do. A concrete or asphalt base is perfectly adequate, and even a soil base can be adequately consolidated by ramming gravel well in—though this will probably have to be repeated every year. If you are considering the heavier type of carport shown in Figs.1 and 4, then you will have to lay a suitable strip foundation; or if you want to build a garage eventually, a strip and raft foundation. So the method you use depends on your plans for the future.

One convenient method for a base is to lay concrete paving slabs on a 2in. or 50mm bed of well compacted sand; or two lines of slabs as wheel tracks with a centre strip of dark gravel to hide any oil drips from the car.

The choice of walls or support will depend on the degree of protection required. If you already have a garage and will use the carport as an additional convenient parking space, then simple side struts could be sufficient. On the other hand, if the carport is to be used as a permanent parking space, then you will require a greater degree of protection with side walls, something like the one in Fig.1. The aspect is also important; for example in Britain a carport that is exposed to north and east winds needs greater protection than one which faces south or west.

Building considerations

It is impossible to give detailed instructions for building a wide range of carports, but there are many points that must be mentioned here because they are not dealt with anywhere else in this publication.

If you are using struts or timber members for supporting the roof, then these must be of sufficient strength to do their job. Timber members must be at least 4in. or 100mm square; mild steel rod about 1½in. or 38mm in diameter; and aluminium support tubing about 3in. or 75mm in diameter. In each case, place the struts at about 9ft or 3m centres.

Supports do more than take a compressive strain (the weight of the roof pressing down);

Fig.1. *Screen blocks provide a very attractive walling for a carport, but the blocks themselves require strengthening if the wall is more than 3ft or 1m high. This is achieved by placing piers—which are specially made blocks—at approximately 6ft or 2m intervals, and making a short return wall at one or both of the ends.*

Fig.2. *Sturdy timbers provide excellent support for a light roof. The base of each timber is encased in a short brick pier, which eliminates the necessity of bedding it into the foundation concrete, where it would be permanently damp and rot away. For extra protection a window framework can be built between the supports and glazed.*

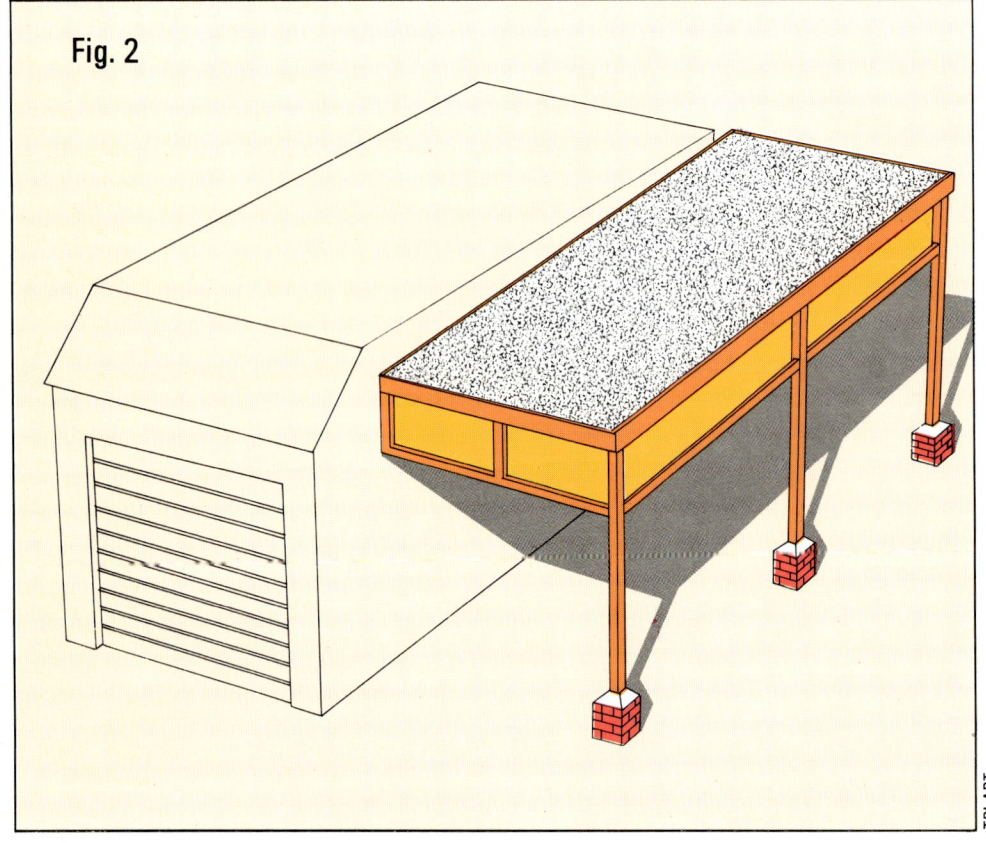

they also have to stand the 'stretching' action that takes place when the wind gusts underneath the roof and tries to lift it. For this reason supports must be very securely fixed at both ends.

Metal supports can be obtained with 6in. or 150mm square base plates welded on so that they can be bedded in concrete or brickwork. If you can't obtain such supports, have plates welded on. It is easier to fit base plates on to timber members, but bear in mind that all such wood must be well soaked in creosote or a similar wood preservative, particularly the part underground where it can rot without being seen.

Brick piers as in Fig.4, whether filled in between or not, have tremendous strength, but walls and piers of lightweight screen blocks are nowhere near as strong. For this reason they must never be built in a straight run of wall. This is why the carport in Fig.1 has return corners at each end (and an extra pier) to give it maximum strength. These return corners obviously take up drive-in space and must be taken into account when planning the carport.

If the carport is to be attached to your house, there will probably be laws or regulations that limit the materials used to those that are most fire resistant. Bitumastic felted roofs, timber, glass and asbestos come well within the scope of most regulations, but some of the cheaper forms of plastic do not. So it is essential to seek the advice of your local authority to find out whether there are any materials that you are not permitted to use.

There are several different methods of butting or fixing the roof joists to the house wall. Screwing or bolting a wall plate to it is the most common, but metal 'shoes' or joist hangers, while requiring more care in setting and alignment, give a much neater finish to the job. Whatever method is used, try to avoid cutting out brickwork to receive the ends of the joists. Wood enclosed in brickwork tends to rot, and if you ever want to remove or re-site the carport you will have to make good the brickwork instead of just filling in a few bolt holes.

The next section deals in detail with the construction of the more usual types of carport.

Fig.3. *Metal struts are the most convenient form of support. You can use either mild steel rods or aluminium support tubing. The struts must be placed in pairs, slightly splayed as shown, with each pair at 9ft or 3m intervals. A carport like this is not only easy to construct—it is also easy to remove if you want to replace it with a more substantial garage at a later date.*

Fig.4. *Brick piers have enormous strength and are another convenient form of support; but make sure the bricks match, or at least harmonize, with the house brickwork. Piers can also provide a basis for several different designs. For instance the spaces between the piers can be filled with screen blocks, or battening can be fixed vertically on the outside of each pier and boarding such as weatherboard fixed across them.*

Right. *If brick walls are alternated with sections of screen blocks, this will avoid a monotonous run of walling.*

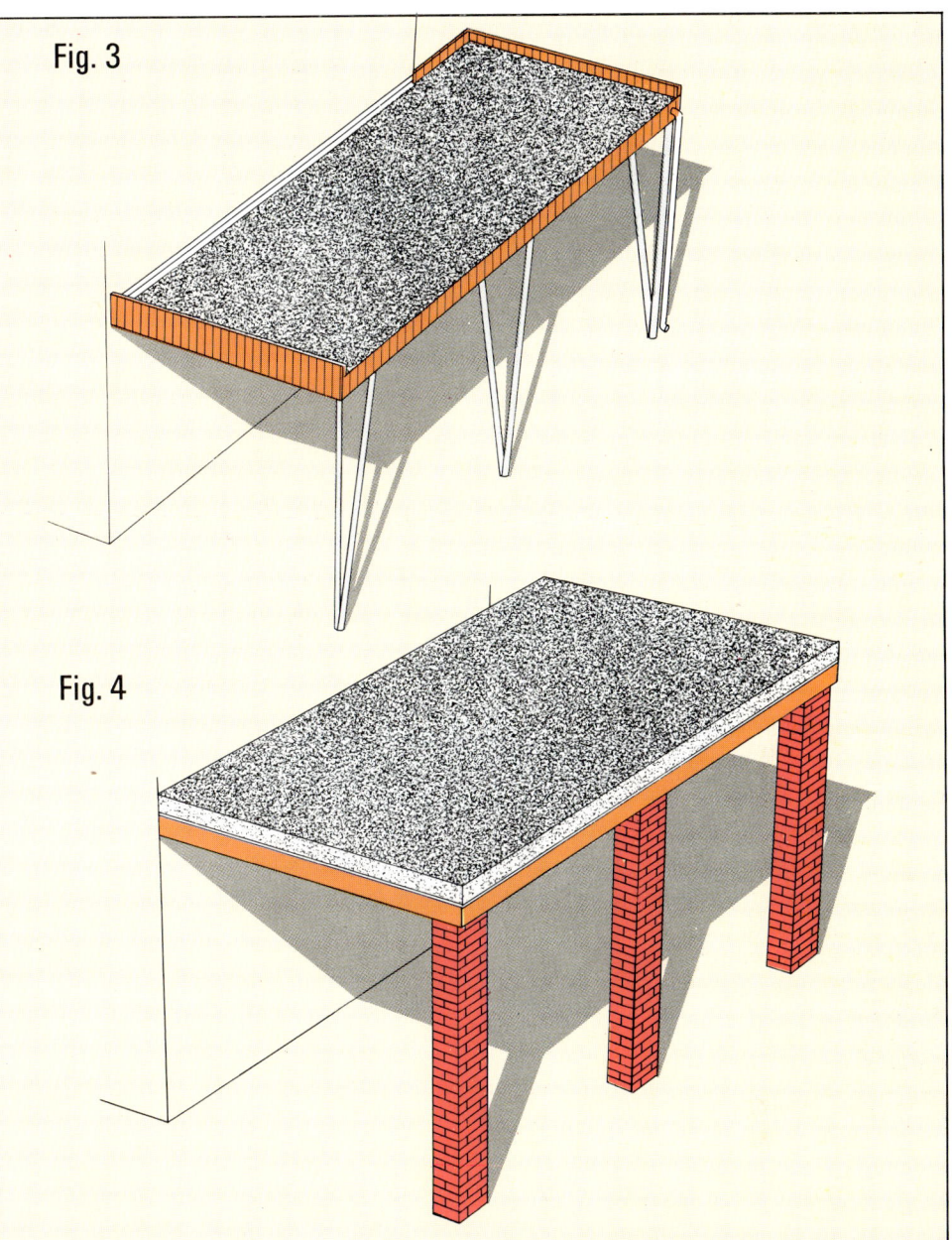

Fig. 3

Fig. 4

Above. This carport is an example of attractive simplicity. Garden walling has been used to support one side, and the other side is supported by a masonry pier of blocks of the type shown in Fig.9.

How to put up a carport: 2

Once you have decided whether a carport or a garage will suit you best, and have come down in favour of a carport, the next step is to sit down with pencil and paper and decide on the type that will best suit your house.

The right design is important at this stage. After all you don't want the carport to *look* as though it has been added almost as an afterthought. It should, ideally, look as though it has been designed and built as part of the house. Get the most artistic member of the family, or a friend, to draw a three-quarter view of your house, (i.e. seen from the corner) at about 45 degrees on the side where the carport is to go.

Then use a pencil to draw in the various carports shown here, one at a time. You should soon find the design that looks best with your house.

General construction details

Two types of carport are described here, one with metal or timber supports for the roof and the other with masonry supports, in this case brick piers or screen walling. But although the methods of support are different, the roof is virtually identical in each, the construction conforming the outline illustrated in Fig. 8 on page 24.

The roof can be either boarded over and covered with roofing felt, or covered with trans-lucent corrugated roofing plastic sheet. The second method is more popular because it is quicker to lay and allows in more light—particularly important if you are working on the car, or if the carport would otherwise blot out a window.

The roof joists butting against the house can be fixed in many ways, and three of the most popular—a wall plate, joist hangers and metal angle strip, are shown in Fig.1. The angle strip is not to be recommended in structures such as this, particularly if you are building a lightweight carport. The reason for this is that wind will gust into a carport and under the roof, causing a lifting effect. And as you can see in Fig.1, it is very difficult to secure joist ends to angle strip in such a way as to resist a lifting force.

Don't forget the drainage. You will have to provide some means of getting rid of rainwater. This means either running a trough or channel along the ground to an existing gulley trap, or making a soakaway. The former method entails less hard labour.

22

The dimensions of the structure should, ideally, be designed to accommodate at least a medium-sized car. It is no use having a space that will protect a tiny car, and then buying something much larger at a later date, and finding that it doesn't fit in. And don't forget the height. The internal height should be great enough to take a medium-sized car with a laden roof rack on top. This could easily be about 6ft or 1.8m high, so to give yourself sufficient working space the height from floor to rafters should be at least 7ft or 2m. The length of an average car, in Britain at least, is about 14ft or 4.3m, so you should aim for a carport at least 20ft or 6m in length. Some American cars are nearly 21ft (6.4m) long and will need a huge carport 26ft (8m) long.

The lightweight carport

Two types of roof support are described here, a strutted version, supported by mild steel rod or aluminium tubing, and one with vertical timbers. Both these types have an advantage over, say, masonry supports, in that they do not require extensive foundations because of their relatively light weight.

For a lightweight carport, the base requires a minimum of reconstruction. Foundation concrete will have to be laid at the base of the timbers or struts, but apart from this you can leave the base as it is unless it consists of sand or something else unsuitable for parking on. An existing concrete or asphalt surface is fine. If the base is soil, then a good layer (at least 1in. or 25mm thick) of gravel can be rolled or rammed in, but this process will have to be repeated from time to time as the car tyres scour grooves in the gravel and soil.

First (and this applies to any of the carports) mark out the outline of the carport on the ground and the walls of the house. This means drawing a line along the house wall to indicate the top level of the wall plate, or the bottom of the joist hangers, and further lines down the walls and round the base area.

Unless the base or foundation is already sufficiently strong, you will have to excavate foundation trenches in the area immediately under the struts or timbers. Excavate an area about 16in. or 400mm square, and 12in. or 300mm deep if you are using metal struts, or alternatively 9in. or 225mm deep if using timber supports.

If you already have a solid floor, this will mean chiselling out some of it ; this is best done with a cold chisel and 3lb or 1.5 kg club hammer.

When this has been done, fill the trench with a good stiff concrete mix. If you are using struts, leave the top two-thirds of the trench unfilled because the bases of the struts will have to be set into this foundation, and it will be filled at this later stage.

The *timber supports* for the structure shown in Fig.2 are of 4in. x 4in. or 100mm x 100mm solid timber. To erect them, cut the three vertical supports to their finished lengths, and then cut the top plate and the two end joists slightly oversize. Paint all the wooden parts with preservative, and soak the foot of each support in a bucket of preservative.

Cut, then fit, the wall plate or joist hangers on the house wall. Whichever you use, they should

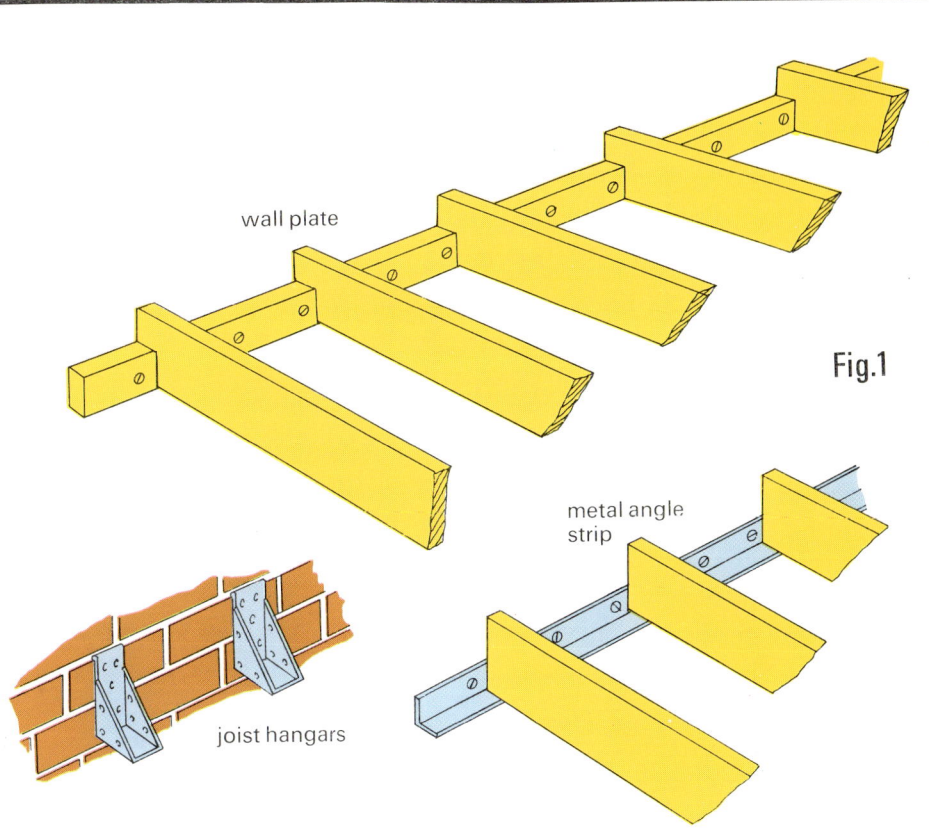

wall plate

metal angle strip

joist hangers

Fig.1. *Three methods of butting the roof joists against a house wall. Angle strip is difficult to secure and is not recommended.*

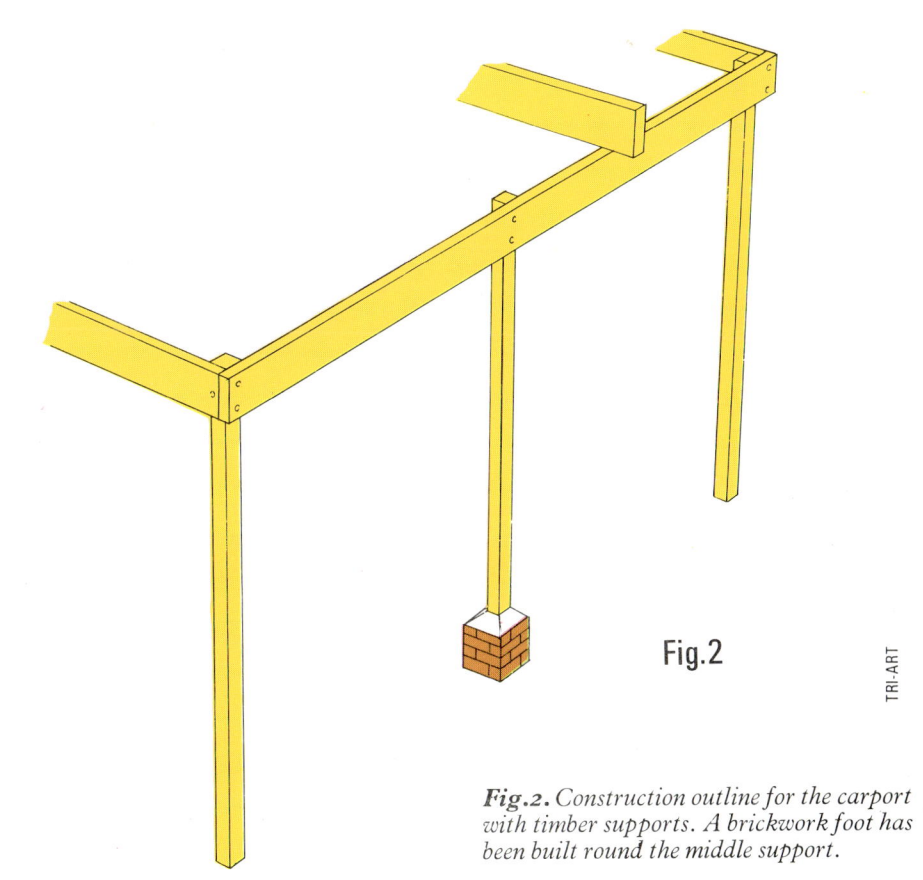

Fig.2

TRI-ART

Fig.2. *Construction outline for the carport with timber supports. A brickwork foot has been built round the middle support.*

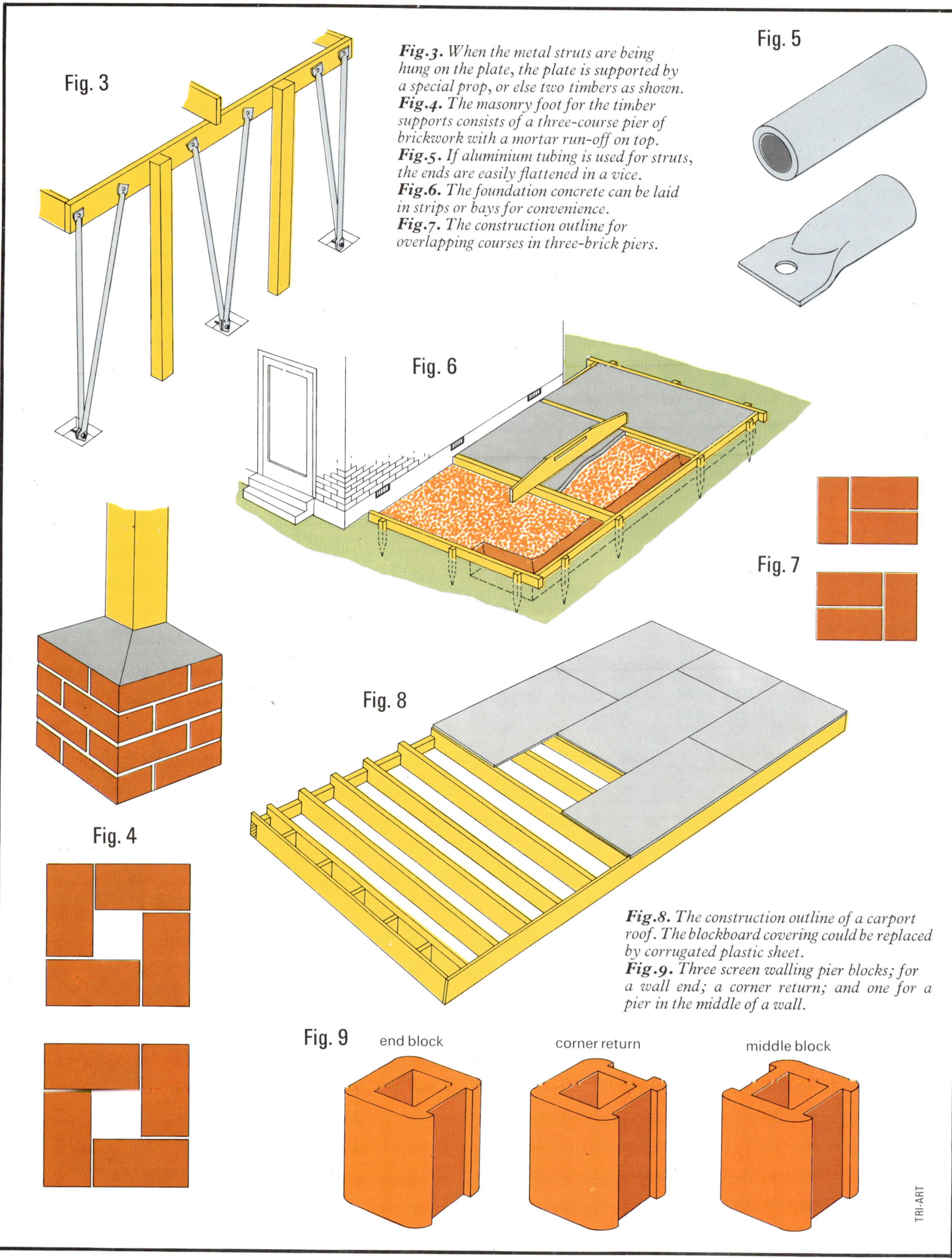

Fig. 3

Fig. 5

Fig.3. *When the metal struts are being hung on the plate, the plate is supported by a special prop, or else two timbers as shown.*
Fig.4. *The masonry foot for the timber supports consists of a three-course pier of brickwork with a mortar run-off on top.*
Fig.5. *If aluminium tubing is used for struts, the ends are easily flattened in a vice.*
Fig.6. *The foundation concrete can be laid in strips or bays for convenience.*
Fig.7. *The construction outline for overlapping courses in three-brick piers.*

Fig. 6

Fig. 7

Fig. 8

Fig. 4

Fig.8. *The construction outline of a carport roof. The blockboard covering could be replaced by corrugated plastic sheet.*
Fig.9. *Three screen walling pier blocks; for a wall end; a corner return; and one for a pier in the middle of a wall.*

Fig. 9   end block   corner return   middle block

TRI-ART

be fixed on with No. 10 screws and plastic plugs set in drilled holes.

Lay the three support timbers down on a flat surface—the base of the carport is ideal if it is flat and solid—and nail the joist plate across the tops. You will probably need assistance for the next stage.

Lift the frame upright where it will be housed, nailing bracing struts to hold it temporarily in place if necessary, square it up, then nail the two oversize joists in place, one to each end. Square it again, and it is ready for the brickwork base or foot to be built.

The foot is extremely simple to make; it is only a brickwork box built round the base of the timber, as shown in Fig.4. Build this up for three courses, filling in any inside space between the brickwork and timber with mortar. When this is complete, build a shoulder of mortar at the top, sloping downwards from the timber, so that rain will run off.

When the brickwork mortar has set thoroughly, you can fit the remaining joists in position and complete the rest of the roof.

Strut supports require a slightly different method of construction because they are actually set into the foundation concrete.

The struts can be of $\frac{1}{2}$in. or 35mm mild steel rod, flattened at each end and drilled to take bolts, or of 3in or 75mm aluminium support tube treated in the same way. Steel rod has one great disadvantage—it is hard to cut to length and flatten the ends and this will normally have to be done professionally, whereas aluminium tube can be ordered slightly overlength and cut and shaped on site with equipment no more complicated than a metal vice and a drill, as shown in Fig.5. For this reason the DIY fan will find the tube much more convenient.

It is almost impossible to set the struts in concrete so that they are properly lined up. So the top plate is suspended in its final place, and then the struts are bolted to the plate and dropped into the foundation recess. The lower ends of the struts are then concreted over, embedding them in the correct position.

The main problem is how to support the plate while you are fitting the struts. The best way is to nail the end pair of joists to the wall plate, then lift the other end of the joists and fix them to the house-wall plate with one temporary nail each, so that they pivot. Then you lift the assembly, and hold it in position with proprietary fittings such as Acrow Props. These devices, which are used by builders, are really giant versions of a car jack. In most places they can be hired, and if this is possible take advantage of it; you will need three. Failing this, you can fit two temporary timber supports as shown in Fig.3.

Nail the feet of the props to a length of timber to keep them steady while you draw the temporary nails, push the ends of the rafters into their correct position, and nail them home. When you have tested the roof for level, you can fit the struts. These should have their ends flattened and bolt holes pre-drilled in them.

Hold one of the end vertical struts in position against the plate, and drill a bolt hole through the plate. Push the bolt through, tightening the nut and securing the strut to the plate, and repeat the process with the next strut, which will be located 12in. or 300mm away from the

Above. The design of this carport, and the materials used, have been carefully selected and harmonize perfectly with the house.

previous strut on the plate, but which will touch it at the bottom, where both enter the same foundation recess.

The struts are flattened and drilled for bolts at each end (see Fig.5). At the bottom, each pair should be touching and bolted together, but if your measuring is slightly out don't worry, this is not essential. If the bolt holes do match, secure the struts with a bolt at least 4in. or 100mm long. The idea is to provide a cross-piece so that it will hold in the concrete. If they don't match, fit a 4in. bolt through each hole and place the ends as near as possible.

When you have finished this, the struts will be securely bolted to the top plate and hanging in the foundation recesses underneath, with sturdy bolts fitted through the bottom bolt holes. All that remains to be done is to fill the recesses with concrete—of the same mix as the rest of the the area—and leave this to set. After this, the props or temporary supports can be removed and the rest of the roof fitted.

The heavyweight carport

If you use masonry—bricks, screen walling or whatever—for your roof supports, then you will have to dig more extensive foundations because of the greater weight involved.

One possibility is a strip foundation running under the walls, or under and between piers. But it is much better to do the job thoroughly and lay a strip and raft foundation over the whole area, as shown in Fig.6. A strip foundation presents no great problem, but covering the whole area is quite a task. You can do it in one go, with some very careful planning, or you can do it a bit at a time in bays or panels, as shown in Fig.6. Coat the edge of each panel with a concrete bonding agent before you pour the next one.

Brick piers are a popular form of roof support.

If you use this method, build the piers up to the full height of the plates, inserting rag bolts in the top course. The top plate can then be secured to the rag bolts, and the joists and roof fitted.

These piers are of a simple three-brick construction, as shown in Fig.4. They must not be spaced wider apart than 10ft or 3m, but they can be built nearer if you prefer. For example, four piers along a 20ft or 6m carport can look quite attractive with some houses. Decide the number of piers that looks best by means of drawing, as described above.

Screen walling is a very attractive way of providing support for the carport roof. The main disadvantage with this material is that it does not have the strength of brickwork, and the piers—which are specially designed blocks, as shown in Fig.9—must be erected at intervals not exceeding 7ft or 2.1m. And for maximum strength, straight runs of walling are to be avoided. This is the reason for the short return wall of the version in the previous chapter.

Rag bolts for walls are fitted to the top pier block. This is done by placing the block on a flat surface and filling the bottom three-quarters of the hollow in the middle with crumpled newspapers. The remaining third is filled with a concrete or mortar mix in which the rag bolts are suspended during setting, to provide a roof rim or plates.

Variations

There are innumerable variations of the four basic carports shown here. For example, brick piers could be used with the screen walling for extra strength. Or a brick plinth could be built under the screen wall, as shown in the first part of this project. Or if you are using timber supports, you could fit four or five timbers, screw cross braces across or nogging in between them, and board the side over. This arrangement would offer better protection to the car, while avoiding the condensation problem of a garage, which can cause premature rust.

The pot-planter's paradise

A lean-to greenhouse or conservatory is an asset to any home; and it has certain advantages over a house extension in that it requires less work to build, and isn't nearly as expensive.

It will enable you to sit 'outside' and relax even when a sharp wind is blowing; and to grow plants that would not normally survive in your garden.

General construction details

This conservatory consists of four frames—door gable end, plain gable end, side section and roof—which can be assembled in either of two ways. The four frames can be made up separately, then bolted together and screwed to the wall. Or the wall timbers or studs can be screwed to the wall first, and the frame-work constructed in situ.

The former, which is the pre-fabricated method, depends on the wall of the receiving structure being absolutely vertical. If the house wall 'leans' more than, say, half an inch in either direction, the prefabricated end frames will not locate flush against the wall, and the gap will have to be filled either with mortar or suitably shaped timber (see below).

Although a brick base or plinth wall about two or three courses high can be built for this design, matching bricks to existing house brickwork is very difficult and a deep foundation will be required. But a complete wooden structure, as shown, is both easier and quicker to build.

The greenhouse can be made from ordinary soft wood, in which case it should be treated with a horticultural grade of preservative containing copper napthenate such as Cuprinol. Special attention should be paid to joints and those parts of the building which are in contact with the ground. These should be soaked for a few hours in a container of the solution. Long timbers such as bottom plates can be laid on a long sheet of polythene gathered along the corners and edges to form a receptacle or bag into which preservative is poured.

Although it costs about 50% more, cedar wood is a timber which requires little treatment or maintenance because it has a natural oil which resists decay and it is ideal for outdoor use.

Glazing bar sizes and designs vary from supplier to supplier, but the type suggested here is generally available. Another important point to

An example of the conservatory described here. This one has been extended outwards, adding one third to the floor area.

DON KIDMAN

note is the small tolerance for glazing. About $\frac{1}{8}$in. (3mm) has been allowed in the width between all glazing bars to facilitate easy insertion of the glass.

Throughout the design two main glass widths —18in. and 24in. (460mm and 610mm)—are used. The window and roof glass, it must be noted, is installed in 'modules' as nearly square as possible. This means in effect that the glass is panelled. For instance, on the roof each run of glass between timbers consists of three panes of overlapping glass. A great deal of experience is needed to install large panes of glass without breaking them, so the method described here is advised.

Consult your glass supplier regarding the necessary thickness required for the glass as the requirements for minimum thicknesses may vary, depending on the local authorities.

It is best to order the glass cut to size unless you are experienced in cutting it yourself. In any case, this job is best left until the frame has been completed, so that any deviations in dimensions can be taken into account.

From the aspect of safety, you should consider the possibilities of using some of the plastic sheeting on the market as panes for the roof. This would be more expensive, but it does eliminate the danger of falling glass should a roof pane accidentally shatter.

The design

This structure has been designed as simply as possible, so that construction can be completed with a minimum of time and effort. The generous eaves height of 5ft (1.52m) and a ridge height of 7ft (2.13m) ensures adequate headroom, especially round the edges at bench or staging level where plants are sited. And the width of 7ft 8in. (2.33m) allows considerable freedom of movement.

The measurements can be adapted according to your requirements, especially the length. If the design is extended in this way, some extra reinforcing will be necessary mid-way along the roof and side. A glazing bar can be replaced by a 2in. x 3in. (50mm x 76mm) timber and a cross bar at the side would add rigidity and strength. A similar stout piece of timber should be inserted mid-way along the side section.

Some form of sealing is required at the surfaces of all butting edges (the outside edges of the two end frames and the side frame, and the back of the roof frame where it butts against the wall). In the past this has been done with a mastic compound, but now there are many proprietory sealing preparations on the market that do a better job. Your local dealer will tell you what is available.

Timber required for door gable end section

Part	No. required	Length	Size
Rear corner stud	1	7ft	2in. x 2in.
Front corner stud	1	5ft	2in. x 2in.
Top plate	1	8ft $\frac{3}{4}$in.	2in. x 2in.
Mid-rail	1	5ft 3in.	2in. x 2in·
Bottom plate	1	7ft 8$\frac{5}{8}$in.	2in. x 2in.
Centre stud	1	6ft 6in.	2in. x 2in.
Glazing bars	1	3ft 1$\frac{1}{2}$in.	2in. x 2in.
	1	3ft 6in.	2in. x 2in.
Door centre bar (for glazing purposes but *not* a moulded bar)	1	2ft 6in.	2in. x 2in.
Door posts	2	6ft	3in. x 2in.
Door mid-rail	1	2ft 6in.	2in. x 2in.
Door top-rail	1	2ft 6in.	2in. x 2in.
Door bottom rail	1	2ft 6in.	2in. x 2in.
Rail above door	1	2ft 6in.	2in. x 2in.
Base boarding	1	2ft 3in.	4in. x $\frac{3}{4}$in.
" "	11	2ft 3in.	6in. x $\frac{3}{4}$in.
Base door boarding	5	2ft 8in.	6in. x $\frac{3}{4}$in.
Door battens	2	4ft	1in. x 1in.
" "	2	3ft	1in. x 1in.
Battens	2	5ft 3in.	1in. x 1in.
Glazing beading	—	18ft	$\frac{1}{2}$in. x $\frac{1}{2}$in.

Note: All sizes pertain to timber which has not been planed. When planed there is a reduction in thickness and width of about $\frac{1}{8}$in. for Deal, and $\frac{3}{16}$in. for Cedar. Boarding covers $\frac{1}{2}$in. less because of the rebates.

All joints are secured with rustproof screws (not nails), and a woodworking adhesive.

Preliminary planning

The placing of the structure is the first consideration, and ideally, though not necessarily, this should be in the warmest and sunniest place—eg against a south-facing wall.

You may wish to site the structure over french windows to give easier access to the conservatory and extend the lounge in summer. If your french windows face north, there is no reason why you should drop the idea. The area within will still be warmer than usual in the winter, and provide a cool place, out of the wind, in the summer. And provided you only grow shade loving plants you will still have a good floral display.

To obtain the maximum value from your conservatory, you must install lighting and heating. For the heating, something like an oil heater could be placed in one corner. If you have central heating it might be easy to have an additional radiator fitted in the structure. Alternatively, you could fit, or have fitted, a power point for an electric heater.

Planning permission

In most countries planning permission will have to be obtained for the erection of this structure, and an application must be made to the appropriate authority. Under no circumstances must work be commenced before permission has been granted. A site plan and details of the structure will have to accompany your application. A copy of the illustrations shown here should suffice for the details, although you will have to draw your own plan.

Local authorities, especially in Britain, are particularly concerned about the fire risk and the close proximity of such a structure to your neighbour's property.

Foundations

The base of the conservatory must be raised above the ground level, to keep it clear of water running along the ground when it rains.

If you are building on soil, then you will have to dig a foundation to provide a base, the top of which should be at least 1in. (25mm) above ground level. This is to ensure that rain water runs off and does not rot the woodwork.

It may be that there will be an existing foundation of sorts, in the form of a driveway, path or patio. Provided that this consists of paving slabs or concrete laid over a hardcore base, it will be adequate, although the level will still have to be raised to the proper height.

One way of doing this is to fit a formwork of 1in. x 1in. or 25mm x 25mm battening round the base and fill it with concrete. If you use this method, you must ensure that the new concrete bonds well to the existing surface by using one of the cement bonding agents such as Uni Bond. The agent is diluted with water, and this solution is spread over the surface to be concreted. Then more agent is added to the water that is worked into the concrete mix. The bond between surfaces is surprisingly strong, and by using this method it is possible to lay very thin cement screeds over old concrete without the danger of it flaking off.

An alternative is to 'build' the base by laying paving slabs or a layer of bricks—suitably mortared in between of course—on the existing surface.

Whichever method you choose, the finished surface must be painted with a proprietary sealing compound such as Aquaseal to damp proof it.

The base must be absolutely level when finished. It makes no difference whether the ground or patio outside slopes in one direction or another, you *must* lay a level stage. Otherwise the wooden frames will be at staggered heights when you come to assemble them and they will not fit.

The receiving wall

The wall to which the conservatory is attached should, ideally, be absolutely vertical. Unfortunately, few walls are. If the wall is less than half an inch out of plumb, the gap can be filled with a bricklaying mortar. But if it is more than half an inch, or you don't want a wedge-shaped mortar gap, then you will have to shape three lengths of 2in. x 2in. or 50mm x 50mm timber (for both ends and the roof) so that they form a vertical surface to which the conservatory frame will be attached.

One method of doing this is very simple. A piece of 2in. x 2in. (50mm x 50mm) timber is placed vertically against the wall so that it is touching the wall at one end. A block of wood is placed between the timber and the wall where the space is at the opposite end. Use a plumb line or builder's 1yd or 1m spirit level to ensure that the timber is absolutely vertical. Now measure the gap between the edge of the timber nearest the wall and the wall itself at regular intervals and lightly mark the timber at these points. Lay the timber on the ground and mark off each measurement along the timber. Draw a line between the ends of these with a straight length of timber, and cut the timber along this line. When the cut-away portion that has the markings is turned around, it should fit the contours or incline of the wall perfectly. Repeat this procedure with the remaining two timbers.

When all three timbers have been cut to shape, they are drilled to take size 10 screws at each end and at approximately 18in. (460mm) intervals. Place one timber against the wall, ensure that it is vertical, and mark the wall through the screw holes. Drill screw holes in the wall at the locations marked, insert plugs to take the screws, run a thick layer of sealing mastic or compound along the wall and the timber where the surfaces, will meet, and screw the timber firmly to the wall. Repeat with the remaining timbers.

You will now have a timber frame firmly secured to the wall onto which the conservatory will be anchored.

Door gable end

If you have a level area, the door gable frame can be made on the ground. When it is finished it can be used as a template for the plain gable end. If the ground is not sufficiently flat, each end and side frame can be built in situ, providing you have a large enough step ladder and plenty of bracing timbers to hold the frame upright until it has been bolted to its adjacent frame.

If you have to use the latter method, first cut the joints for both ends of the wall stud and the bottom plate (Fig.1, B and D). Drill five holes—one of them at each end, about 2$\frac{1}{2}$in. (64mm) inwards, and the rest spaced equally—down the middle of B, to take the wall screws. Hang a plumb line down the wall where B will be located, and assuming that the wall is in plumb within a half inch, mark each end so that the

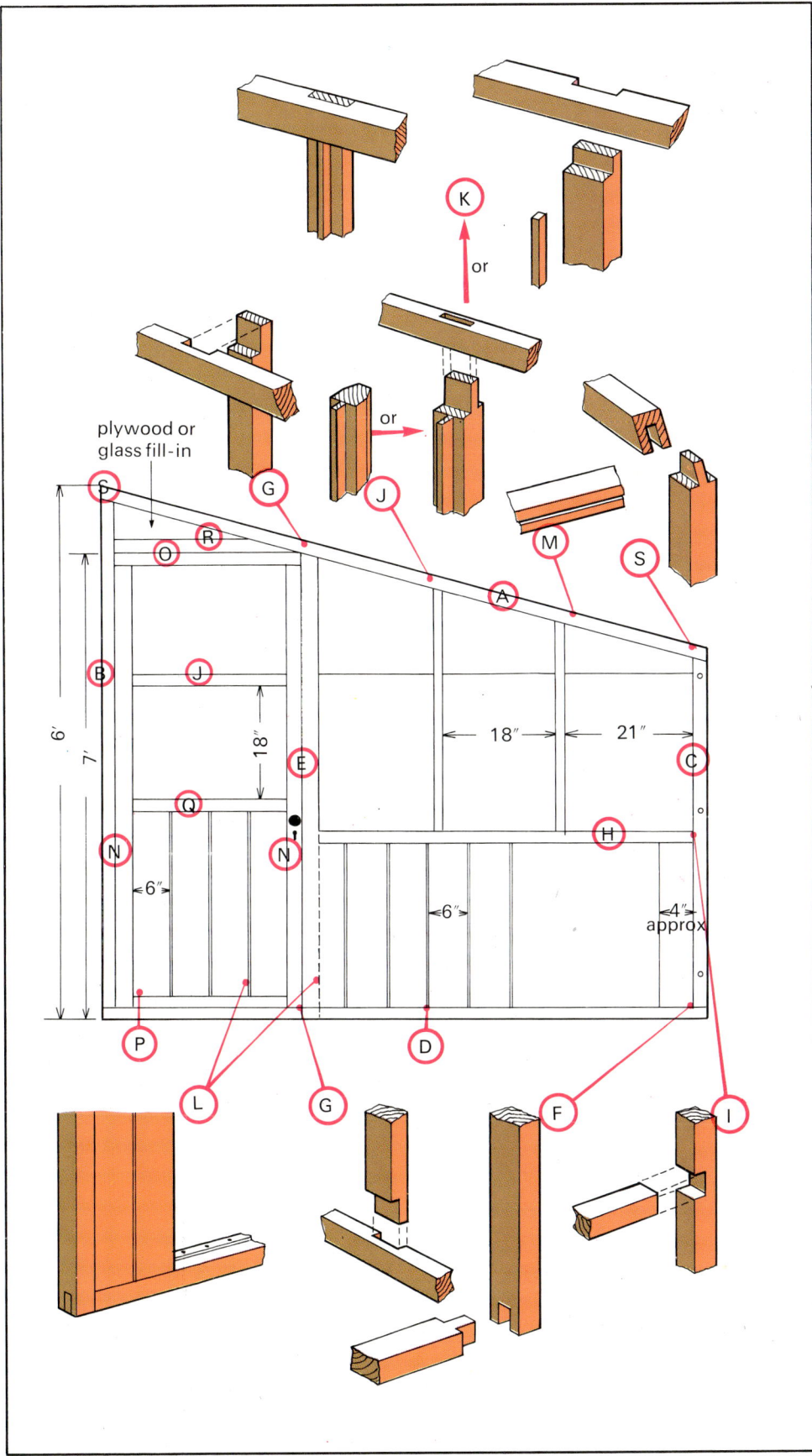

plywood or
glass fill-in

Fig.1 *Construction outline of the door gable end. Inset J shows two types of ready-made glazing bars, and K shows how to make one up yourself. Although the boarding is a 6in. or 150mm width, one of the end boards will probably have to be trimmed vertically by an inch or two to fit into the end of the partition.*

The middle rail H is cut and joined to the corner stud C and centre rail E by the joint shown in I. The two glazing bars are carefully positioned and checked for spacing and joints are cut out to meet up with the top plate A. Joints for these bars are shown in J.

If a very simple glazing bar system is required (which will reduce complex cutting of moulded timber such as prefabricated glazing bars), then home-made bars can be provided by a $\frac{1}{2}$in. (13mm) square strip of batten nailed or screwed to the centre as shown in K. This system could be used for all the glazing bars in this design.

The timber boarding for the base is fastened to two 1in. x 1in. (25mm x 25mm) battens which are nailed to the middle rail H and the bottom plate D. Details are shown in L. It may be necessary to cut the end piece of boarding down its length in order to fit it in.

Two $\frac{1}{4}$in. (6mm) bolt holes are drilled through the top and lower parts of the post, C, for the threaded bolts which will join this frame to the side frame later on if you are making prefabricated sections. Alternatively, drill holes for size 10 screws at 1ft (305mm) intervals if you are building in situ and will screw the structure together.

Rebates for the glass are made in timbers A, C, E and H by nailing in lengths of $\frac{1}{2}$in. x $\frac{1}{2}$in. (13mm x 13mm) batten. These battens will not be necessary in the top plate A, if a glazing groove is taken out as shown in the drawing M. The groove can be made with a rough plane if you possess this useful instrument, or with an electric drill fitted with one of the several attachments on the market designed to cut grooves. A depth of $\frac{1}{4}$in. (6mm) is all that is necessary. The groove is filled with putty before the glass is pushed into it, and any surplus putty squeezed out is wiped off.

The door is best left until the whole structure is up. But as it is part of the door gable end, the construction is described here.

This is quite a substantial section and is made up of two posts N, which are joined together by the top rail O and bottom rail P. Joints are as in illustration S but without the angled cuts. The middle rail Q is slotted into the two posts as in I. The glazing bar is positioned and slotted in as in K. This bar is *not* a moulded glazing bar but is made up as in K, 1in. x 1in. (25mm x 25mm) battens are nailed round the inside of timbers N, P and Q, and the boarding for the bottom door panel is nailed to these battens.

Three heavy duty hinges are used to hang the door, which closes on to an internal 'stop' made from a 2$\frac{1}{2}$in. x $\frac{1}{2}$in. (64mm x 13mm) batten screwed to the *inside* of post E

Finally, add $\frac{1}{2}$in. x $\frac{1}{2}$in. (13mm x 13mm) battening around the inside of section R to form a rebate, and fill in with plywood, glass, or sheet plastic cut to shape.

post, when fixed, will also be plumb. Stand the post against the wall, and with a large nail mark the wall through the screw holes. Lay the post down and drill the holes in the wall, then insert the plugs or fittings to take the screws. Stand the post up against the wall again, and screw in

position.

Start the construction with the main framing, using the plan in Fig.1. This comprises the top plate A, rear corner stud C, bottom plate D and the centre rail E. The joints for these are shown in illustrations S, F and G.

HARRY SMITH

Opposite page. *A conservatory will allow you to grow an exotic selection of plants that would not survive in your garden.*
Top left. *Optunna lindheimeri 'Louisianna'. There are hundreds of species of cactus, in a variety of shapes, and, although better known for their spikes, they often produce exotic flowers each year.*
Top right. *Passiflora caerulea, better known as the passion flower. The egg-shaped fruits are often produced in a*

greenhouse, particularly after a hot summer. The fruit is fleshy and inedible. In southern Britain the plant can be moved outside in summer.
Bottom. *Aphelandra brockfeld. This is a very exotic evergreen from the tropics, and it reaches a height of 3 ft. The flowers possess a sculptured quality, and, when they stop blooming, the leaves make a strikingly decorative feature on their own. This alone makes them well worth growing.*

Above. *The extra space created by a conservatory will enable you to carry out projects that might otherwise be impossible. And if the addition proves successful, it is relatively easy to extend it and almost double the area, creating still more space for living in or growing plants—or both. This delightful scene shows what can be achieved in a conservatory. You can sit 'outside' surrounded by plants that might be impossible to grow in your garden.*

Having completed the gable door end (without, as yet, inserting the glass for the windows and the door) the next step is to build the opposite side—the plain gable end.

Construction

If you are building the structure in pre-fabricated frames or sections, the most accurate method would be to leave the frame you have just made on the ground, and make the second section, which must be identical in outline, over the first.

If on the other hand you are building the structure in situ, you must still ensure that the frame for this end is identical to the opposite end. This is relatively simple provided the floor is absolutely level and the support wall is in plumb.

First cut the top and bottom plates and end studs to the same lengths as their opposites. For instance the bottom plate for the door gable end must be identical in length with the bottom plate of the plain gable end. Then cut the joints for these timbers. You can now trial assemble the outline framework immediately next to the door gable end, using it as a template. When you are certain that the outlines of the frames are identical, you can dismantle the framework and continue construction.

All the joints are the same as for the door gable end, and are shown in part 1 of this Project. The construction outline is shown in Fig.3. The main difference is that this section does not have a door. This means that the middle rail is longer and, consequently, liable to sag a fraction at the middle before the boarding is inserted. To prevent this, once the middle rail has been housed, lightly nail one piece of board, cut to the correct length, at a point roughly in the middle of the base section. This is removed and repositioned when the boarding is finally fitted.

Side section

Illustrated details of construction for the side frame are shown in Fig.2.

Cut the four timbers comprising the top and bottom plates and the end studs of the side section. Do this by direct marking, laying the plates along between the two end sections, so that the length will be absolutely accurate. Then mark and cut all recesses for the joints in these timbers. It is now possible to trial assemble the rectangular outline frame to ensure an accurate fit before completing the frame.

The above procedure must be followed whether you are using the prefabricated method or not, but whereas the prefabricated frame will be continued on the ground, building the structure on site from here on will be slightly different.

Erect the outline of the side frame between the ends, glue and screw the joints, then drill No. 10 screw holes through the inside of the studs at approximately 18in. or 460mm intervals, drill countersunk recesses, then insert 3in. or 75mm wood screws and fix each stud firmly to the inside edges of the studs or posts of the two end frames.

Nail the battening for the boarding along the underside of the middle rail. House the rail into the recesses in each stud and immediately cut and fit the intermediate stud, shown by a dotted line in Fig.2, between the bottom plate and the middle rail. Next cut and fit the four 2ft 6in. (760mm) glazing bars in the top half between the middle rail and top plate. This will create five spaces or partitions, the end ones containing the opening windows. When these have been fitted, nail the battening for the boards along the bottom plate. The next job is to nail the boards into position along the bottom half of the frame as shown in Fig.2. Mark them for length, by 'direct measuring'—that is, holding a length against the *outside* while you mark from the *inside*—and use galvanized or other rustless nails to fix them on.

The construction of the opening windows is shown in Fig.2B, but it is not necessary to make them at this stage. The corner joints are simply lapped at the corners, as shown, and glazing battening for the glass is nailed round the inside. In Fig.2C, a batten is shown fitted to the 2in. x 2in. (50mm x 50mm) battening of the main frame, behind the window itself, to act as a window-stop. This battening is carried right round the inside of each window partition, and also acts as a seal against wind and rain.

The roof section

This is designed to overlap the front section by approximately 1½in. or 37mm in order to allow 3in. or 75mm guttering to be fixed underneath: if you cannot buy 3in. guttering make the overhang proportionately larger.

The frame consists mainly of 2in. x 2in. (50mm x 50mm) timbers, as shown in Fig.1, except for the front rail, Fig.1C, which, when joined to the ends of the glazing bars as in H and F, allows rainwater to run off freely. The opposite ends of the glazing bars and side rails are joined to the wall rails as shown in G.

The ventilator rests on top of the roof frame, the side rails along the outside glazing bars and the top and bottom rails along two ventilator cross rails which are housed across the glazing bars at the bottom and top. The top ventilator cross rail is also screwed to the top or wall rail of the main frame.

The top edges of the wall rail should, if possible, be angled slightly as shown in Fig.1G, but this is not essential because the rail will be covered by roofing felt. However the top ventilator cross rail (the one screwed to the wall rail) must be angled, as shown in G, to the slope of the glazing bars. To ensure an accurate fit it is best to house the ventilator cross rail first, then plane the protruding corner down level with the glazing bars.

The ventilator is hinged at the top cross rail with three 2in. or 50mm brass flap hinges; ordinary hinges will rust too easily at this point. The ventilator frame is sealed with a strip of foam neoprene, 1in. or 25mm wide, running round the bottom of the frame and glued to the frame with an impact adhesive such as Evostik Impact. Foam neoprene can be obtained from most water-sports shops as it is the material used for skin-divers' wet suits. Avoid natural rubber, which perishes and becomes sticky. If you can't get foam neoprene, your supplier will be able to suggest some of the many proprietary sealing strips that are on the market.

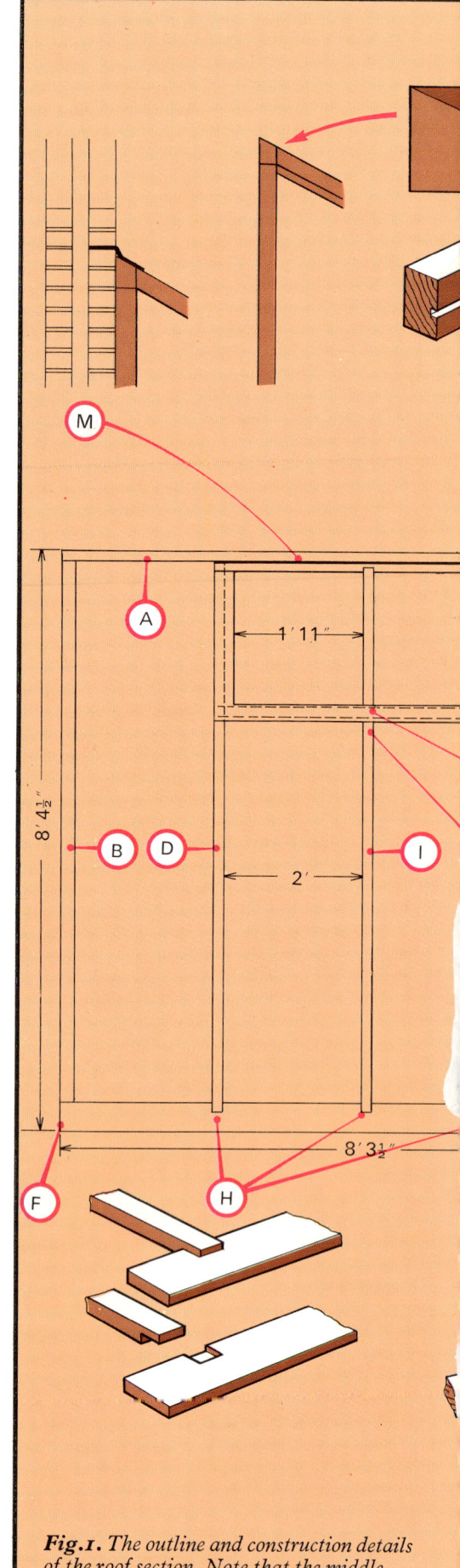

Fig.1. The outline and construction details of the roof section. Note that the middle member runs from top to bottom under the

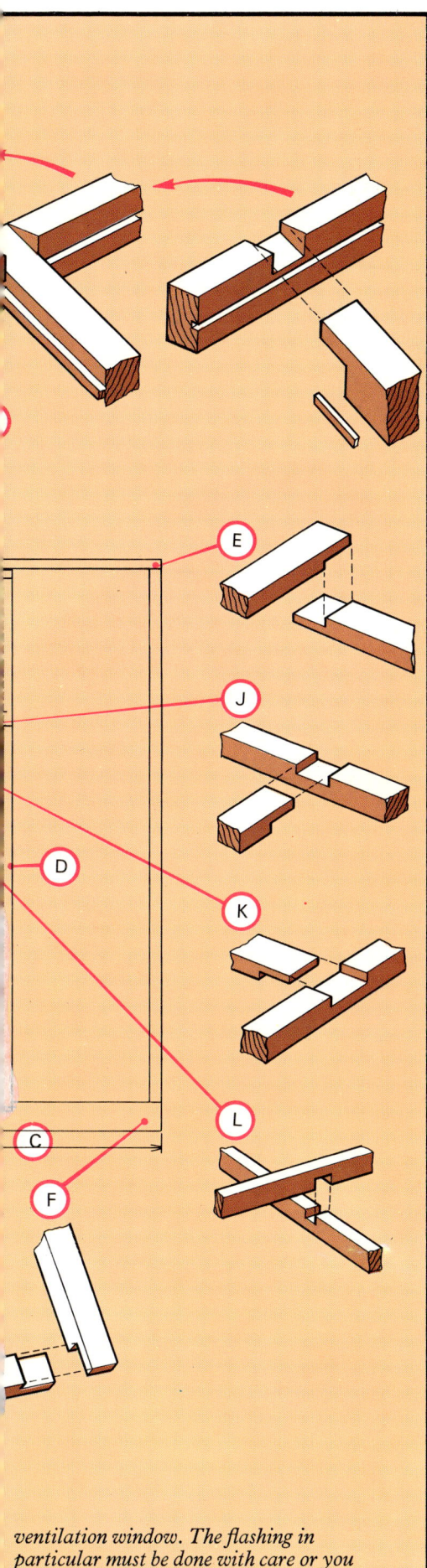

Timber for plain gable end section

Part	No. Required	Length	Size
Rear corner stud	1	7ft	2in. x 2in.
Front corner stud	1	5ft	2in. x 2in.
Top plate	1	8ft $\frac{3}{4}$in.	2in. x 2in.
Mid-rail	1	7ft 8$\frac{5}{8}$in.	2in. x 2in.
Bottom plate	1	7ft 8$\frac{5}{8}$in.	2in. x 2in.
Glazing bars	1	4ft 3in.	2in. x 2in.
	1	4ft	2in. x 2in.
	1	3ft 6in.	2in. x 2in.
	1	3ft	2in. x 2in.
Battens for boarding	2	7ft 8$\frac{5}{8}$in.	2in. x 1in.
Glazing beading	—	24ft	$\frac{1}{2}$in. x $\frac{1}{2}$in.
Tongued-and-grooved boarding	16	2ft 3in.	6in. x $\frac{3}{4}$in.

Timber for roof section

Part	No. required	Length	Size
Side rails	2	8ft 4$\frac{1}{2}$in.	2in. x 2in.
Top rail	1	8ft 8$\frac{1}{2}$in.	2in. x 2in.
Bottom rail	1	8ft 8$\frac{1}{2}$in.	4in. x 1$\frac{1}{2}$in.
Glazing bars	3	8ft 4$\frac{1}{2}$in.	2in. x 2in.
Ventilator cross rails	2	4ft 4in.	2in. x 2in.
Ventilator top rail	1	4ft 4in.	2ft. x 1$\frac{1}{2}$in.
Ventilator bottom rail	1	4ft 4in.	3in. x 1$\frac{1}{2}$in.
Ventilator side and middle rail	3	2ft 5in.	2in. x 1$\frac{1}{2}$in.
Glazing beading	—	72ft	$\frac{1}{2}$in. x $\frac{1}{2}$in.

Timber for side section

Part	No. required	Length	Size
End studs	2	5ft	2in. x 2in.
Top plate	1	8ft 3$\frac{1}{2}$in.	2in. x 2in.
Bottom plate	1	8ft 3$\frac{1}{2}$in.	2in. x 2in.
Middle rail	1	8ft 3$\frac{1}{2}$in.	2in. x 2in.
Intermediate stud	1	2ft 6in.	2$\frac{1}{2}$in. x 1$\frac{1}{4}$in.
Glazing bars	4	2ft 6in.	2in. x 2in.
Glazing beading for windows	—	18ft	$\frac{1}{2}$in. x $\frac{1}{2}$in.
Tongued-and-grooved boarding	16	2ft 3in.	6in. x $\frac{3}{4}$in.
Battens for boarding	2	8ft 3$\frac{1}{2}$in.	1in. x 1in.
Windows, framing	4	2ft 6in.	2in. x 1in.
	4	1ft 7in.	2in. x 1in.

ventilation window. The flashing in particular must be done with care or you will have a waterfall when it is raining.

TRI-ART

If you are an experienced handyman, you could probably prefabricate the roof section, but in view of the fact that this section has to be put together more precisely than the lower three frames, and that it would require several people to ease it on to the roof, it is better to construct it on the already assembled frames. This means that you can adopt direct measuring and require no assistance other than that of a suitable stepladder.

First cut and fit the wall rail, drilling holes for No. 10 screws at 18in. or 460mm intervals. Using these holes as a guide, mark the wall, drill holes along the marks and insert wall plugs. Screw the rail firmly to the wall.

Next cut and fit the side rails. Holes will also have to be drilled in these, at 2ft or 610mm intervals, so that the side rails can be screwed to the top plates. This is done as soon as you have cut them to fit.

Cut and fit the bottom rail, screwing it firmly to the top plate of the side frame.

The glazing bars and ventilator cross rails are now simply dropped into place, glued and screwed.

The ventilator does not need to be made at this stage, but you might like to consider it while you have the stepladder out. As shown in Figs.1K and E, the construction requires simple half lap joints.

Glazing

The glazing beading, which forms a rebate to hold the glass, is now nailed in position along all surfaces which will take window glass. Note that the beading, in the case of the ventilator, needs to be located at a depth which will bring the upper surface of the glass flush with the wood frame when bedded in putty. This will allow rain water to run off easily. The glazing beading round the door and opening windows must be at *twice* the depth of the thickness of the glass to take into account a shoulder of putty. The rest of the beading must be located at a depth *three* times the thickness of a pane of glass because the panes will be overlapped at intervals as described in part 1, and you will still need space for the putty shoulder.

Overlapping glass panes are a common feature of D-I-Y greenhouses because of the difficulties of handling large sheets of glass. The method of fitting the panes is quite simple. A bed of putty is pressed in along the glazing beading shelf, and the bottom pane of glass is pressed into the putty. Now hold the next higher pane where it will be fixed, and mark the sides of the structure where the bottom of the pane will be located. Put the pane aside for the time being and drive a 1in. or 25mm nail into each side of the woodwork immediately next to the lower pane, level with the marks, until just about

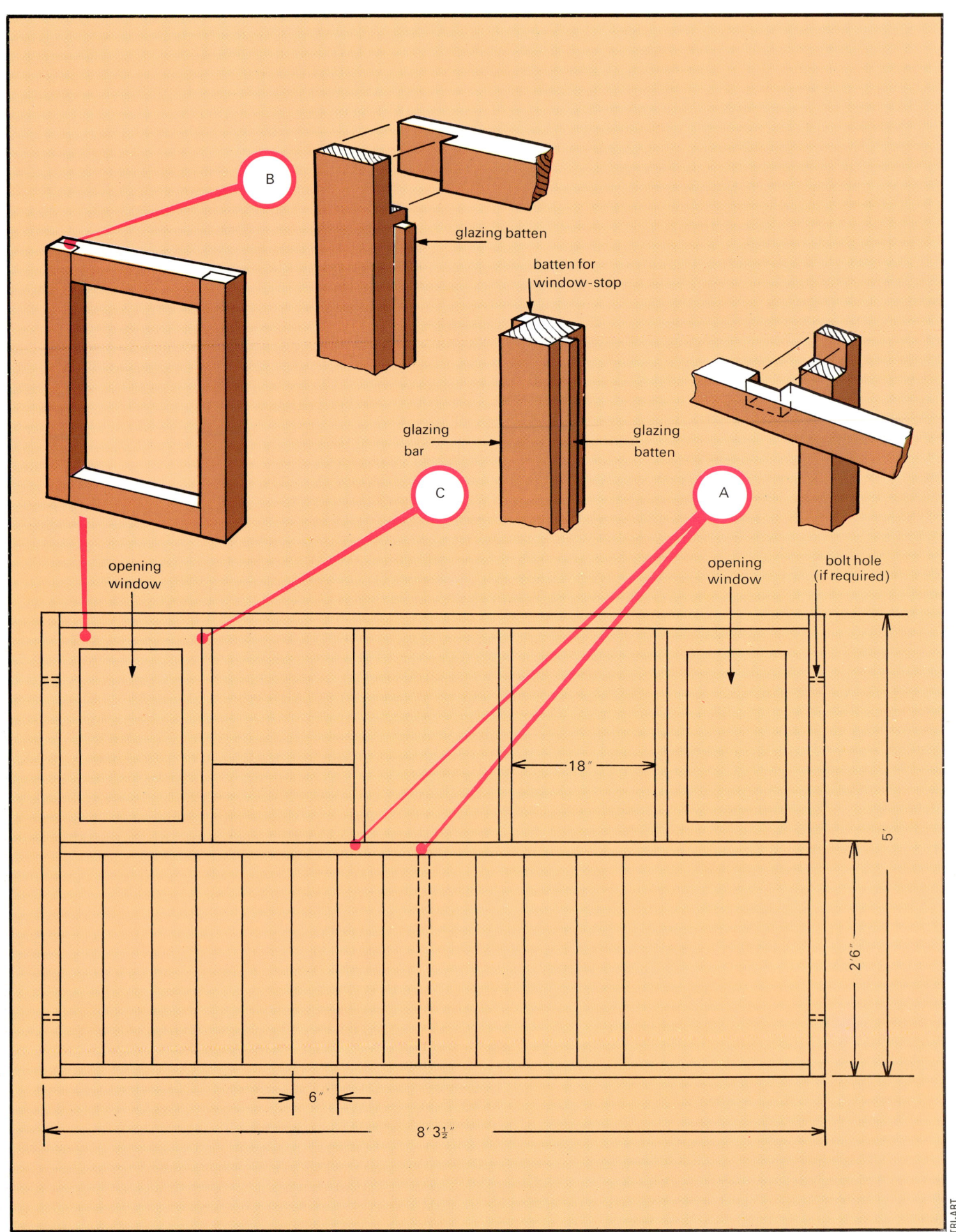

B

glazing batten

batten for
window-stop

glazing
bar

glazing
batten

C

A

opening
window

opening
window

bolt hole
(if required)

18″

5′

2′6″

6″

8′3½″

TRI-ART

¼in. or 6mm of the head is still protruding. You now have two metal 'stops' on which the next pane can rest while it is puttied in position. The process is repeated for successive panes. There are several types of proprietary clips that are made for joining overlapping glass sheets, but they all suffer from the same disadvantage—the final pane sometimes has to be cut to fit. The nail method, on the other hand, allows you as little or as much overlap as you need.

Glazing is not really that difficult, but if you have not tried it before, experiment on some odd pieces of wood and glass. You will soon be able to master the glazing techniques required for this project.

Inserting the flashing

Flashing is the name for a waterproof strip of material that is inserted into the mortar course of a wall, providing a run-off for rainwater. This is shown in Fig.1M.

Flashing can consist of roofing felt, zinc, lead or copper. Although roofing felt is the cheapest, it is also the most perishable, and as renewing the flashing also entails removing a strip of mortar course at least 1in. or 2.5mm deep, it is a worthwhile economy, both in terms of money and labour, to fit one of the metal strips.

With a club hammer and cold chisel, rake out the mortar course immediately above the conservatory to a depth of 1in. or 25mm. Now ease in a 4in. or 100mm wide strip of flashing, along the length of the recess, wedging it at intervals, if necessary, with small pieces of stone or brick to hold it in place.

Make up a mix of bricklaying mortar, and trowel this into the course to refill the recess. Press the mortar in, then run the trowel along to remove any surplus cement. Leave it for at least two days to set.

Fig.3 (below). *The plain gable end. This must be identical in outline to the opposite end. Although it has no door, one could be fitted if required by using the construction diagram for the door gable end as described previously and shown on page 685.*

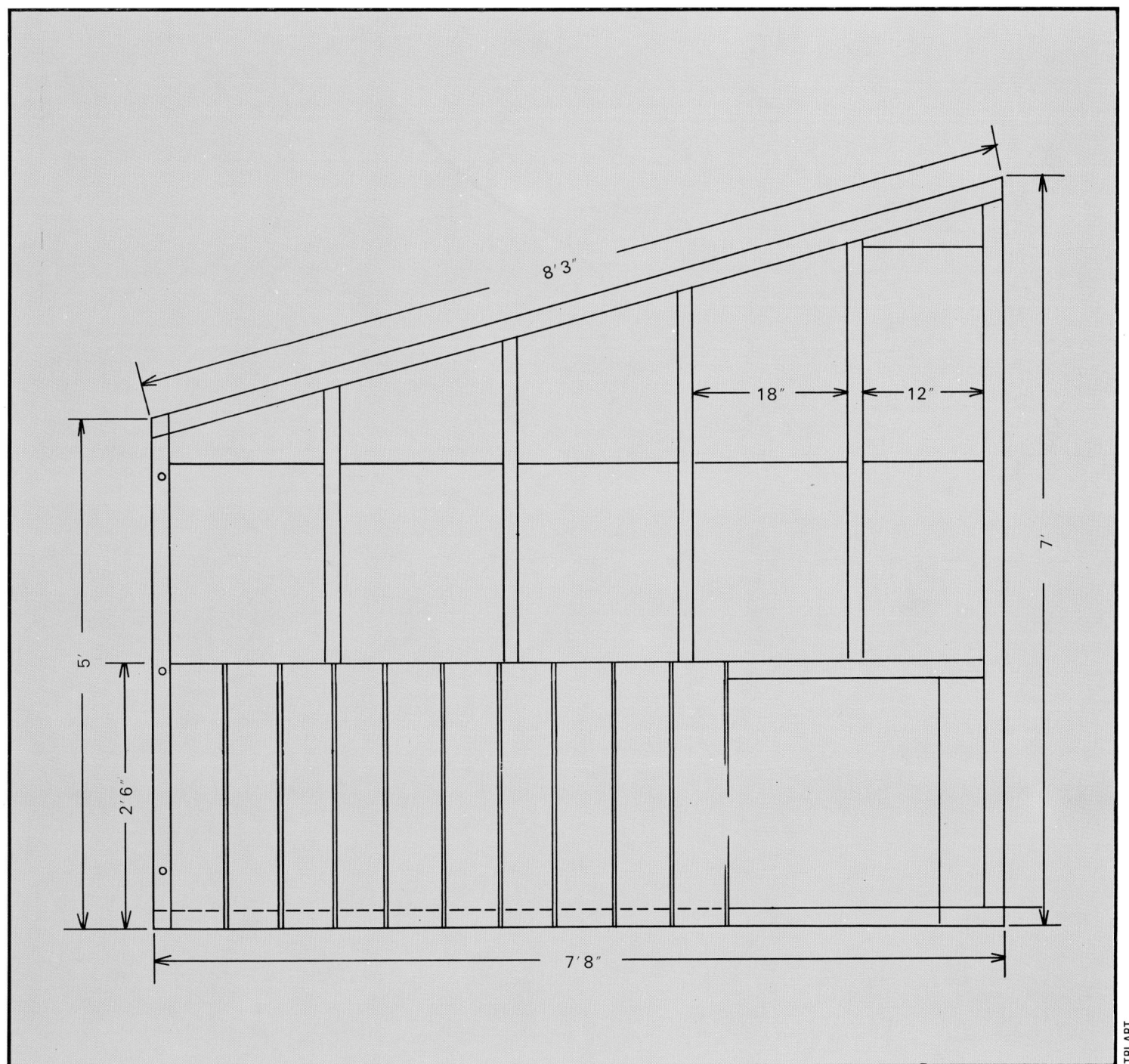

TRI-ART

An unusual tree house

This tree house is made for adventure. Its geometric shape, wide 'look-out' platform, rope ladders and rigging allow full scope for a child's imagination—creating, perhaps, a pirate ship or a jungle hideaway. But the best aspect of the tree house is that it is easy to build and original in design.

The basic construction of the tree house is quite simple. It consists of two timber triangles, stood on their apex and bolted together through the short side of the triangles—the top member in the finished construction. The apex of each triangle is fixed to a concrete block, set into the ground. The structure is braced by *metal* cables, fixed to the top member of the triangles and running to the ground, where they are attached to hooks set in concrete blocks.

A look-out platform is placed between the timber members and the metal guy ropes, about halfway up the height of the tree house. One end of the platform has a rectangular opening—this acts as a kind of trap door to the platform. At the opposite end there is a triangular wall, with an opening in the base of it which acts as another door. Nylon ropes are strung around the tree house timbers and the metal guys. These act as 'safety rails' around the platform.

The platform is reached by means of 'rope ladders'—in this case made from nylon rope with timber rungs. These are securely fixed at the top and bottom.

Planning considerations

The tree house will occupy an area in your garden measuring 9ft x 9ft 8in. (2.74m x 2.94m). It is worth drawing a scaled plan of your garden to help you position the tree house correctly—it can be moved after it has been erected, but planning will save you the trouble.

The best position for the construction is near to the house where you can keep an eye on the children. Don't build the tree house near an outhouse or tall trees—children are likely to use the tree house to climb into higher, and dangerous, places. Build the tree house on a lawn so that if your children do manage to fall out of it they will land on a fairly soft surface.

The triangular frames

The triangular frames are made from lengths of 4in. x 2in. (100mm x 50mm) timber to the shape shown in Fig.6. The timber that forms the long sides of the triangle is jointed to that which forms the short side with housing joints. At the apex of the triangle the two long sides are butted. The joints are strengthened by plywood fillets bolted in place over the apex of the triangle on both sides of the timbers.

Cut the long sides of the triangle a little over-length. On the ends of these timbers, mark an angle of 156° on the narrow edge of the timbers. You can mark this with a bevel gauge, setting the angle with a protractor. Cut through the timbers, down the marked lines.

Now mark the finished length of the timbers, referring to Fig.6 for dimensions. From the point marking the finished length, mark an angle of 156° on the wide edge of the timbers. Cut through the timbers, down the marked lines. The next step is to cut, in the newly cut slanted ends, a 1in. (25mm) housing to take the ends of the short sides of the triangle.

Cut the plywood fillets that cover the apex of the triangle. These fillets are shown in Fig.6. Bolt these in place over the apex of the triangle with 5in. coach bolts. You now have two V shaped constructions. Cut the short sides of the triangles overlength and lay them between the arms of the V, set into the housing. Direct mark the length of this side of the triangle. Cut it to length and nail it to the two arms of the V shaped constructions. This gives you the two triangular frames.

The next step is to cut housings in the frame members for the two timbers that form the side struts of the look-out platform. The position and all the necessary dimensions of these are shown in Fig.6. Nail these side struts in place in the housings.

Now bolt the two triangles together through the short sides. Use 7in. coach bolts for this, spaced about 1ft (305mm) apart along the timber. At the end use two coach bolts, one underneath the other. The top one should be 7in. long, the bottom one 10in. long.

The concrete bases

With the two triangles bolted together, you can now determine the exact position for the concrete bases for the legs and guy ropes. To do this you will have to hold the construction up in its finished position—you will need at least two helpers for this.

With the helpers holding the triangles upright, mark round the point on the ground where the legs of the tree house rest. The guy ropes run to points on the ground almost underneath the ends of the short sides of the triangles—see Fig.11. You can estimate the position of the blocks here or mark out the ground plan with wooden pegs.

Once you have determined the position of the bases you can dig the holes for the concrete blocks. These should be about 12in. (305mm) deep. The holes for the guy rope blocks should

Left. The geometric design of this tree house and its wide 'look out' platform, rope ladders and rigging allows full scope for your child's imagination.

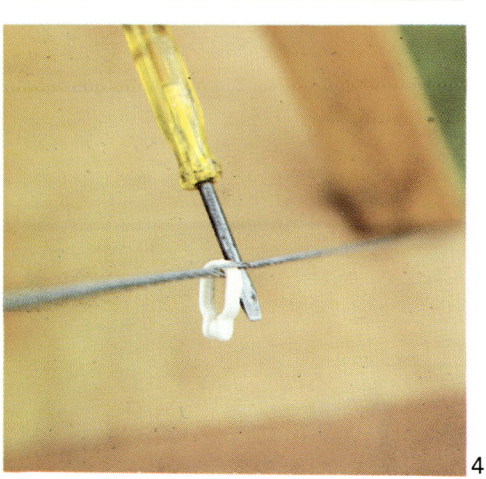

be wider at the bottom than at the top—the strain exerted here is an upward pull, whereas the pressure exerted by the legs is downwards—the blocks for these can, therefore, be straight-sided. All four blocks stand proud of the ground by 4in. (102mm) so you will need some simple formwork. One of the concrete blocks is shown in Fig.3.

As a fixing for the guy ropes, a metal hook with a 1in. (25mm) diameter eye on the top is set into the block. You can make these yourself from lengths of 10in. x $\frac{3}{8}$in. (254mm x 9.5mm) mild steel rod. They are bedded in the block so that just the eye stands proud. The fixing for the timber legs of the tree house is a 12in. x 1$\frac{1}{2}$in. (305mm x 38mm) diameter pipe, bedded in concrete to a depth of 6in. (152mm). A flange joint is slipped over the pipe so that it sits on the top of the block.

Pour the concrete for the blocks and push the fixings into it. Leave the concrete to set.

The look-out platform

This consists of a framework of 3in. x 1in. (75mm x 25mm) PAR timber, boarded over with 9mm plywood. The platform is bolted to the inside edge of the long sides of the triangles, at the points where the side struts of the platform wall are housed into the triangular frame members. The platform has a rectangular opening at one end to act as a door to the platform. Construct the platform to the shape and dimensions shown in Fig.12.

To bolt the square-sided platform to the sloping sides of the triangles, you will first have to cut four wedges. Lightly nail these in place on the triangle members. The platform is bolted in place with 8in. (203mm) fence stretchers—these are bolts with an eye at the head. These also give a fixing for the guy ropes that are positioned later. Bolt the platform in place.

Fig.1. *All the components and the fixtures of the tree house, prior to assembly.*
Fig.2. *The top members of the two triangular frames are fixed together with coach bolts.*
Fig.3. *The flange joint, set in the concrete base. This supplies a ground fixing for the timber legs of the tree house.*
Fig.4. *The nylon rope that forms the 'safety rail' around the platform is secured to the guy ropes with these fixtures. The 'threads' of the cable are separated with a screwdriver and the fixtures inserted.*

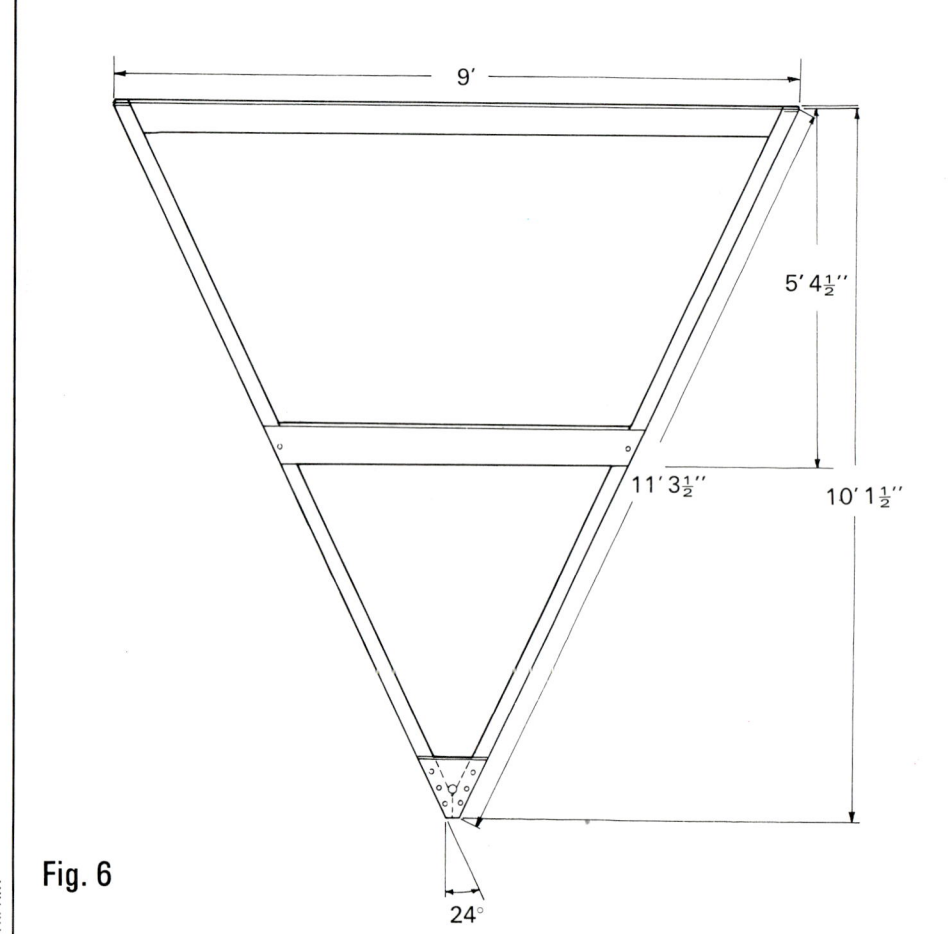

Fig. 6

9'

5' 4$\frac{1}{2}$''

11' 3$\frac{1}{2}$''

10' 1$\frac{1}{2}$''

24°

Fig.5. *The joint between the sloping members of the triangular frames and the 'look out' platform. Fence stretchers are used to bolt the components together and to carry the metal guy cables at these points.*

Fig.6. *The shape and dimensions of the frames of the tree house. The plywood fillet at the bottom of the frame braces the joint between the mitred ends of the sloping frame members.*

Fig.7. *The metal hook that supplies a ground fixing for the rigging and the rope ladders.*

Fig.8. *The rope ladders are made from nylon rope with lengths of timber as the rungs. When you have made the ladders, hang them up for a few days before you fix them to the tree house. Put some weights on the end of the ladders—this will fully stretch the rope. The ends of the metal guy cables are attached to cable stretchers.*

Fig.9. *At the top members of the two triangular frames, in the centre of their length, the metal guy cables are attached to this fixing. The ends of the cables are looped over, through the fixing, and the loose ends bound with pvc adhesive tape.*

Fig.10. *The finished tree house. All you have to do now is deck out the construction with decorations of your choice.*

Fig.11. *A side view and an end view of the tree house with all the necessary information and dimensions. The Bowden cable that runs from the top member of the triangular frames to the concrete blocks set in the ground are essential supports. These must be metal —children might cut through rope.*

7

8

9

10

NELSON HARGREAVES

Fig. 11

nylon ropes

6mm ply

screw eyes

26°

9mm ply

9'

3″ x 1″ PAR

4″ x 2″ PAR

nylon rope

nylon rope

wedges

Bowden cable

64°

TRI-ART

Use 9mm plywood for the side wall of the look-out platform. This is nailed to the platform and to the side struts fixed earlier. Before you do this though, cut an opening at the base of the panel to be used for the side wall—this acts as another door. The shape of the opening and the position of the extra timbers that frame it are shown in Fig.11.

The rigging

The rigging that runs to the two concrete blocks set in the ground is ½in. (13mm) steel cable, known as Bowden cable. You must use steel cable rather than rope or nylon—you can't run the risk of children cutting through these essential supports.

You will need four lengths of cable, each about 11ft (3.35m) long. These run from a fixing, shown in Fig.9, which is fixed through the top member of the two triangles, in the centre of their length. They then pass through the eye of the fence stretchers on the sides of the look-out platform and round the triangle member to the concrete blocks. At the top the cable itself is attached to U bolts or Bowden clips, and at the bottom to cable stretchers.

Drill a 1½in. (38mm) hole up through the bottom of the timber legs. Do this with a brace and expansive bit. These holes allow the legs to be fitted over the metal pipes set in the concrete. Drill a ½in. (13mm) hole in the bottom of the plywood fillets also—this will allow rainwater to drain out of the base of the legs.

The safety rail

This consists of nylon rope, strung from the ends of the top member of the triangles and fanning out to plastic fittings on the guy ropes. The arrangement of the nylon rope is shown in Fig.11 and the plastic fittings in Fig.4.

Erecting the tree house

Again you will need two helpers for this. First, fix the guy ropes to the fixing in the top triangle member and thread them through the eyes of the fence stretchers in the platform sides. Get your helpers to lift the tree house in place, with the timber legs over the metal pipe fittings. Attach the cable stretchers on the end of the guy ropes to the eye fittings in the concrete blocks. Tighten the guy ropes.

Fig.12. A view of the tree house from directly underneath. The dimensions of the 'look out' platform are given and the 'trap door' at one end of the platform is shown.
Fig.13. Two alternative designs of a tree house, using basically the same construction described in this chapter. String nylon rope around the platform area to act as a 'safety rail'. The top member of the triangles must protrude beyond the end timber members, so that you can provide adequate fixing. You must not screw directly into end grain here, as the fixing will work loose in time and the tree house will collapse. Use coach bolts to fix the tree house members together.

The rope ladders

The rope ladders are made from lengths of 12in. x 1½in. x ¾in. (305mm x 38mm x 19mm) timber, strung on to nylon ropes. The ladders are shown in Fig.8. Drill ½in. (13mm) holes through the 1½in. (38mm) edge of the timbers, about 1in. (25mm) from their ends. Take a length of nylon rope. Tie a knot in it. Do the same with another length of rope. Repeat this process, spacing the rungs every 9in. (229mm) apart until the ladders are complete.

Both ladders are fixed at the bottom to the guy ropes, 9in. (229mm) from the ground. Fix them to the guys with the plastic eye clips used to fix the nylon safety rail to the guys above the platform. These are shown in Fig.4. One ladder is vertical and runs through the opening in the platform floor. At the top, about 12in. (305mm) from the top triangle member, the two lengths of rope are tied to size 14 screw eyes. The other ladder runs up to the opening in the platform wall. It is tied to the side of the platform, through size 14 screw eyes.

Finishing

You can coat all the timbers with a wood preservative, or paint them in the colour of your choice. This will weatherproof the timbers. Decoration of the tree house—decking the guy ropes with coloured pennants for example—is up to you and your children.

The tree house will last for years, and give your children hours of fun.

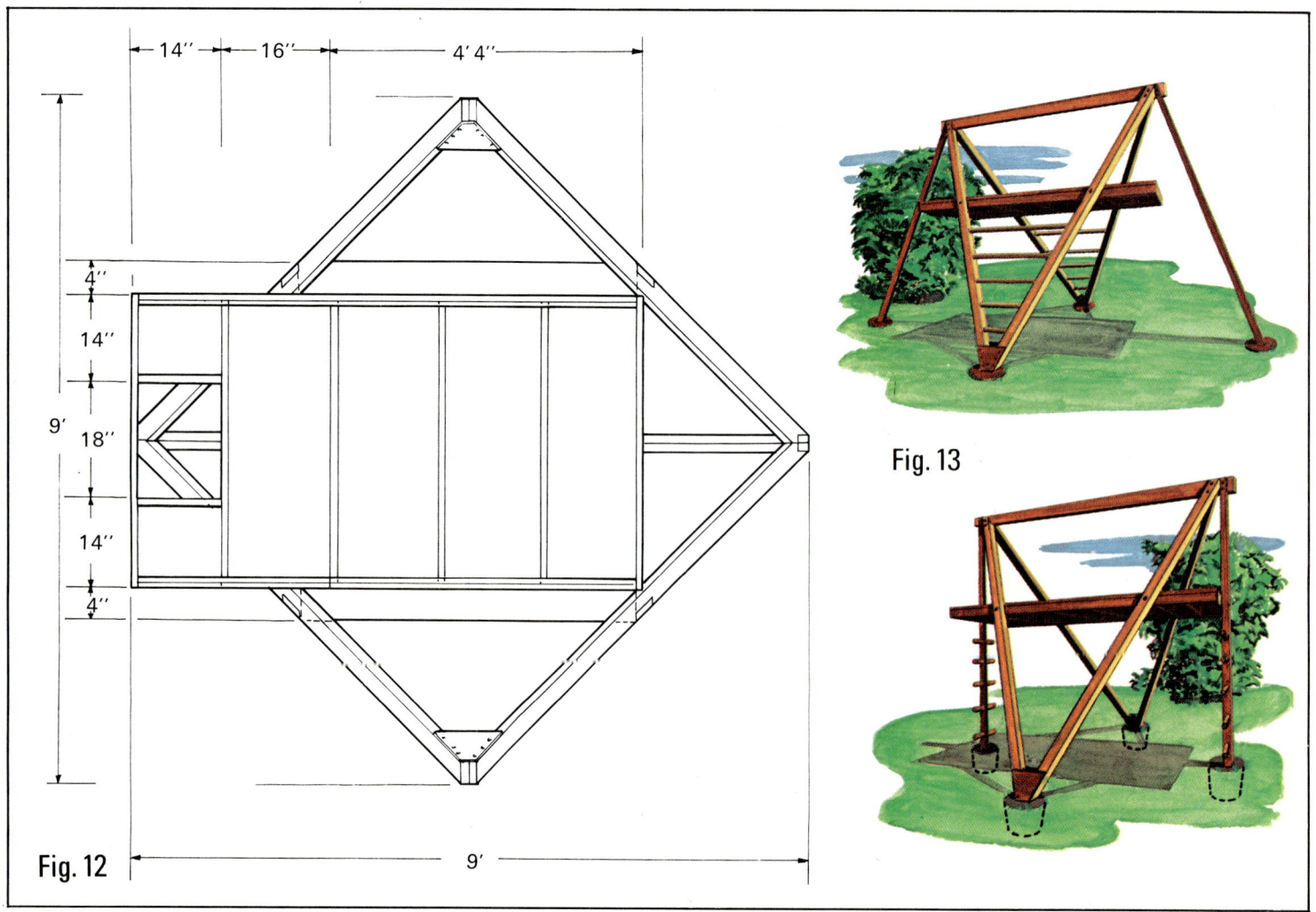

Fig. 13

TRI-ART

Fig. 12

Making a grand entrance

One of the most noticeable features of a house with a front garden is the garden gate—but when people renovate the outside of their houses, they often neglect this important feature.

Wooden garden gates, however well made and painted, inevitably decay and need replacing after a few years. Wood merchants generally stock replacements in a range of sizes. Unfortunately, gate posts, particularly those of old houses, do not always conform to the standard

sizes. If you want a new gate for such a place, you will either have to have one purpose-built—which can be expensive—or make one yourself.

If you do choose to make your own gate, you will have complete control over the design instead of having to make do with what you can buy. A few variations on a simple, basic design are given here, but all use the same woodworking techniques, and so will almost any version you design yourself.

A garden gate has to stand up to considerable wear and tear, including children swinging on it. So it must be stoutly made, with the same standards of accuracy and finish as you would use for a piece of indoor furniture. Only then will it last for a reasonable length of time.

This project introduces the *stopped rebate,* a groove cut in the edge of a piece of wood but not reaching to the ends, and the *mortise-and-tenon joint,* one of the strongest and most useful joints in carpentry.

Materials needed

The cheapest way of making a gate is to use ordinary softwood. Provided it is properly primed and painted, it should last for years. But the more you are prepared to spend on timber, the longer-lasting the job will be. Oak, at three or four times the price of softwood, and teak, which is even more expensive, are particularly durable.

The gate design given here uses tongued-and-grooved boarding, which is often not obtainable in hardwood. Fortunately its use is not essential. You can use plain boards, or build a gate of a design not using boarding at all.

The quantities given below are for a gate 4ft (1.2m) wide and 3ft (914mm) high, exclusive of the size of the gateposts. Use planed timber, which will be slightly narrower than the dimensions stated. You will need :

For the frame : 20ft or 6m of 4in. x 2in. or 100mm x 50mm.

For the diagonal brace : 4ft or 1.2m of 4in. x 1½in. or 100mm x 40mm.

T & G boarding : 11ft or 33m of 6in. x ½in. or 150mm x 12.5mm.

If you are putting in new gateposts at the time, you will also need 10ft or 3m of 3in. x 3in. or 75mm x 75mm timber—or you can use 4in. x 4in. or 100mm x 100mm, which is stronger.

You will also need 'knotting', primer, undercoat and paint to make the gate weatherproof.

Nails used for outdoor work should be sherardized or galvanized to resist rust, and screws should be of the black japanned type. This is particularly important if you are making a hardwood gate, because the natural acids in the wood attack bare steel. Use oval nails 1½in. (38mm) long.

The hinges for the gate can be of several types (see Fig.3). Ordinary 'tee' hinges are quite strong enough for a medium-sized gate. A larger gate—more than about 5ft or 1.5m wide—will need the stronger cast-iron hinges. These are available with either normal fixings for wooden posts or special flat plates for sticking into the mortar joints of brick pillars.

If you want your gate to fold back flat against the wall, 'Parliament' hinges with offset pivots should be used. These are not very strong, and suitable only for light gates. The gate must be made with roughly an inch (25mm) clearance between it and the gatepost on the lock side, since 'Parliament' hinges cause gates to swing at an unusual angle when opened.

Measurement and planning

The first step is to measure the site and note the condition of the existing gateposts. They will probably need replacing at the same time as an old gate. If you are installing a new gate between existing posts, the total width of the gate must be about half an inch (13mm) narrower than the space between the posts, and more for a large gate. This gap allows for the fact that at a slight angle (say, as you begin to open it) the gate needs extra room if it is not to jam. (Doors, but not gates, are bevelled to allow for this). If you are using 'Parliament' hinges, the gap should be proportionately larger.

Once you know the height and width of the gate, draw up a plan of the design you want. This need not be full size, but it enables you to work out the dimensions of everything.

Note that planed 4in. x 2in. or 100mm x 50mm timber is actually about 3½in. x 1¾in. or 89mm x 44mm, and that other sizes are proportionately smaller.

Whether you are adapting the gate shown in Fig.1 or designing one of your own, some dimensions will be the same in all cases. These include the sizes of the mortise-and-tenon joints and of the rebates into which the tongued-and-grooved boards are set. The only thing that might affect the size of the mortises is your not having a chisel of the right size to cut them. In this case, either buy a chisel the same size as the mortise ($\frac{9}{16}$in. or 14mm) or make a slightly smaller mortise. It must not be larger; the size of a mortise should not exceed one third of the thickness of the wood.

Once you have everything planned to your satisfaction, buy the timber, mark out the length of each piece and cut it ¼in. (6mm) over length at each end to allow for waste. Also cut twelve small wooden wedges from scrap timber to fit into the mortise-and-tenon joints.

The mortise-and-tenon joint

This joint is very strong and reasonably simple to make. But it must be made accurately, for it is worse than useless if it is a loose fit. Most mortise-and-tenon joints, including the ones here, are held tight with small wooden wedges.

The top rail (horizontal member) of the gate has the simplest type of through mortise-and-tenon joint, so make it first. Begin with the mortise, or slot. Find its position on the stile

Top. The gate is raised to the correct height with a piece of scrap wood.

Second from top. Once the gate is propped in place, holes are drilled in the post for the hinge mounting screws.

Third from top. The other gatepost is set upright before being mortared in place.

Bottom. The finished gate—a sturdy piece of work that will last for years.

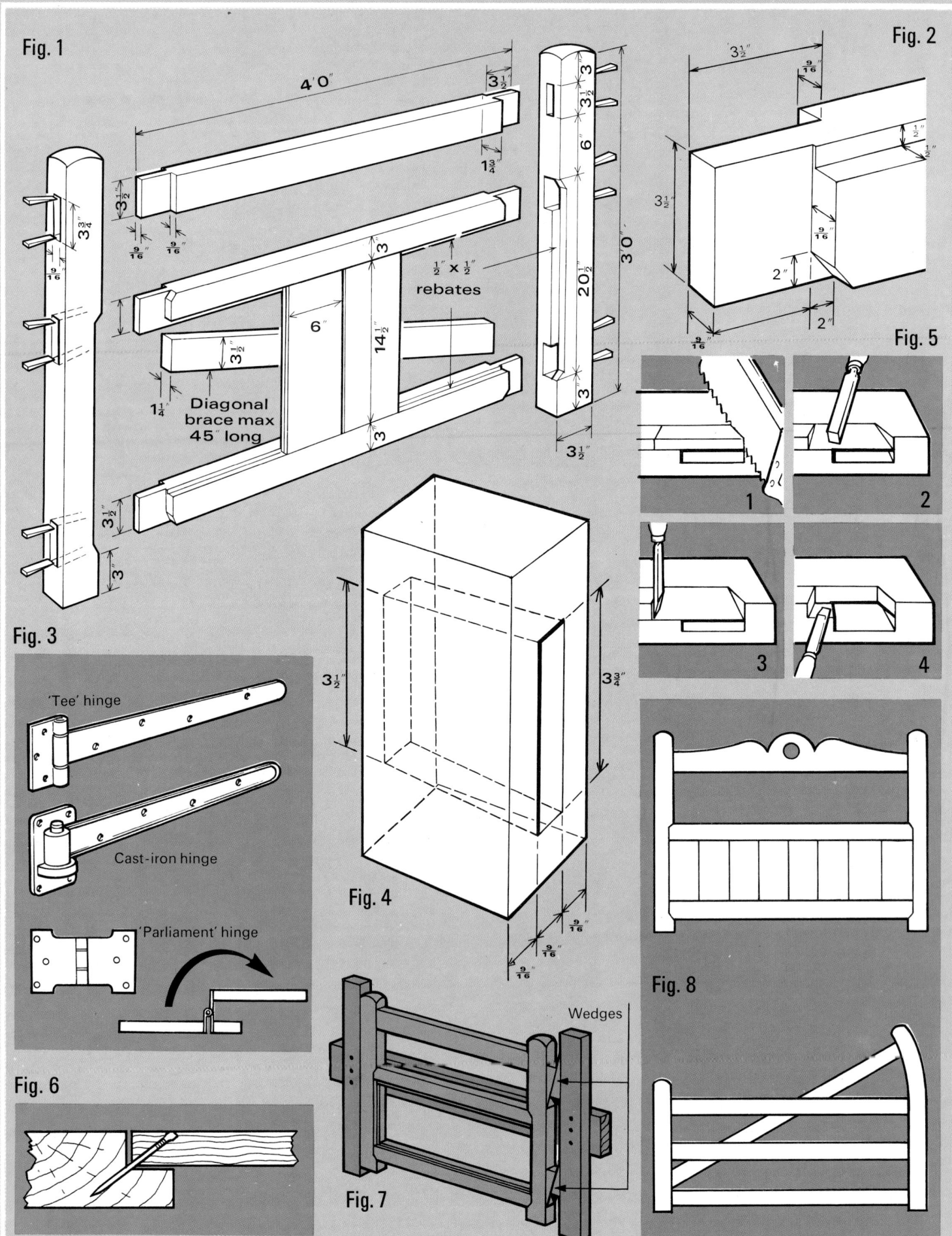

Fig. 1

4' 0"

3½"

3½"

3¾"

9/16"

9/16"

1¾"

6"

3"

½" x ½" rebates

6"

14½"

3½"

1¼"

Diagonal brace max 45" long

3"

3"

3½"

20½"

30"

3½"

3"

Fig. 2

3½"

9/16"

½"

½"

3½"

9/16"

2"

9/16"

2"

Fig. 5

1

2

3

4

Fig. 3

'Tee' hinge

Cast-iron hinge

'Parliament' hinge

Fig. 4

3½"

3¾"

9/16"

9/16"

9/16"

Fig. 8

Fig. 6

Wedges

Fig. 7

TRI·ART

44

(upright) of the gate from your design and mark the top and bottom—which should be the same distance apart as the width of the tenon, or tongue—on both edges of the stile. Then set your marking gauge to $\frac{9}{16}$in. or 15mm (or the width of your chisel), and scribe two short test lines on the edge of one piece of timber, one from each side. Check carefully that they are $\frac{9}{16}$in. apart (or 14mm—the 1mm difference in the metric figure is due to the thickness of the wood, 44mm, not being divisible by 3).

Special mortise gauges are available which scribe both sides of a mortise at once, but unless you plan to make a lot of mortises, this type of gauge is an unnecessary luxury.

When you are satisfied that your gauge is set accurately, mark all the mortises with it on both edges of the wood.

Now take a $\frac{9}{16}$in. drill (or a drill the width of your chisel) and drill through the stile from edge to edge inside the marks for the mortise. Drill one hole at each end, and one between the first two holes. Take particular care to keep the drill straight, so that the exit holes fall inside the marks on the far edge of the wood. When the point of the drill begins to come through the far edge, stop drilling and finish the hole from the other side.

Then take a chisel the same width as the mortise and cut out the wood between the holes and in the corners, so that the mortise takes on a rectangular shape.

Finally, lengthen the mortise slot on the outer edge of each stile (the edge away from the rails) by $\frac{1}{8}$in. (3mm) at each end of the rectangle, so that its length increases from $3\frac{1}{2}$in. (89mm) to $3\frac{3}{4}$in. (96mm) as shown in Fig.4. Do not lengthen the slot at the inner edge, but slope the end 'wall' of the inside of the mortise towards it, so that the ends of the cutout are slightly slanted. When the tenon is inserted into the mortise, wedges will be driven into the triangular gap formed by this slope.

The tenons are marked out with the gauge set the same as for the mortises. Scribe from both faces of the wood to mark a central tongue $\frac{9}{16}$in. (14mm) wide. Then set the rail upright in a vice and carefully saw down the outside of the marked lines for a distance of $3\frac{1}{2}$in. (89mm). It will improve the accuracy of the saw cuts if you tilt the saw blade slightly downwards to allow you to see. Then finish the tendons by sawing across the grain to detach the side pieces from the central tongue.

Fit the tenons into the mortises to make sure they will go. Do not insert any wedges at this stage. If the joint is too tight-fitting, minor adjustments can be made to either side with a chisel. If it is too loose, there is not much you can do except start again on another piece of wood.

The mortise-and-tenon joints for the lower two rails have a more complex shape. They should be started before the rebates are cut in the stiles, but finished after. This apparently complicated method actually simplifies cutting the rebates.

Cut the mortises as before, making sure the widest part of the hole is on the same edge of the timber as that of the top mortises. The tenons are not quite the same: the wood should be removed only 3in. (76mm) from the end on one

side, and the normal $3\frac{1}{2}$in. (89mm) on the other (see Fig.2). This means that the tenons cannot be completely inserted into their mortises, but do not cut off any more wood for the time being. The overall length of the rails, from tenon-tip to tenon-tip, is the same as for the top rail.

Stopped rebates

The front corners of both stiles and the lower two rails are rebated, or cut away, to enable the tongued-and-grooved boards to fit neatly into them and keep the surface of the gate flush.

The rebates in the rails can be made by following the outline of construction in Fig. 1. They must be cut on the side of the wood where only 3in. (76mm) has been removed to make the tenon. All the rebates in this gate are $\frac{1}{2}$in. × $\frac{1}{2}$in. (13mm × 13mm).

The rebates in the stiles are *stopped*—that is, they do not reach all the way to the ends of the wood. Stopped rebates are rather hard to make with either an ordinary rebate plane or a plough plane, because the body of the plane projects about 3in. or 75mm in front of the blade and 5in. or 130mm behind it. This means that you cannot plane right to the end of the rebate. A special type of rebate plane, called a *bullnose rebate plane*, is specially made for stopped rebates, but it is not worth buying one just for one job.

If you are using an ordinary plough or rebate plane, you can overcome the difficulty by cutting out the ends of the rebates with a chisel to make room for the body of the plane. Cut out enough wood to allow the plane blade to run clear into the chiselled section.

The ends of the rebates on the stiles are mitred—cut at an angle of 45°—so that the rails can fit into them neatly. Mark out the full extent of the rebates accurately, using a bevel for the mitre, and make a short tenon saw cut up each end along the line of the mitre (see Fig.5). This cut will not go to the full depth of the rebate because it only cuts across the corner of the wood, but it gives you a starting point for chiselling out the rebate end. Make a similar cut four inches (100mm) further along the rebate, at both ends or however far you need to go to clear a space for the body of the plane. Then chisel out the wood between each pair of cuts, working slowly and accurately to keep the rebate straight and level. As wood comes away from the ends of the rebate, chop down deeper past the saw cuts, with a chisel held vertically, to expose more end surface. When all the wood is chiselled out, finish the rebates with the plough plane.

Finishing the parts

Insert the tenons of each of the lower two rails into the appropriate mortises of each stile, taking care that the rails are the right way round as shown in Fig.1. The tenons will still not go all the way in, because the mitres have not been cut on the front corners. Chisel these mitres slowly and carefully, taking off only a little wood at a time to make sure that they fit snugly against the mitres at the end of the rebates. Then fit the whole framework of the gate together dry, without inserting wedges into the mortises. Plane the stiles and rails to their final length.

Check that the frame is square by measuring the diagonals (each diagonal should measure the

same distance across). Then carefully measure the distance between the rebated front edges of the two lower rails. Cut your tongued-and-grooved boards slightly over this measurement, and plane them to the exact length. This should ensure that they fit neatly into their rebates without a gap.

The boarded area on the front of the gate is unlikely to be made up of an exact number of board widths. To give the gate a symmetrical appearance, the edges should be planed off *both* outside boards to bring the boarding down to width. This process also removes the tongues and grooves, which are not needed because the outside edges of the boarding fit into the plain rebates on the stiles. The boards must not be too tight a fit across the grain; you need to allow for expansion in wet weather.

The only job that remains in the construction of the gate is to make the diagonal brace. This has to be made after the rest of the gate has been completed, because its exact length controls the squareness of the frame. Saw and plane its ends to the right length and angle by measuring them against the frame itself—constantly checking that the frame is still square. The brace does not need a mortise-and-tenon joint to hold it in place, because it is compressed when the gate is hung. But you must put it in the right way round, with its lower end next to the 'hanging' stile to which the hinges are attached.

Form a slightly domed top on the two stiles (and the gateposts, if you are replacing them) to stop rainwater from collecting on them and rotting the wood. This is best done with a Surform or similar tool, working from the edge of the post to the centre to avoid snagging the tool on the grain.

Assembling the gate

The gate is now ready for assembly, but before putting it together it is a good idea to start painting it. In this way the layer of paint will extend into the joints, giving some degree of weather protection if water should seep into them.

Apply two coats of knotting to any knots in the wood to stop the resin in them from discolouring the paint. Then apply primer and undercoat according to the manufacturer's instructions.

Do not apply any primer or undercoat to those surfaces that are going to be glued, since it will stop the glue from sticking to them. The paint should extend a short way into each joint for weather protection, but most of the surfaces of the mortises, tenons, rebates and the ends of the T&G boards should be left unpainted. If you use urea formaldehyde glue (which is strongly recommended for a long-lasting job) it will waterproof the glued surfaces as well as fasten them together. Do not paint the wedges at all; soak them in the same glue.

Before assembling the gate, make sure that you have some means of holding the frame together while the glue dries. Sash cramps are ideal. If you have none, you can nail two battens to a stout plank and jam the gate between them with two large wooden wedges (see Fig.6). Make sure the battens are mounted at right angles to the plank and parallel to each other.

Above left. A creosoted farm-type gate suitable for a wide drive. Above. A classically simple wicket gate painted white. Below. The same type of gate in a pair. Their rustic charm is enhanced by their curved tops. Bottom. A full-sized farm gate with diagonal bracing. This design has enormous strength.

Apply adhesive to all six tenons and mortises —not an excessive amount, but don't leave any bare patches. Then push the stiles on to the rails as far as you can get them by hand and knock them home with a mallet. Put adhesive on the wedges and push them into the mortises on either side of the tenons. Knock them in the rest of the way with a mallet, hitting each wedge of each pair alternately to keep the tenon straight. Retest the frame for squareness.

Cramp the frame up with rebates at the front and leave the glue to set. While it is setting, you can install the tongued-and-grooved boarding in the rebates. To avoid splitting the ends of the boards, use oval nails set end-on with the grain of the wood, and drive the nails into the rebates in the rails at an angle, as shown in Fig.7. Use two nails for each end of each board if the gate is to be painted, but only one for an unpainted hardwood gate, to allow the boards to widen in wet weather.

When the glue is dry, take the gate out of the cramps and turn it over. Put the diagonal brace in from the back, making sure that it is the right way round. Glue it to the frame at each end, hold it in place with two temporary nails, and then turn the gate front upward again and nail all the boards to the brace. This keeps both the brace and the boards from warping. No other form of fixing is necessary.

When you have completed the priming coat of paint, screw the hinges to the gate and place it between the gateposts. Raise the gate on blocks or bricks to the height it will be, then get a helper to hold it steady while you screw the other side of each hinge to the gatepost.

If you are installing new gateposts, they should preferably be set 2ft (0.6m) deep in concrete, and at least a week should be allowed (more in cold weather) before putting any weight on them. Posts set in hardcore alone tend to sag unless the hardcore is rammed down with considerable force.

The only two things that remain to be done are to install a latch on the gate and give it its final coats of paint. After that, the gate is complete.

Other gates

If you find the design of the gate given here too plain, there are a lot of variations on the basic gate that do not add too much to the difficulty of building it. For example, for the top rail, you can substitute a piece of 6in. x 2in. or 150mm x 50mm timber cut to any shape with a jigsaw (see Fig.8). The boarding can also be cut into decorative shapes.

The farm-type gate also shown is made in the same way as the basic gate, but the diagonal brace runs the other way, so that the weight of the gate stretches it. As a result, the brace must be firmly anchored with mortise-and-tenon joints at each end, strengthened by screws. This type of gate looks best without boarding, so the brace should be as thick as the rails and stiles. Angled halving joints should be made where the brace crosses the rails—it is best to make these while you are actually assembling the frame, to ensure that the angle is correct. The curved stile to which the brace is attached is cut out of a piece of 8in. x 2in. or 200mm x 50mm timber, using a jigsaw. If you can find a board with a grain that naturally follows the curve you are going to cut, the stile will be much stronger.

If you are prepared to be more adventurous with techniques, the only limit on the designs you can build will be set by your imagination.

JOHN HOVEL

Above. *A light and spacious workshop is a must if you undertake any reasonably advanced do-it-yourself projects because you need room to work in comfort and safety. The workshop described here combines all the best design features—and it is very easy to build.*

A workshop or playroom to make

If you do any do-it-yourself jobs, you need a workshop—to house your tools and keep them in good condition and to allow you to work whatever the weather. This workshop is good-looking, easy to build and spacious inside. With a workshop like this—and the right tools—there is virtually no limit to the kinds of projects you can undertake.

The design of this workshop is based upon the availability of reasonably priced standard components—louvre windows, matching double doors and braced doors with tongued and grooved matching. Using these eliminates the really time-consuming work in a project of this kind—making all these items yourself. All these components are available in ready-made form and at a price that is competitive with the price

you would pay for the raw materials at a builders' merchant.

Buy all these ready-made components before you start work. The frames for the sides of the workshop can then be made with the right sized openings for the doors and windows.

The dimensions given in the diagrams are for the workshop shown here. You can of course scale these up or down depending on the size of workshop you want, and what will fit your garden.

Construction details

The four walls of the workshop consist of a timber framework covered with shiplap boarding. The workshop has two entrances, one set of glazed double doors in the front short wall and a ledged and braced door in the back short wall. Both of the long walls of the workshop are made from two identical frames which are bolted together. The facing wall of the workshop, as shown, has two windows. The top part of both are louvred windows. The back long wall is plain shiplap boarding.

The workshop has a gable roof with a fairly gentle pitch. The floor consists of tongued and grooved boards which are tightly cramped together. The construction does not involve the cutting of complicated joints—the only joints used are simple housings and butted joints.

Planning considerations

The first step is to decide exactly where to put

Left. The workshop has large windows along one wall to give plenty of light inside. The double doors in one short wall are glazed also. The workshop is not only a place where you can work in comfort though—it looks good as well.

Fig.1. The dimensions of the frames of the two long walls of the workshop. Two frames are made for each wall and these are bolted together later. Frame A is for the back wall and frame B is for the window wall.

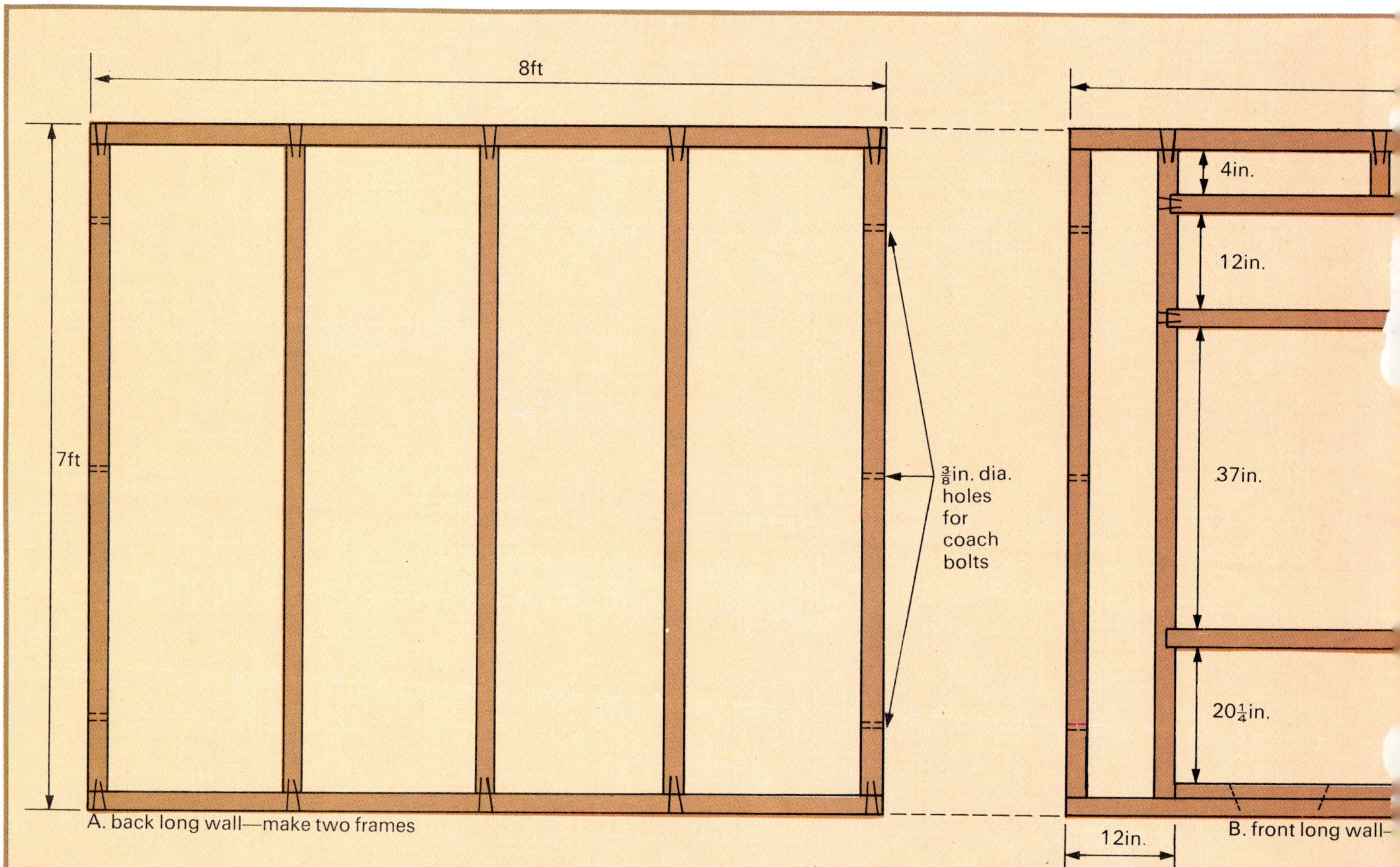

8ft

7ft

$\frac{3}{8}$in. dia. holes for coach bolts

4in.

12in.

37in.

20$\frac{1}{4}$in.

A. back long wall—make two frames

12in.

B. front long wall—

Fig. 1

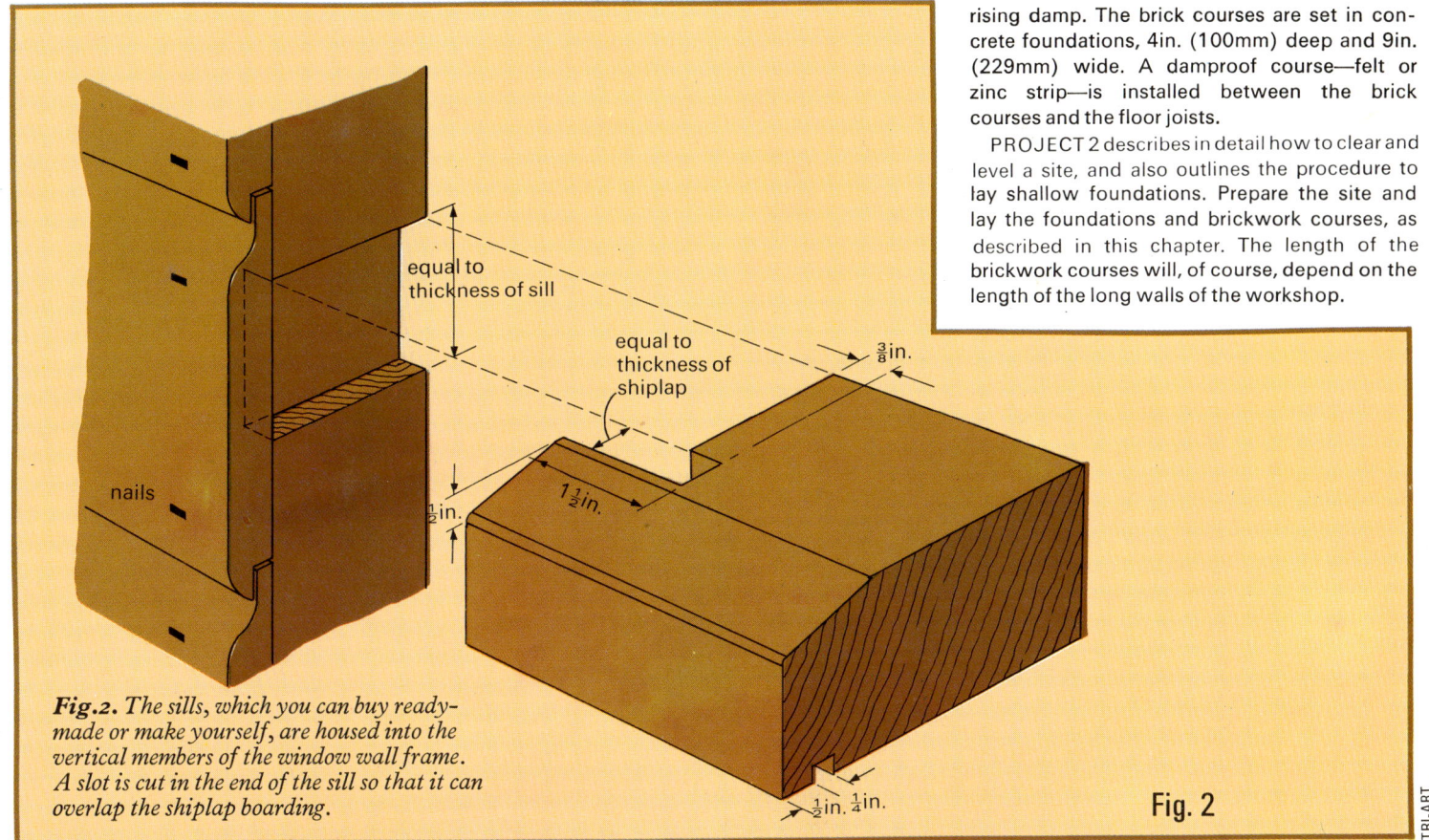

rising damp. The brick courses are set in concrete foundations, 4in. (100mm) deep and 9in. (229mm) wide. A damproof course—felt or zinc strip—is installed between the brick courses and the floor joists.

PROJECT 2 describes in detail how to clear and level a site, and also outlines the procedure to lay shallow foundations. Prepare the site and lay the foundations and brickwork courses, as described in this chapter. The length of the brickwork courses will, of course, depend on the length of the long walls of the workshop.

Fig.2. *The sills, which you can buy ready-made or make yourself, are housed into the vertical members of the window wall frame. A slot is cut in the end of the sill so that it can overlap the shiplap boarding.*

your workshop. Choose a site that will give you the maximum available space—a cramped workshop not only restricts the type of project you can undertake but it can also be dangerous.

Remember, also, that advanced do-it-yourself projects often require advanced tools. You may, at some stage, require a radial arm saw, a lathe or even a small planing machine (although these won't be required in this project). You need space to house these and to work them safely. Within reason, therefore, opt for the largest building your garden—and pocket—can accommodate.

The position you choose for the workshop will depend on the size and shape of your garden. Try to place the workshop so that the noise of hammering or of your electric tools won't disturb the neighbours.

Lighting in the workshop is an important consideration. Too much bright sunlight streaming into a workshop can cause eye strain and fatigue—and is therefore both uncomfortable and dangerous. Place the workshop so that its windows are away from the direct rays of the noon/afternoon sun but so that you receive a good natural light.

A final point: this project takes time even if you can work continuously on it, so have some large polythene sheets ready to cover the work area and keep the materials dry in between construction periods.

Site preparation

The workshop floor rests on three single brickwork courses, one supporting each end of the joists at the long walls and one supporting the centre of the joists. The bricks lift the joists off the ground and this helps prevent damage by

Laying the floor

The floor consists of 4in. x $\frac{3}{4}$in. (100mm x 19mm) tongued and grooved boards. These are cramped tightly together and dovetail nailed to the floor joists which are of 3in. x 2in. or 75mm x 50mm timber. The joists are laid at right angles to the brickwork courses and are placed at equal centres. The joists are placed 23in. (585mm) apart in the workshop shown here, but if you have altered the proportions of the building to suit your needs you can reduce this distance to keep all the spaces between the joists equal. The floor is made in two sections, each 8ft 2in. x 8ft (2.49m x 2.44m). This makes the workshop easy to dismantle if you wish to change its position or move house.

The first step is to cut all the floor joists to size. Then treat the joists with a timber preservative such as Green Emprinol. Stand the ends of the timber in preservative to allow it to soak into the end grain. Then lay the joists in place across the brick courses and the dpc.

You can now cut all the tongued and grooved floorboards to the right length. Dovetail nail one board in place, at right angles to the joists, with its edge flush with the joist ends. The subsequent boards can now be laid but they must be cramped tightly together.

To do this, lay four boards in place across the joists. Cut six wedges, about 7in. (178mm) long, from 2in. x 2in. (51mm x 51mm) prepared timber. Then nail a piece of scrap timber across the joists, with a gap of under 4in. (100mm) between this and the last board. Knock the wedges, used in pairs, into the gap—this gives firm cramping pressure. Dovetail nail the boards to each joist and punch the nail heads well in.

Remove the scrap timber, lay down four more

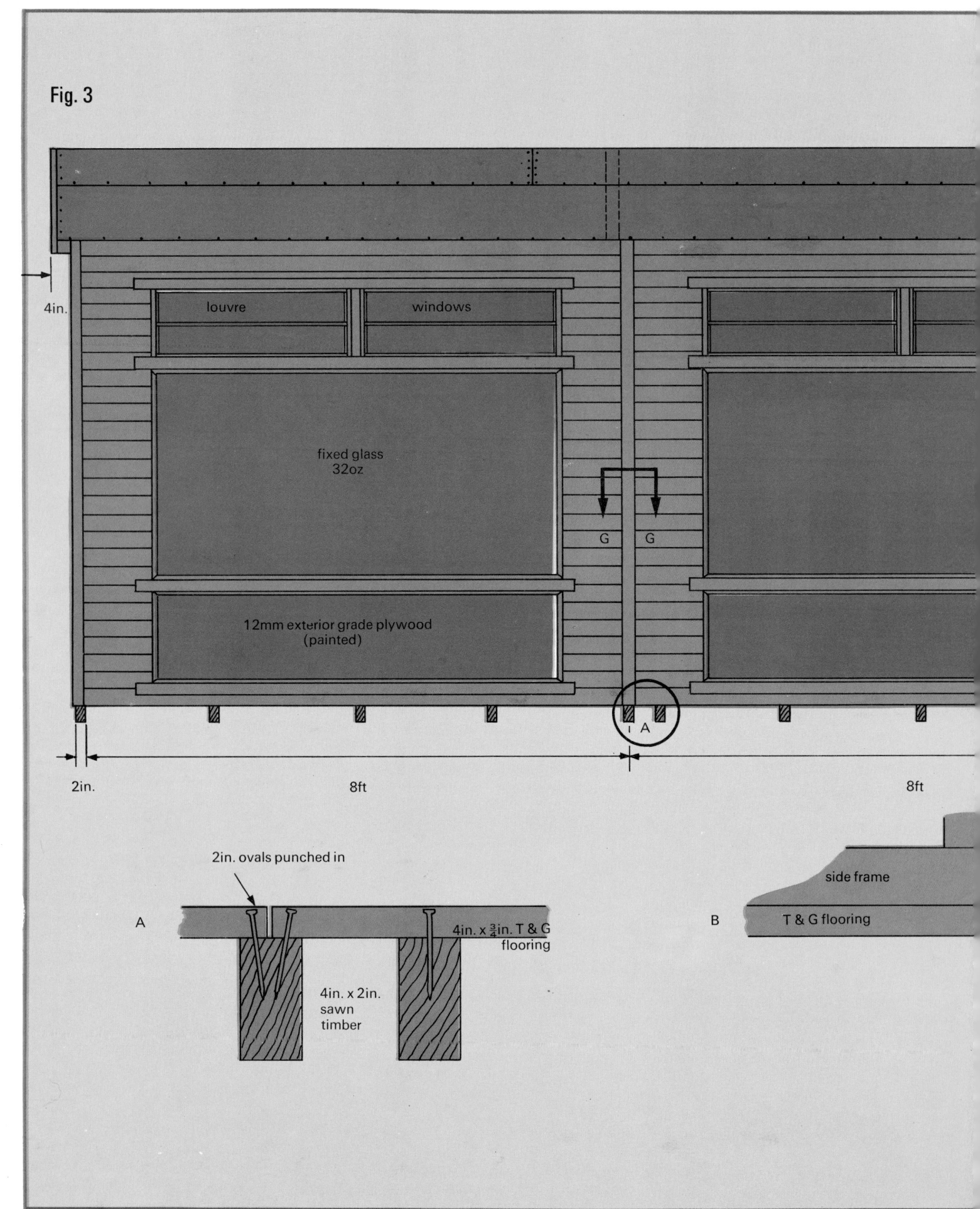

Fig. 3

4in.

louvre   windows

fixed glass
32oz

12mm exterior grade plywood
(painted)

G   G

I A

2in.   8ft   8ft

2in. ovals punched in

A   4in. x ¾in. T & G
                                                     flooring

                    4in. x 2in.
                    sawn
                    timber

                                          side frame

B   T & G flooring

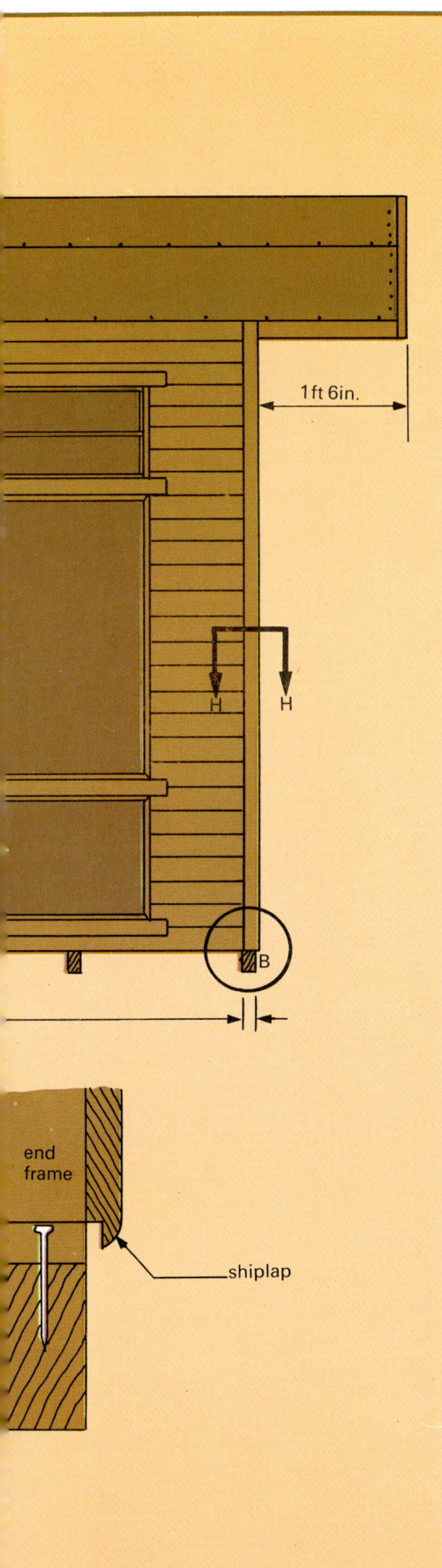

1ft 6in.

H H

B

end
frame

shiplap

TRI-ART

boards and repeat the process. If you are using good quality timber you may be able to lay and fix more than four boards at a time—but do not try to fix too many or they may bow upwards and spring out of position.

When the whole floor is fixed you can use it as a work surface to mark out and make the frames for the workshop walls.

Making the long wall frames

The long wall frames are made in two identical halves which are bolted together. One long wall is boarded over completely with shiplap while the other, the facing side, has two large windows.

At this stage you can cut all the frame members to size except the window sills. The dimensions for this workshop are shown in Fig.1. The two components of each of the long walls have the same dimensions as the front and back walls though these walls have a shallow gable as well.

Make the two frames for the back long wall, marked A in Fig.1. This will give you the frame for the long wall that is boarded over later. All the joints here are dovetail nailed. Make sure that the vertical members are an equal distance apart and that the corners are flush and even. Lay one frame on top of the other and check that they are square by measuring the diagonals.

The shiplap boarding, shown in Fig.3, can now be nailed in place. At the meeting rail of each frame (the rails that butt each other in the finished construction) the boarding is left ½in. (13mm) short—this allows a cover strip of wood moulding to be fixed in place later to disguise and weatherproof the join between the meeting rails.

Nail the shiplap in place with 1½in. (38mm) oval nails, knocking each board up against the preceding one. Then punch in all the nail heads. When you have fixed the boarding to the two halves of the back long wall put the components to one side.

The two parts of the long window wall can now be built. The dimensions of the frames, for this workshop are given in Fig.1. The two inside vertical rails of each part of the wall have three housings cut in them for the horizontal members that frame the windows.

The first step is to mark out the housings on the four vertical rails. Lay the rails together to do this and refer to Fig.1 for the position of the housings. The depth of the housings should match the thickness of the sill material. You can buy ready-made sills (type 5), ask at your nearest builders merchant or make them yourself from 4in. x 2in. (100mm x 50mm) prepared timber. Cut out the housings and assemble the frames.

Now prepare the timber for the window sills, according to the dimensions shown in Fig.2. If you are making the sills yourself you will have to plane a bevel on the top outside corner of the timber. You must also plane a drip groove in the underside of the timber. This helps rainwater to drip to the ground rather than run onto the timber beneath the sill.

The sills that frame the windows are jointed to the vertical members of the frames. Cut these joints to the shape shown in Fig.2. The sill ends protrude beyond the vertical sides of the window frame, so a slot is cut into the sills to allow for this. The width of the slot depends on the thickness of the shiplap boarding you are using—the size may vary from supplier to supplier.

The window wall has another sill. This is nailed to the bottom horizontal member, as shown in Fig.3.

Assemble the two frames, as shown in Fig.1, check that they are square and then apply boarding to the areas to be covered. You will need to cut several short lengths of boarding to do this. To save time in measuring and marking you can make a sawing jig – this is like a mitre box with a stop at one end.

Remember that the boards running to the meeting rails are fixed ½in. (13mm) away from the outside edge of the rails. This is so a weatherproofing cover strip can be fixed later. When you have assembled the long window wall, put it to one side. Do not put the windows in yet.

The next step in making the workshop is assembly of the short gable walls. This, and the rest of the steps necessary to complete the workshop, is described in the next part.

Fig.3. *The window wall of the workshop as it looks in the finished construction with the shiplap, roofing felt and glazing in place. Detail A shows how the floor is fixed to the joists in the middle of the window wall. Detail B shows the floor fixing at the corner.*

Fig.4. *The two cross sections marked on Fig.3. Section GG shows how the two parts of the long walls are bolted together with coach bolts and the join covered with a strip of moulding for weatherproofing. Section HH shows how long walls are bolted to the short walls.*

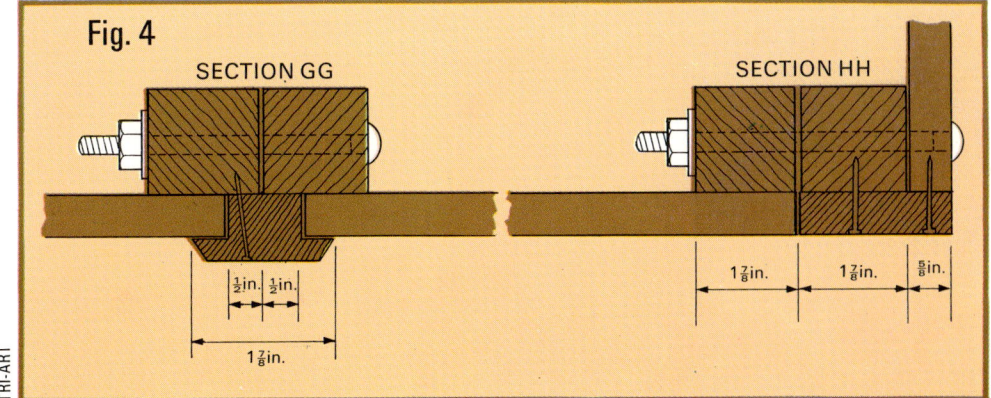

Fig. 4

SECTION GG

SECTION HH

½in. ½in.

1⅞in.

1⅞in. 1⅞in. ⅝in.

TRI-ART

51

This well planned workshop provides room for a wide range of do-it-yourself projects and storage space for all your tools. The preparatory work and initial construction stages were described in the first part of this chapter. Here full instructions for the final construction stages are given.

The dimensions given in this chapter are for the workshop shown in the photograph. You can scale these up or down to give you a workshop that fits your garden and suits your pocket.

Making the short walls

Prepare the timber for the frames of the short walls and mark out the position of the door on the top and bottom frame members (Fig.1). The workshop has two doors, both of which are bought ready made. One end has a ledged and braced door and the other has double doors that are glazed later. Make sure, when you mark up the timber, that the openings for the doors are the right size.

Both short wall frames have a gable construction fixed to the top of them. The centre post of the gables is housed into the top horizontal member of each end frame as shown in Fig.1. The housing is ¾in. (19mm) deep and the centre post is 13¾in. (349mm) high. Assemble the frames and lay one on top of the other to make sure they are identical. Then fix the gable centre posts in place.

The next step is to cut the sloping members that are fixed to the end frames and which give the workshop roof its pitch. Mark inwards from the ends of the top member of each frame a distance of 7in. (178mm). From the top of each gable centre post mark a distance of 2in. (51mm) downwards. The gable members run between, and to, these points. The best method of marking the necessary angles on the ends of these members is to lay the timber you are going to use between these points and 'direct mark'. You will need four of these gable members—they can now be cut and fixed in place. Put the frames for the short walls to one side.

Left. The workshop is placed to receive as much light as possible through its two large windows and glazed double doors. It should not receive direct sunlight though, as this may distract you while working inside, and will also cause eye strain and fatigue—which could be dangerous.

NIGEL MESSETT

The central roof truss

The roof of the workshop must be supported in the middle of its length. This support is provided by a central truss, the shape and dimensions of which are shown in Fig.3. It is the same shape as the gable ends but because it rests on top of the long side walls it is not as high as the gables. It is the thickness of the top member of the long side wall frame shorter than the gable ends.

The truss has a plywood fillet covering the apex of the triangle (Fig.3). This helps prevent the truss sagging. Construct the truss and compare it with the gable ends to make sure the angles are identical.

Boarding over the short wall frames

Fix shiplap boarding to the front short wall frame. The boarding does not run right up to the door opening here and a 1in. x ¾in. (25mm x 19mm) fillet is glued and pinned around the door frame. This neatens the appearance of the door opening (see Fig.2). The doors in this wall open outwards so a door stop is fixed around the opening, near the inside edge of the frame member.

On the back short wall the boards come right up to the door opening (Fig.2). The door stop, fixed to the outer edge of the frame members because the door opens inwards, disguises the sawn ends of the boards.

When you have fixed the shiplap boarding, the doors can be hung. The ledged and braced door is hung with tee hinges, the double doors with butt hinges. Fit locks, bolts and latches of your choice to the doors.

The roof

The roof is made from four panels, each one consisting of 4in. x ¾in. (100mm x 19mm) T & G boards. These are fixed to two strips of prepared timber for each panel. These timbers are 2in. x 2in. (50mm x 50mm) in size and act as the purlins of the finished roof. The panels are shown in Fig.4.

The panels are cramped together and then nailed to the purlins. They are given extra support by triangular wedges which are nailed to each side of the gables and to the central truss construction. Two wedges are nailed to each sloping member so you will need to make twelve. They can be cut from offcuts from the workshop frame and should be about 6in. (152mm) in length.

These wedges are nailed to the gables and to the truss before the roof panels are made. The purlins of the roof rest against the triangular wedges so you must take great care to position the purlins correctly.

The purlins are halved at the point where each pair of roof panels meet in the middle. There are two pairs of roof panels, a left and a right hand one for each side of the roof, so do not produce a matching pair or they will not fit together. Make the roof panels, referring to Fig.4. On the two short wall gables, make cut outs for the purlin ends.

Assembly of the workshop

The two panels of each of the long walls are bolted together (Fig.4, page 1797), through the meeting rails, with three 4½in. x ⅜in. (114mm x 9.5mm) coach bolts. And the walls of the workshop are bolted together at each corner with three 5in. x ⅜in. (127mm x 9.5mm) coach bolts. The roof is lightly fixed in place and then the walls are nailed to the floorboards and joists with 4in. (100mm) wire nails. The roof is then nailed

more securely in place. The moulded weather strips, which disguise the join between the two parts of each long wall, can now be glued and nailed in place.

Finishing

The roof is covered with roofing felt. Before you apply the felt, unroll it and leave it to stretch for a few days. This prevents the felt stretching and creasing when it is in place on the roof. Nail the felt in place, working from the roof eaves up towards the 'ridge', with ½in. (13mm) clout nails at 3in. (75mm) centres. The strips of felt must overlap and the overlap should point downwards. In Britain, the building regulations specify that shed roofs must be covered with at least two layers of roofing felt.

Fit the plywood panels that occupy the gaps under the main windows on the facing long wall. Fit the proprietary units for the louvred windows, following the manufacturers' instructions. Have all the glass required cut to size by a glass merchant.

Coat the workshop timbers with a wood

preservative and then carry out all the glazing. PROJECT 4, on pps. 33 & 35, tells you how to do this. Apply a strip of 3in. x ¾in. (75mm x 19mm) timber under the roof eaves along the long walls of the workshop. Fix a plastic rainwater gutter to each of these and connect the gutters to plastic downpipes, bracketed to the workshop walls.

You now have an outhouse that, although a separate structure, is really an extension of your home.

Fig.1. The shape and dimensions of the short wall frames, with the gables in place. Note the wedges on the sloping gable members. These provide extra fixing for the roof. The exact position of the members that frame the doors depends on the size of door you use. The doors are bought ready made so sizes may vary. *Fig.2.* The short walls with the shiplap boarding in place, and the door hung. The frame on the right shows the roof and the rainwater gutter in place also. The cross sections show the arrangements of the workshop members and components around the frames of the two doors.

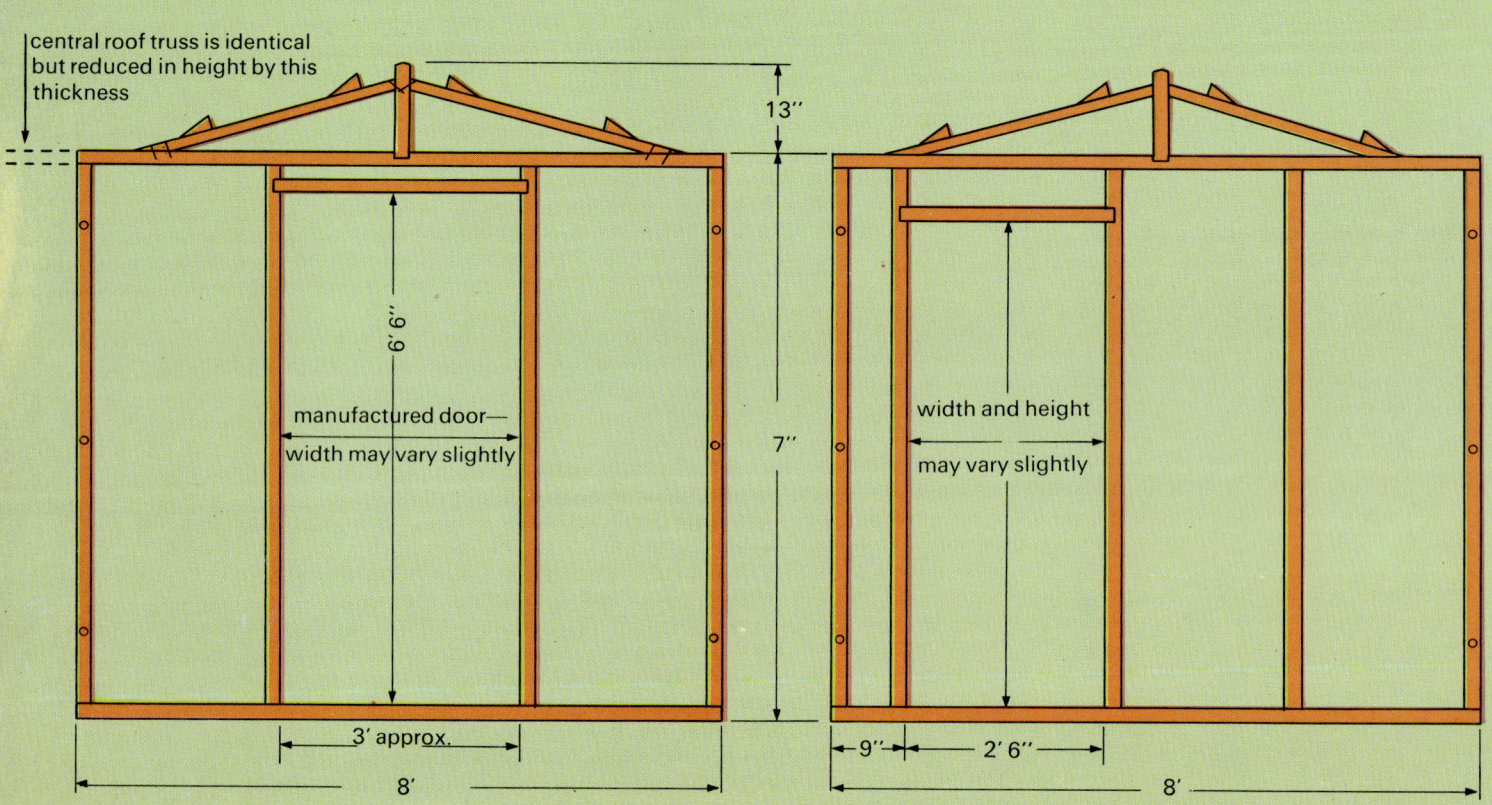

Fig. 1

central roof truss is identical but reduced in height by this thickness

13"

6' 6"

manufactured door— width may vary slightly

7"

width and height may vary slightly

3' approx.

8'

9" 2' 6"

8'

front short wall frame—make one

back short wall frame—make one

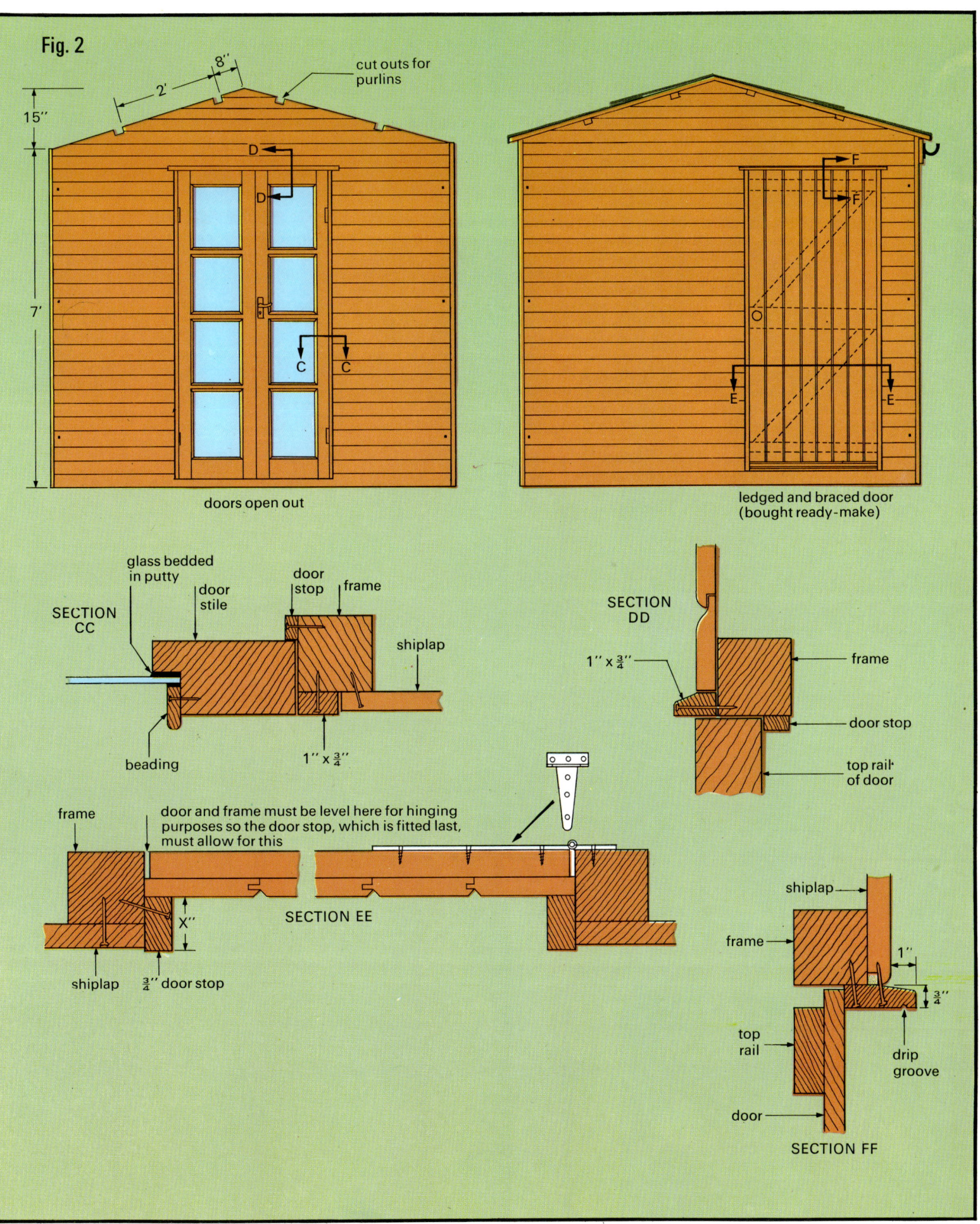

Fig. 2

15''

7'

8''

2'

cut outs for purlins

D

D

C   C

doors open out

F

F

O

E   E

ledged and braced door
(bought ready-make)

SECTION CC

glass bedded in putty

door stile

door stop

frame

shiplap

beading

1'' x ¾''

SECTION DD

1'' x ¾''

frame

door stop

top rail of door

frame

door and frame must be level here for hinging purposes so the door stop, which is fitted last, must allow for this

X''

shiplap

¾'' door stop

SECTION EE

shiplap

frame

top rail

door

1''

¾''

drip groove

SECTION FF

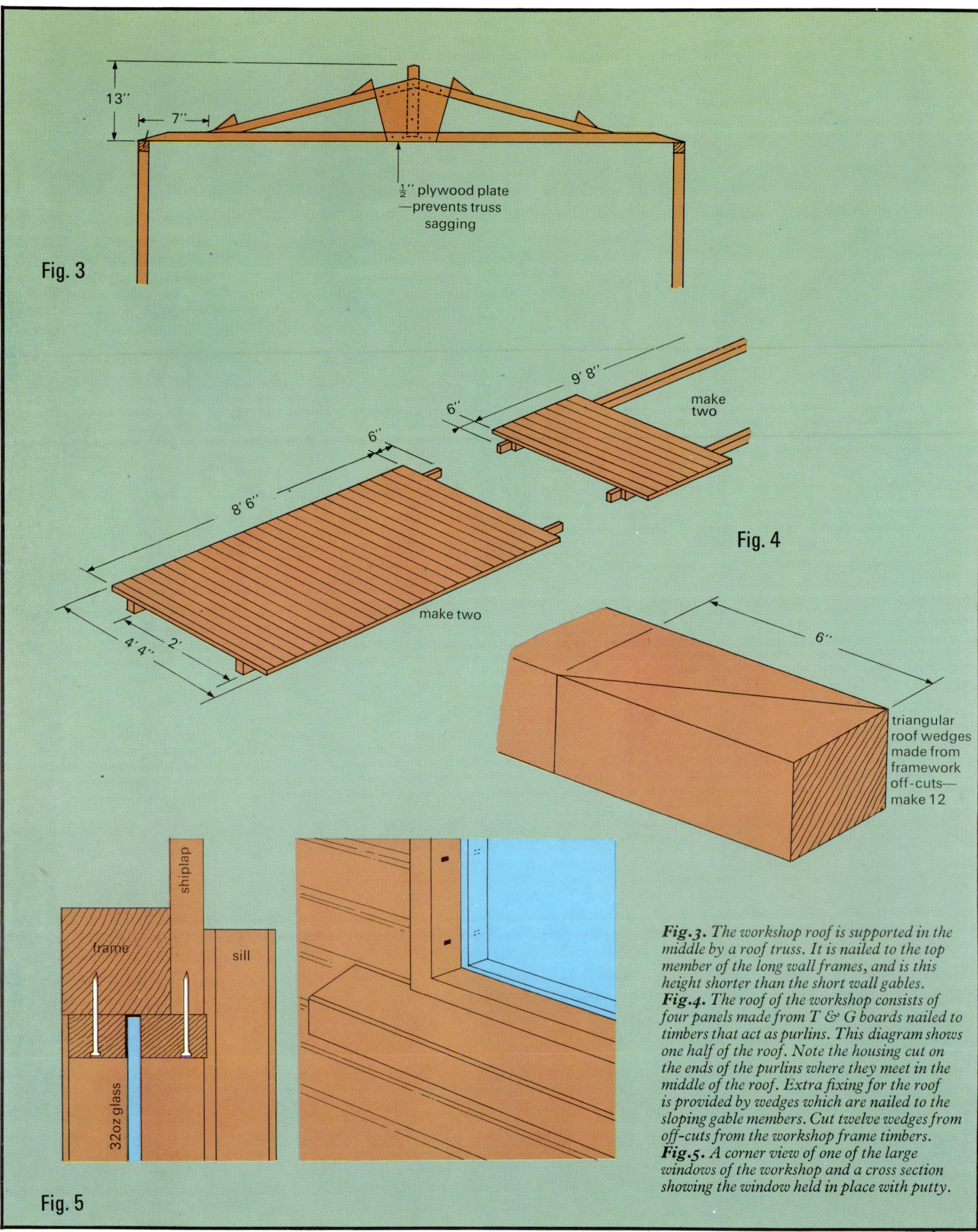

13"

7"

½" plywood plate
—prevents truss
sagging

Fig. 3

9' 8"

6"

make
two

6"

8' 6"

make two

4' 4" 2"

6"

Fig. 4

triangular
roof wedges
made from
framework
off-cuts—
make 12

shiplap

frame

sill

32oz glass

Fig. 5

Fig.3. The workshop roof is supported in the middle by a roof truss. It is nailed to the top member of the long wall frames, and is this height shorter than the short wall gables.

Fig.4. The roof of the workshop consists of four panels made from T & G boards nailed to timbers that act as purlins. This diagram shows one half of the roof. Note the housing cut on the ends of the purlins where they meet in the middle of the roof. Extra fixing for the roof is provided by wedges which are nailed to the sloping gable members. Cut twelve wedges from off-cuts from the workshop frame timbers.

Fig.5. A corner view of one of the large windows of the workshop and a cross section showing the window held in place with putty.

PROJECT 8

A swimming pool to make: 1

A swimming pool adds enormously to your recreational facilities and to the value of your home. A pool also rapidly becomes a focal point of social activities, where you can entertain your friends and family. To have a pool built by a specialist is expensive but you can build a pool yourself and drastically reduce the cost involved. This four part chapter tells you how to do it right through, from preparing the site to adding the finishing touches, to the landscaping of the finished pool. At the end, you will have a leisure feature your friends will envy.

This project gives you full instructions on how to build a swimming pool of classical design. The pool can be built over a reasonable number of days or over weekends and will look as good as any specialist-built pool—yet will involve less than half the cost.

The structural design is the same as that used by the majority of specialist pool contractors. Local builders can be used to do some sections of the work to speed up the project—as your plans become more detailed you have the choice of saving time or expense. The design and construction of the pool described here is as good as that of any specialist built pool—in fact, some of the better aspects of pool design are included, and alternative ideas which may be more practical in your case.

And PROJECT 1, which concentrates on free-standing swimming pools, should be read in conjunction with this chapter.

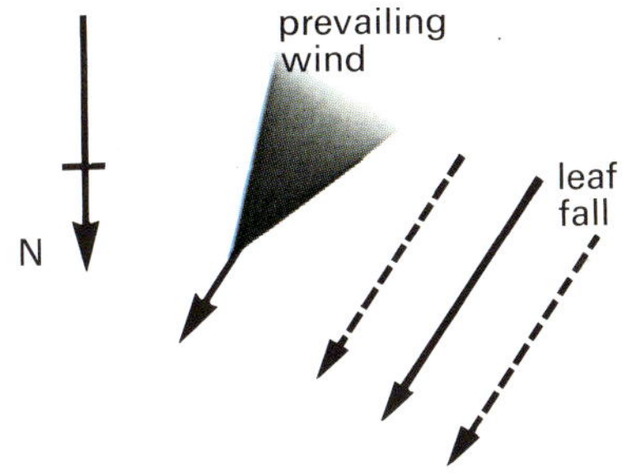

prevailing wind

N

leaf fall

This swimming pool has a classical design that looks good in a well planned setting. This illustration shows the layout of all the pool components and circulation system. The perspective view below gives an impression of the finished pool.

TRI-ART

Programme and Schedule

No. of Days	Job/Materials Guide	Quantity
1-2	Site clearance and setting out	
2-4	EXCAVATION	
	Hire of excavator/mixer/barrow/cartage to tip	
5-8	BASE	
	2in. land drains	50ft
	1in.-2in. drainage beach	4 cu yds
	Waterproof paper/polythene	50 sq yds
	Ready-mix blinding screed (if paper not firm enough)	1½ cu yds
	6in. ready-mix base and 9in. wall foundations	10 cu yds
	alternatively hand mix 4:2:1 (coarse aggregate)	
	⅜in. mild steel rod (no rust scale) and walls	3,000 ft
	⅜in. mild steel rod starters (3ft 6in. approx.)	150
	alternative 6 lb per sq yd 6in. mesh reinforcement	
	(delete 1,200ft rod)	
10-14	WALLS/BACKFILL	
	18in. x 9in. x 9in. 2-core hollow concrete blocks	330
	⅜in. block fill aggregate	4 cu yds
	Sharp sand (clean)—and coping/render	8 cu yds
	Grey cement—and coping/render	50 cwt
	(Block mix 4:2:1)	
	(Building mix 4:1)	
10-12	RENDER/COPING	
	Waterproofing powder (non-staining)	24lbs
	Cement render mix 3:1 (plus waterproofer)	
	Terrazzo render—⅛in. marble granules	12 cwt
	—fine marble powder	6 cwt
	—white cement	7 cwt
	(terrazzo mix 5:2½:3)	
	6in. mosaics tiling band (frost-proof)	45 sq ft
	24in. swimming pool coping edging—straight	54ft
	—5ft radius	14ft
	—17ft 6in. radius	12ft
	—internal corner	4
	—external corner	2
5-10	PAVING ⎫ as required	
10-20	LANDSCAPING ⎬	
7-10	PLUMBING/EQUIPMENT. Detailed in part 3	

50-80 workdays

If you are using metric measurements, work from these approximate equivalents of the imperial measurements given above.

1ft equals 0.03m or 305mm, 5ft equals 1.52m or 1525mm
1 sq ft equals 0.09 sq m, 5 sq ft equals 0.45 sq m
1 sq yd equals 0.84 sq m, 5 sq yd equals 4.18 sq m
1 cu yd equals 0.77 cu m, 5 cu yd equals 3.85 cu m
1 cwt equals 50.8 kg, 5 cwt equals 554 kg

Design selection

The most important point to remember is that an 'in-ground' swimming pool is a 'one-off' job which is affected by a variety of factors. These include:
—budget, personal taste and the quality of workmanship.
—siting, main services and facilities for equipment.
—access, nearest tip (for disposal of excavated material) and availability of building materials.
—type of ground, subsoil and weather conditions.
—type of landscape features.
—byelaws and safety requirements.
As long as you consider these factors carefully, building the swimming pool presents no more problems than any other home improvement scheme.

Time factor

You will need at least three months for this project but ideally you should allow yourself six months for the whole project, from the planning stage right through to the final landscaping. A useful work scheme allows two months for the construction of the tank, two months for installing plumbing and equipment, and two months for landscaping. This scheme is based on mainly weekend working. The programme schedule gives greater detail of the time required for the various design and construction steps.

Types of structure

There are a variety of in-ground tank structures. Type A includes concrete, aluminium or steel panels, glassfibre, and gunite (a kind of ferro-cement) structures. Type B includes reinforced concrete, and concrete blocks with marble terrazzo rendering or pvc liner designs.

For type A, excavation for the tank has to be carried out according to the manufacturers' instructions and you may need specialist sub-contractors to build the tank. These types of tank are useful where the construction has to be done relatively quickly in hillside or wet areas, or where the pool is irregularly shaped.

The tanks in type B are more suitable if you can only work intermittently on the project because they can be built in stages. You will need formwork for reinforced shuttered concrete tanks and this is usually expensive. These tanks present a further problem because, unless you can cast the whole tank in one go, you will have the difficult problem of making sealing joints between the older and newer concrete. If you can obtain formwork, then you can build a tank with 6in. to 8in. (152mm to 203mm) concrete walls and floors, strengthened with either reinforced steel matting (about 6lbs per sq yd) of ⅜in. mild steel reinforced rod. Steel suppliers will give further information on reinforcing materials.

The structural design for the pool described in this project will suit almost every site. Where there are special conditions that require a special tank structure though, you should consult a civil or structural engineer. Very special site conditions are listed below and these can be dealt with in a number of ways.

High water table. An empty pool tank, in areas with a high water table such as marshy ground or near to a river bank, will float like a boat. Do not try to build a pool in such an area unless steps have been taken to drain the soil. Land can be drained with special pumps, but these are expensive to hire, so quick construction of the tank is obviously an advantage. Type A structures should be used here, therefore. To prevent the tank floating, provision must be made for an anti-flotation raft (extra weight to hold down and anchor the tank).

Temporary water table. In low lying areas, or areas with a porous sub-soil, you can take the steps outlined above to cope with the special conditions. An alternative is to build a partial out-of-ground pool—this cuts down excavation and construction difficulties. However, if you build a 3ft 6in. (1.07m) deep pool there should not be more than 2ft (0.61mm) of the pool out of the ground or you will have to adjust the reinforcement of the pool. A hydrostatic relief valve, described below, or the pumping of the ground water away to a main drain, will overcome some of the problems associated with this type of soil. If the site is sloping, rainwater causes a problem, but adequate drainage will overcome this.

Unstable or expansive soils. Sand, or sand and water sub-soils, make excavation difficult. The lie of loose soil in the excavated banks makes for considerably more excavation than normal sites. The below floor sub-soil is unstable and a sub-raft and extra reinforcement is needed. Hillside sites on slate, shale or gravel sub-soil areas will impose great forces on a below-ground structure, and extra reinforcing walls may be required. Freezing soil also increases pressure on the pool walls so protection of the tank, and pipes, is required.

Right. *A simple pool design in a well planned setting. A swimming pool quickly becomes the centre of your social activities.*

Corrosive soils. Soils which contain corrosive materials, such as sulphates, will attack concrete. Here, special admixtures are included in the below-ground concrete, and local suppliers will advise on this.

Unusual sites:

—Do not build on a cliff or hilltop site where soil movement may occur.

—Where digging through bedrock is necessary, pneumatic drills or dynamite have to be used— obviously this is not a job you can do yourself.

—Where a pool will be within 10ft (3.05m) of a building, wall or earth bank the pool will need extra reinforcing structures. Do not add to the weight of the tank floor unless you provide extra and deeper foundations for the building or wall.

Remember that these are very special site conditions which will not apply to 99 out of 100 cases. This project describes a pool built on a normal site—if in any doubt consult an expert pool builder, a civil, structural or soil engineer, the local authority and building and water authorities. You should consult the latter two anyway. Construction of the pool is not difficult or hazardous providing the pool is planned carefully and care is taken in the construction.

Sources of information

There are a variety of sources of information about swimming pools. You should consult your local authority. In Britain you do not normally need planning permission to build a pool, unless it is to be enclosed, but you should check with the local byelaws that there are no restrictions on, or special requirements for, the building of a swimming pool. You should also consult the electricity and water authority for information and advice.

You can usually get lists of specialist pool builders, a range of advisory booklets and construction and filtration standards, from national pool associations. In Britain the association is the Swimming Pool and Allied Trades Association. Pool specialists themselves can help you with literature, design advice and information about specialist equipment.

There are several swimming pool periodicals on the market and these can be obtained through newsagents. And you can get books about swimming pools from your library or bookseller. Concrete trade associations can supply pool construction booklets and address lists for building and equipment supplies. In Britain, the body to get in touch with is the Cement and Concrete Association.

Fig.1 (top). *A plan view of the pool, showing the overall dimensions. You can, of course, alter the dimensions of the pool to suit your garden and budget. Try to maintain the same proportions though, and don't plan too small a pool—its cost will be high compared to its usefulness.*

Fig.1 (centre). *A cross section of the pool showing the required levels and the depth of water at different levels.*

Fig.1 (bottom). *A plan view of the pool showing the radius of each curve.*

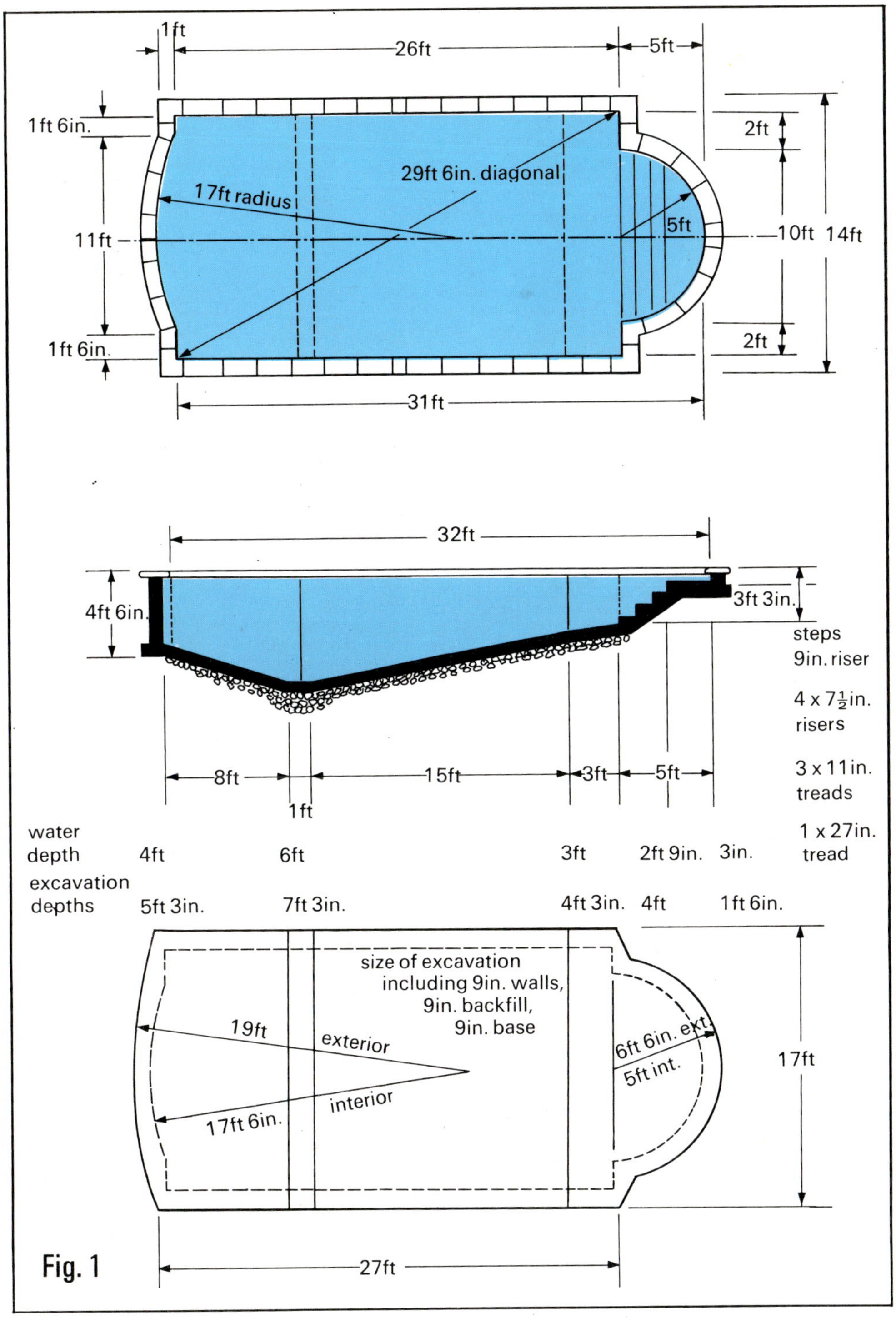

Fig. 1

TRI-ART

Fig. 2

straight-edge and
spirit level

datum
peg

proposed level

existing level

depth pegs

Fig. 3

bank cut
back

finished level

previous level

bank
drain

bank built up

Fig. 4

levelling pegs

equal tee piece siting to
provide level base

Fig.2. *To set the levels for the excavation of the pool tank, a datum peg is set in concrete near the site, and required levels transferred from it with a straight-edge and spirit level.*
Fig.3. *To dig the hole for the pool tank, you may have to cut back some earth*

banks and make up other levels. Land drains, at the base of earth banks, will prevent surface water draining into the finished excavation.
Fig.4. *When the excavation has been made, check floor levels back to the datum peg with three 4ft tee pieces.*

Above. *A swimming pool becomes the focal point of any garden, and adds a new dimension to your family's leisure activities.*

Siting

The size and shape of your garden will obviously influence the siting of your pool. The 32ft x 14ft (9.75m x 4.27m) pool described in this project takes up about 500 sq ft of ground area and you will need at least this much again for an adequate pool surround. The total minimum land area, therefore, is 45ft x 22ft (13.71m x 6.70m).

The reason you need so much space for the pool surround is that most people spend about 75% of their time around the pool rather than in the water. Plan for a complete pool garden, and think of it as another room to your home. It requires satisfactory access both during construction and use, with pleasant surroundings and decor.

If you plan to use mechanical diggers or dumpers for the excavation work you will need to provide an access path at least 8ft (2.44m) wide for them. Remember also that unless you lay some kind of temporary tracking these machines will inevitably damage the existing lawn and paths.

Don't tuck the pool away out of sight; it is likely to fall into disuse if you do. The pool can be screened, but make sure it receives the maximum sun. The area needs some shade but not too much. The pool should be sheltered from cold breezes but away from overhanging trees—otherwise leaf fall will soon cause cleaning problems. Plan for an open space—a lawn or small paved area—for the children to play on. Site the pool so that you can keep an eye on the children from the house when they are in or near the pool.

Plan the siting of the pool very carefully—*you can't move it afterwards*. If you draw up a plan of your garden, and position cut-outs of the pool and other installations on it, you will soon sort out the planning problems. Page 57 outlines the pool described here, laid out in an average size garden.

Setting

If possible utilize the natural lie of the land and plan for the tank to stand some way out of the ground—a maximum of 2ft (0.61m). This will reduce the amount of excavation that has to be undertaken. A slightly raised pool not only cuts construction costs but provides good opportunities for landscaping rockeries, walled gardens, and so on. Tasteful decor adds style to any pool and some useful ideas are given later (see 'Finishing' in the final part of this chapter).

You will often entertain guests around the pool so comfortable seating, lighting, firm paths, colour and warmth are almost essential. Sunbathing and sitting areas should overlook the pool and look onto attractive parts of the garden, a view of your house, or a favourite flower border. Pool surrounds can be as costly in both time and money, as the pool itself and it is often best to regard it as a second project.

If you have children, your pool should have as large a shallow area as possible, with wide steps that they can use with safety. Useful safety features if lots of children will be using the pool, are a fence around the deep end, and a net in the pool separating the deep from the shallow end. You should also be able to see the water area from the house.

You will want a deep end that is deep enough for diving. You can swim in 2ft 6in. (0.76m) of water, dive from the side in 6ft (1.83m), dive from a diving board in 7ft (2.13m) of water and dive from a springboard in 9ft (2.74m) of water. You should also plan for the maximum possible length so that athletic types can have a long swim.

A simple pool shape and setting looks best, and is easier to construct. Don't have too much changes of level (steps and gradients) as they only add to the expense, and not to the effect, of the pool.

Planning

Careful planning of this project pays dividends. A materials list will save you money, and a work plan, by giving incentive dates, should speed up the project. You will also be able to keep a check on the progress of the project.

Arrange for the delivery of materials close to the working site. About 50 tons of waste material will have to be removed and about the same amount of materials and equipment will arrive. Be careful, though, not to store any heavy materials close to the edge of the excavation—this could cause the walls to cave-in. Make sure that clean materials arrive in the right order and also use your oldest stock first.

Setting out

The first step in setting out the swimming pool is to set a solid timber stake into a small quantity of concrete just outside the excavation area. This peg is the datum position and all measurements and levels are taken from it. Remember, when setting this peg, to allow for the above ground protrusion if you are constructing a tank that is partially out-of-ground.

The dimensions given below are for the pool shown in Fig.1. You can, of course, alter the dimensions to suit your needs. Clear the site and temporarily mark out the internal dimensions of the pool with wooden pegs. Check that the pool

will be in the right position and of the correct area. Then you can mark out the external dimensions of the pool—these allow for 9in. (299mm) block walls plus 9in. of backfill between the pool walls and sides of the excavation. The measurements also allow for a 9in. floor.

The dimensions for the pool described here are :—

Length and width

	Internal dimensions	External dimensions for excavation
overall length	32ft (9.75m)	35ft (10.66m)
rectangular length (exc. deep end curve)	26ft (7.92m)	27ft (approx) (8.23m)
rectangular width	14ft (4.27m)	17ft (5.18m)
diagonal measurement	29ft 6in. (8.88m)	—
semicircular steps	10ft (3.05m)	13ft (3.69m)

Depth

	Water depth	Overall depth	Excavation depth from datum peg at top paving level
shallow end	2ft 9in. (0.83m)	3ft 3in. (1m)	4ft (1.22m)
maximum	6ft (1.83m)	6ft 6in. (1.98m)	7ft 3in. (2.20m)
deep end	4ft (1.22m)	4ft 6in. (1.37m)	5ft 3in. (1.60m)

Fig. 1 gives the pool's dimensions in greater detail. It is a good idea to knock pegs in at the corners and join them with string levels for extra reference (PROJECT 2, Fig. 2 can help you here). Check the diagonals to make sure that the marked out area is 'square'. Check the dimensions of the pool, from the datum point, regularly during construction of the pool.

Excavation

An excavating machine will make short work of the hole, it will do the job in a day on normal sites and as such is an almost essential item. Alternatively, two men can dig the hole in about 14 days. An excavator digs with reasonable precision but do not dig the hole too deep as it will be difficult to make up the level satisfactorily, and avoid sinkage of the pool. If it is absolutely necessary, either increase the pool depth or ram hardcore down into the bottom of the hole and cover it with a blinding screed.

The floor of the hole must be firm if it is to take the considerable weight of the water and the pool, so you must dig down until you reach firm, stable sub-soil.

Once you have dug the hole you must set the floor and get the deep end walls up as soon as possible. Weak areas in the walls of the hole and corners should be shored up. Heavy rainfall will ruin an excavation so you should take these steps as soon as you can.

Refer to the datum pegs regularly to check the

depths of the excavation and check the final floor levels with three 4ft tee pieces, as shown in Fig.4. You will probably need to do some of the final levelling by hand.

A water table presents problems during excavation. A water table refers to the level below which the rock or soil is saturated with water. Whether or not there is a water table within 7ft of the surface, do not dig in wet weather as you will treble the cost and time involved. You could use pumps to keep a wet site reasonably dry but these are expensive to hire and it is probably best, in these circumstances, to opt for rapid pool construction and the services of an expert pool builder. A moderate water table will fluctuate, so carry out the excavation in dry weather.

Digging a sump near the pool excavation is useful as it can be used to pump water away during construction. If you think there may be a water table, then the hole for the sump will act as a test bore hole. Hydrostatic relief valves (valves which operate under water pressure are sometimes fitted to the main drain of the pool, these allow water to seep into the pool, easing any outside pressure that could create an upwards thrust. These valves only assist in the draining off of water, however, and they are not a solution to the problem of water close to the surface. The valves are only about 1in. (25mm) in diameter so they will not cope with a lot of water and they sometimes stick. Professional pool builders, faced with the problem of a high water table, will design for a concrete subraft, 1ft to 2ft thick, that will anchor the pool tank by countering the upward flotation lift of water in the soil. This solution, though, greatly increases the cost of the project.

You may be able to overcome the problem of a high water table by having the tank partially raised out of the ground. Alternatively, opt for a free standing, above ground pool, as described in PROJECT 1.

After the hole for the tank has been dug, some of the excavated soil can be kept to fill the gap between the pool walls (when they are built) and the walls of the excavation. The top 6in. to 12in. (150mm to 305mm) of good soil may be useful elsewhere in the garden.

While you have the excavating machine on site, dig the service trenches to the plant room (details in part 3 of this chapter) and the backwash drain. The trenches should be about 18in. (457mm) deep and 12in. (305mm) wide with an even fall and rise to the plant room. The plant room itself should be no more than 25ft (7.62m) away from the pool and at the manufacturers' recommended height above or below the water level. This can be up to 3ft (0.91m) above or 6ft (1.83m) below the water level, depending on the pump rating. Try to avoid sharp bends in the trenching—every corner reduces the efficiency of the pump. More details are given in the second part of this chapter.

You could dig the foundations for the plant room and dig the backwash soakaway while you have the excavating machine. You could also simply level the topsoil in another part of the garden.

Once you have dug the hole for the pool tank you can set the tank floor and walls. This is described in the second part of this chapter.

A swimming pool to make: 2

The first part of this chapter described how to plan the task of building a swimming pool and how to make the excavation for the pool tank. Here all the steps involved in reinforcing and building the pool walls and floor are given, together with details of under-pool drainage. The work described here is a big step towards completing the pool.

The finished excavation is probably the most crucial stage in the construction of a swimming pool. Bad weather, particularly heavy rain, can ruin the excavation, so it is important to get the floor and walls of the pool built as soon as possible. If you can't do this job soon after the hole has been dug you may save time and money by having a contractor do it for you. A contractor will take about a week to do the job.

Protecting the excavation

There are several steps you can take to protect the excavation from the weather. On sloping sites you should dig trenches to divert surface water round, rather than into, the excavation. You should also lay temporary land drains around the base of banks of excavated earth. Land drains consist of porous pipes that let water in through their sides and at the joins along the pipework. If possible, install drainage lines running downhill from the deepest point of the excavation.

Other steps you can take are to round the top edge of the excavation—simply hit the earth with the flat of a shovel. Rounded edges crumble less easily than angular ones. Lay polythene sheets over the walls of the excavation to reduce the risk of cave-ins. The sheets will protect the earth walls from the effects of rain water. If you have to delay construction of the walls, take steps to shore up the earth walls at any weak points.

DOUGLAS SIMMONDS

Drainage

There must not be any water trapped underneath the finished pool, so effective drainage beneath the tank is essential. The first thing to do is to see where sub-soil water seeping into the excavation can drain to—this could be a ditch, a main drain or simply along the ground, away from the excavation. This point will, of course, be below the level of the deepest part of the excavation. This type of drainage is a gravity outlet which is described fully in the third part of this chapter.

Land drains beneath the pool should lead to a main drain connected to the gravity outlet, as

Left. The ideal place for a pool is close to the house. This helps make the pool into an 'extra room' where much of your entertaining will be done. You can keep an eye on the children too—a useful safety factor.
Below. Simple pool designs are the best choice for the do-it-yourself pool builder.

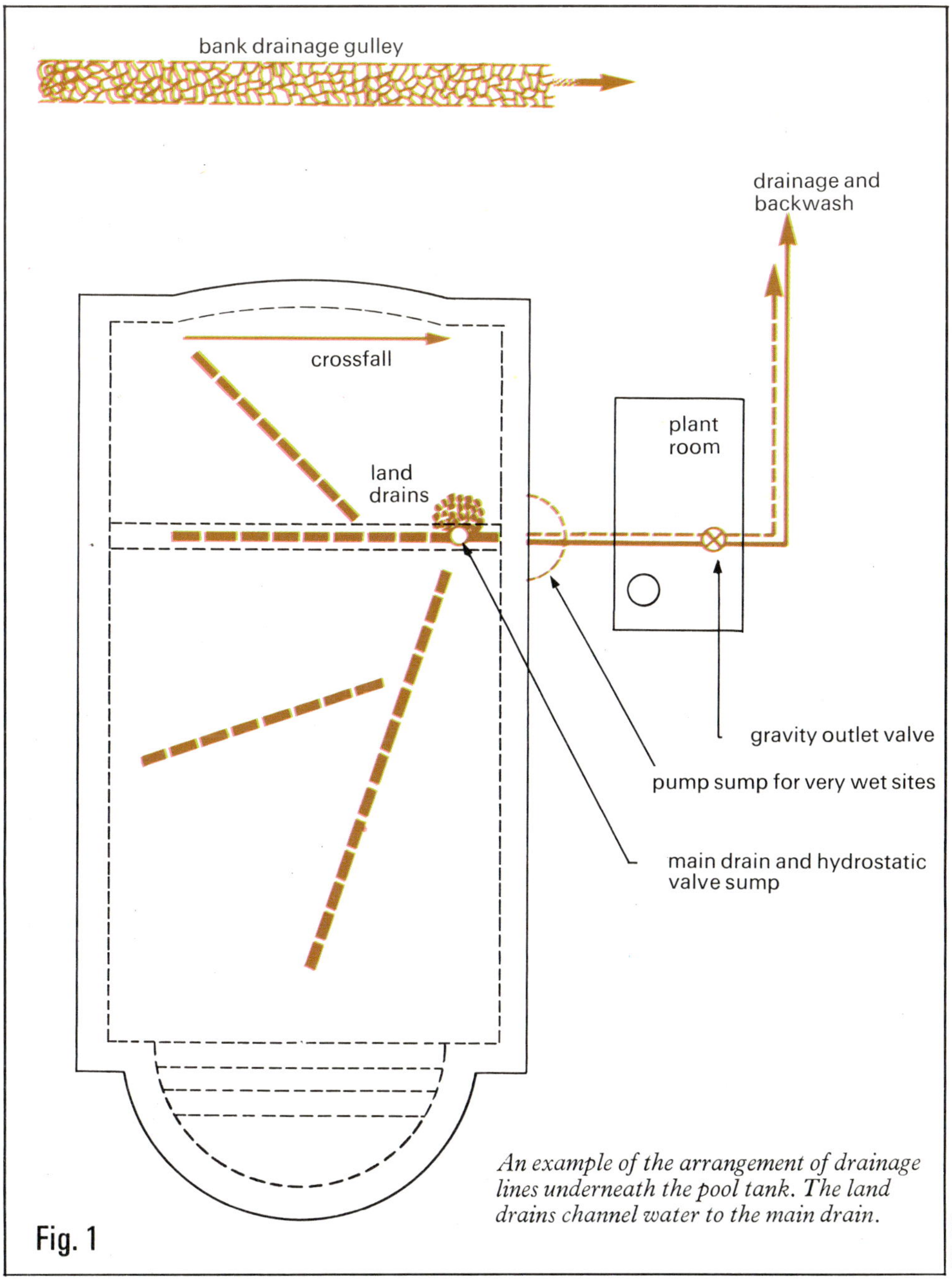

shown in Fig.2. They should be arranged in a pattern similar to that shown in Fig.1. If a gravity outlet is not practical—where, for example, the bottom of the excavation is below the level of the lowest point of your garden—you can install a hydrostatic relief valve inside the main drain. This will reduce below-ground water pressure. A hydrostatic relief valve is a device with a one way valve that opens when below-ground water pressure rises, letting water into the excavation to be pumped away. When the pool is full, the pressure of pool water will always exceed outside water pressure.

A hydrostatic valve is some protection against an empty pool tank starting to float under the pressure of below-ground water, but it does not solve the problem of a high water table. These valves are limited in size, so they cannot cope with a large volume of water and they sometimes stick. Where there is a high water table, hydrostatic valves are not an alternative to the concrete sub-floor raft that pool contractors

would use to prevent flotation of an empty tank.

Lay the land drains end to end in channels scooped out of the floor of the excavation. Make sure they are firmly bedded. Cover the floor area, except about 2ft (610mm) around the perimeter of the hole, with 1in.—2in. (25mm—51mm) pebbles (sometimes called 'beach') to a depth of about 3ft (915mm). Press these down lightly. These pebbles help to drain water from the hole. They are not laid to the edges of the excavation—this allows the walls to be built on a layer of concrete thicker than the floor concrete. This gives the wall its foundations, or footings.

A hydrostatic relief valve can be positioned inside the main drain so that it will be $\frac{3}{4}$in. (19mm) proud of the finished floor. Set it in the drainage pebbles. Alternatively, fit a gravity outlet drain, running downhill, to clear water from the excavation and from the finished pool. This should also be positioned so that it will be about $\frac{3}{4}$in. (19mm) proud of the finished floor.

The main drain is also set about $\frac{3}{4}$in. (19mm)

bank drainage gulley

drainage and backwash

crossfall

plant room

land drains

gravity outlet valve

pump sump for very wet sites

main drain and hydrostatic valve sump

An example of the arrangement of drainage lines underneath the pool tank. The land drains channel water to the main drain.

Fig. 1

TRI-ART

proud of the finished level of the floor. The suction/up pipe is securely fixed in position with steel rod—used as fixing pins—and wire, ready for connection to the pipework that runs to the filter. All these fittings are discussed in the third part of this chapter and their arrangement is shown in Fig.2. Make sure you plug the ends of pipes and outlets so that they don't become blocked with concrete when you come to lay the floor of the pool.

The next step is to cover the pebbles with 500 gauge polythene sheeting or waterproof paper. Do not, of course, cover the floor fittings. If you can keep this covering, or membrane, clean, you can lay the floor directly onto it. If the covering does get dirty, apply a 1 in. (25mm) thick concrete screed over it.

Reinforcement

The concrete walls and floor of the pool must be reinforced with steel. This, of course, is put in place before the walls and floor are built. You can use either $\frac{3}{8}$in. (9.5mm) steel rod for the reinforcement, or steel mesh with a weight of 6.2lbs per sq yd. Mesh is only used where the walls of the pool are cavity walls, the mesh being placed between the two 'skins' of the wall. This makes the whole project more expensive than one using single skin walls, though cavity walls are stronger and non-porous.

The pool described here has walls made of hollow core concrete blocks, reinforced with mild steel rod. The 6in. (150mm) concrete floor is similarly reinforced. Note that the spacings of the reinforcement used in the pool described

here are for pools on normal sites, not for pools built in special sites (see the first part of this chapter).

Reinforcement for the pool consists of a 'steel basket skeleton'. The structure described here is suitable for pools in normal sites and caters for a 6ft 6in. (1.98m) depth of water.

Floor reinforcement

The steel rods for the floor reinforcement are arranged in a pattern of squares set at 12in. (305mm) centres. The ends of the rods are overlapped by 15in. (380mm). The rods are positioned on top of 4½in. (114mm) bricks—this ensures that the reinforcement is covered with 1½in. (38mm) of concrete when the 6in. (150mm) floor is laid. You can build the steel framework on top of the waterproof membrane if it has been kept clean—if it has not, cover it with a 1in. (25mm) concrete blinding screed.

Lay the steel rods for the floor in a pattern of squares, on top of the bricks (see Fig.3). At the the edges of the excavation, stop the rods about 2in. (51mm) short of where the pool walls will be. Overlap the rods by 15in. at their ends and bend over the 2in. to 3in. (51mm to 75mm) of each rod to give a stronger reinforcement. Where the rods cross, bind them together with 18 gauge steel wire.

Wall reinforcement

The reinforcement for the walls of the pool is formed with $\frac{3}{8}$in. (9.5mm) steel rod, set at 9in. (229mm) centres up to a pool depth of 4ft (1220mm) and at 4½in. (114mm) centres

towards the deep end. The hollow core concrete blocks for the pool walls are placed over these rods.

The wall reinforcement is built up from the base of the walls with 'starter' rods, 3ft to 4ft (915mm to 1220mm) in length. These are bent at 90° in the middle so that part of them rests on the floor and are tied to the floor reinforcement with wire. The wall reinforcement is held away from the sides of the excavation with support pins made from $\frac{3}{8}$in. (9.5mm) rods, hooked over at one end and pushed into the earth wall at the other.

Position the starter rods carefully, remembering to allow for ½in. (13mm) width of mortar joint between the blocks. Bind vertical rods to the starters with 18 gauge wire. Push support pins in place where necessary. Do not position all the deep end rods at once—this will cut down the amount of lifting of the hollow core concrete

Fig.2. A cross section of the under tank drainage necessary for the pool described in this chapter. The hydrostatic relief valve allows below ground water to seep into the pool tank when it is empty. The water is then pumped away. The valve is used where water cannot be drained to a point in the garden lower than the main drain in the tank floor.
Fig.3. Details of the steel reinforcement of the concrete swimming pool tank. The vertical rods in the pool walls are put in place after each course of concrete blocks is laid. The detail (top right) shows the step reinforcement (see Fig.1 in part 1 of this chapter).

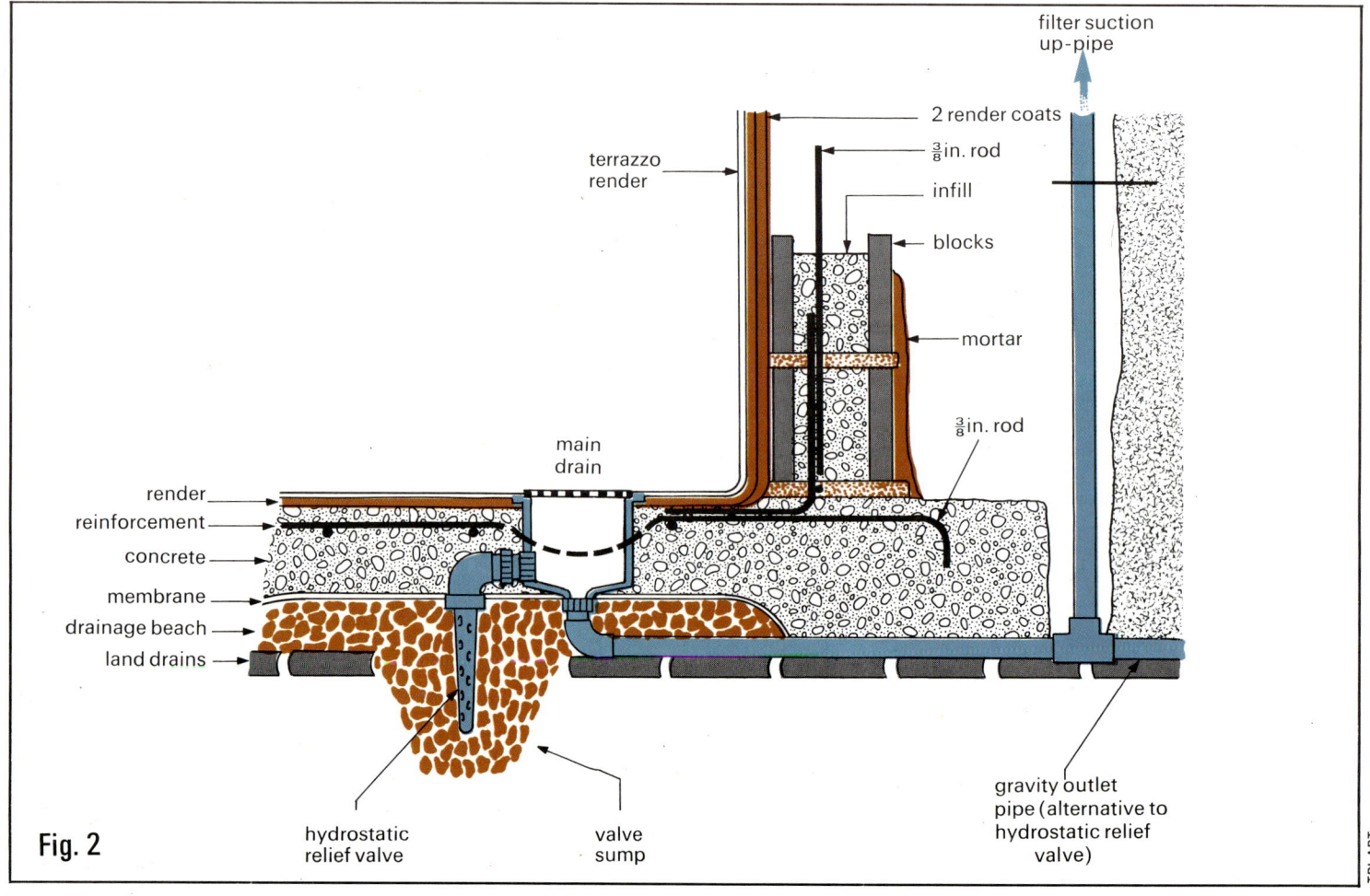

Fig. 2

filter suction up-pipe

2 render coats
$\frac{3}{8}$in. rod
infill
blocks

terrazzo render

mortar

$\frac{3}{8}$in. rod

main drain

render
reinforcement
concrete
membrane
drainage beach
land drains

hydrostatic relief valve

valve sump

gravity outlet pipe (alternative to hydrostatic relief valve)

TRI-ART

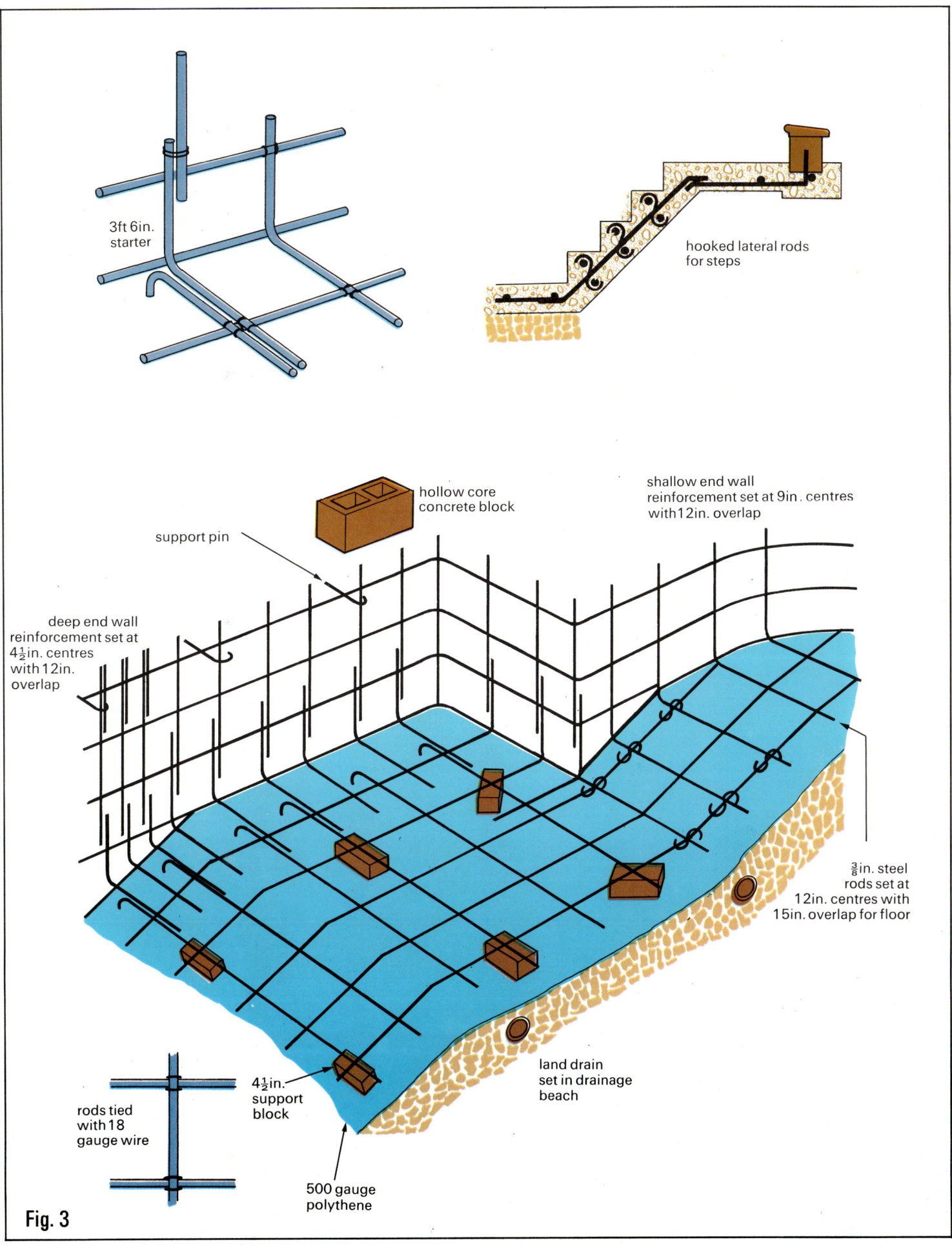

3ft 6in.
starter

hooked lateral rods
for steps

support pin

hollow core
concrete block

shallow end wall
reinforcement set at 9in. centres
with 12in. overlap

deep end wall
reinforcement set at
$4\frac{1}{2}$in. centres
with 12in.
overlap

$\frac{3}{8}$in. steel
rods set at
12in. centres with
15in. overlap for floor

rods tied
with 18
gauge wire

$4\frac{1}{2}$in.
support
block

land drain
set in drainage
beach

500 gauge
polythene

Fig. 3

TRI-ART

Fig. 4

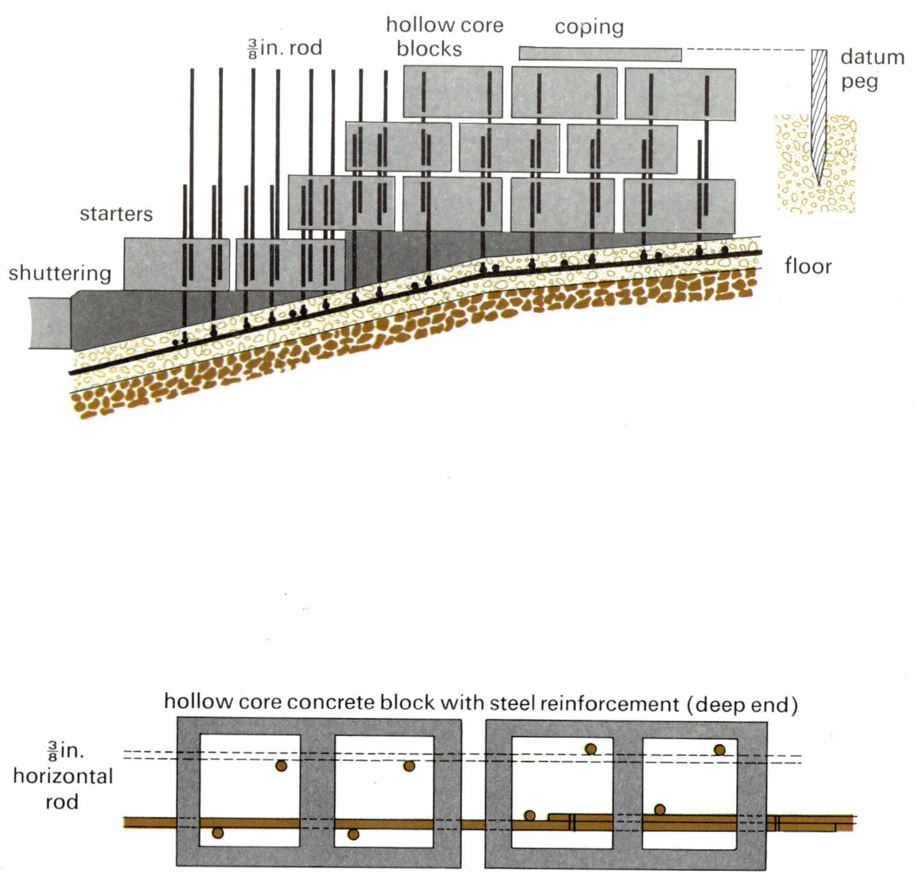

TRI-ART

Fig.4. The pool walls, built of hollow core concrete blocks. Make sure that each block-work course is level by referring back to the datum peg. The lower diagram shows the position of the vertical reinforcing rods, one in opposite corners of each hollow core.

blocks that you will have to do later.

Make sure that all the steel rods used in the reinforcement are free from rust and scale. Also clear any fallen earth from around the steel framework as this will reduce the strength of the concrete that is used later to fill the hollow cores of the wall blocks.

Laying the floor

Use a concrete mix of four parts shingle, two parts sharp sand and one part cement. Working from the shallow end, and taking care not to cover the floor fittings, lay 6in. (150mm) of concrete over the steel reinforcement. Remove the blocks from under the steel rods as you go. Firmly tamp down the concrete to give a dense, coarse finish. Check all levels back to the datum peg (see the first part of this chapter).

There are a few points to remember when doing this job. The whole floor and footings should be laid in the same day so make sure you have sufficient help, and a concrete mixer on site. Use only clean, good quality materials. Do not mix the concrete too wet or it will start to compact, or 'slump', before you lay it. Use just enough water to make the concrete workable.

The newly laid floor will take a week to cure and it should be protected from heat and cold during this period with waterproof coverings. You can use the time to build the formwork for the steps and plan their reinforcement. The steps are shown in Fig.3. You could also lay the concrete for the floor of the equipment room.

Building the walls

The walls of the pool are built up with 18in. x 9in. x 9in. (457mm x 229mm x 229mm) hollow core concrete blocks. They are set on the footings, leaving 9in. (229mm) between the pool walls and the walls of the excavation. The blocks are laid with normal semi-block bond throughout (see Fig.4) and the blocks are bonded at the corners as for brickwork. Steel rods are laid horizontally in the ½in. (13mm) mortar course between each course of blocks—these rods are woven in and out of the vertical rods.

The hollow core concrete blocks are porous so impervious render coats or liners are essential for watertightness. Where there is a water table, the back of the blocks (the side facing the excavation walls) must be covered with a ½in. (13mm) coating of render. This back coat is applied as each brickwork course is built. The render stops water seepage from the surrounding earth lifting off the internal render coat which is applied later.

The incline of the excavation floor is levelled off with concrete set in formwork—this job is done in stages as you proceed with setting the blockwork walls.

It is important that the number of block courses from the finished level datum peg be calculated. Allow for ½in. (13mm) mortar courses between the blocks and 2in. (51mm) for coping (described in part 4 of this chapter). A 6ft 6in. (1.98m) depth of water, therefore, requires 7ft (2.13m) of walling, calculated as follows:

8 x 9in. blocks	equals	6ft
8 x ½in. joints	equals	4in.
1 x 2in. coping	equals	2in.
shuttering concrete to level incline		6in. (deepest point)
		7ft 0in.

This calculation is for the size of block given above. Blocks do vary in size by as much as ¾in. (19mm) depending on the manufacturer, so check the size of the block you are using.

Make sure, before and during the construction of the walls, that the levels and lines are correct. Start the job at the deep and and shutter the sloping floor in the corner to give a level base. Pour concrete into the formwork and set the first block in place, sliding it down over the horizontal reinforcement. Continue this process until the first block course is laid, and then install a horizontal rod, on top of the blocks and woven in and out of the vertical reinforcement. Make sure, when laying the first and subsequent block courses, that the vertical rods are clear of the inner sides of the blocks.

Work towards the shallow end. When the wall is level with the foundation for the end wall at the corner, you can start to build up the blockwork at the corners—this will make an accurate guide for subsequent work.

Half fill the hollow core of the blocks in the first course with a 4:2:1 mix of aggregate, sharp sand and cement. Make sure that the steel rods are covered by at least 1½in. (38mm) of concrete all round. Compact the concrete infill without disturbing the setting of the blocks.

Lay the second course of blocks and half fill them with concrete. The first course is now keyed with the second because of the concrete infill. Lay horizontal steel rod between every course. Half fill the blocks in each course, except the last. Leave only a 1in. (25mm) gap here between the top of the infill and the top of the block—this leaves sufficient space to key the coping to the top course.

Throughout this job check levels back to the datum peg. If your final course is not level this will be very obvious when the pool is filled with water, as the water surface will be perfectly true.

When the blocks have set, push excavated soil into the gap between the back of the blocks and the walls of the excavation, compacting the soil thoroughly. If possible, do this after every second course. Do not backfill the final two courses through—use this gap for laying pipework.

Remember to prevent earth entering the hollow cores of the blocks. Earth in the concrete infill will reduce its strength.

The next step is to install the pool wall fittings.

MICHAEL BOYS

A swimming pool to make: 3

The first two parts of this chapter described how to excavate the hole for the swimming pool tank, and how to build the walls and floor of the pool. This part describes the basic equipment needed to get water into and out of the pool, and how to keep the water clean and comfortably warm.

The basic requirement, in a swimming pool of the kind described here, is a circulation and filtration system that will keep the pool water fresh and clean. You cannot simply fill a pool and then empty it when the water starts to stagnate—this is expensive and many water authorities won't allow you to empty thousands of gallons of water into the drains.

A modern circulation system cleanses pool water continuously. The sort of filtration system you choose depends on your pocket—you can install a simple and cheap filter or a sophisticated system of filtration, sterilization, water balancing and heating.

The circulation system for the pool described here consists of lengths of plastic pipe, running from the main drain and the skimmer weir

(see below) to the filter and heater, and back to the pool, through the inlet. The pump provides the power that draws and pushes water along the pipes.

Circulation fittings

The installation of these fittings will vary according to the type you use, and manufacturers supply setting instructions for their models. A general outline of the pool fittings is useful, though.

The layout of the circulation pipework and fittings—the inlet, filter, pump and skimmer weir—is shown in Fig.1. Before you install these however, fit small lengths of plastic pipework to them at the points where the circulation pipework (see below) has to be connected to the fittings. This makes connection to the pipework easier, especially where fittings are set into the pool wall.

The skimmer weir is a device set at water level, in place of one concrete block (see Fig.2). It is set firmly in reinforced concrete.

The skimmer weir draws surface debris from the pool towards the filter. Larger debris is trapped in a basket within the skimmer—this stops it blocking the pipe lines. A floating flap on the skimmer weir rises and falls with the water level. The skimmer has a lid so that you can remove the basket of debris and on most makes this can be adjusted to the level of the paved pool surround. Skimmers do not clear all the scum from the pool so there should be an area of tiles around the top of the pool to make cleaning easier.

Position the skimmer weir away from the corners of the pool, facing the general direction of the wind. One skimmer is adequate for the pool described here, but larger pools may need two.

The main drain is set at the lowest point of the pool. Water goes down the main drain and along a pipe beneath the pool floor to the filter. This pipe line is called the main suction.

The inlet is the point at which filtered water re-enters the pool. It should be large enough to cope with the flow of water—otherwise

Left. A vertical high speed sand filter— a very efficient water cleansing system. These filters do not need recharging.
Below. An attractive and well built pool.

water pressure will build up in the pipe. This will put pressure on the filter and impose a greater workload on the pump.

The inlet is set into one wall of the pool, about two block courses down. To make the hole for the inlet, the corners of two adjacent blocks are knocked off during the building of the pool wall. When the inlet is in place the rest of the hole is carefully filled with concrete.

Fig.1 shows the location of these fittings. Since fitting instructions vary, depending on the type of equipment you are using, you should follow the manufacturers' instructions carefully. Remember, when setting the fittings into the wall, to allow for the depth of the internal rendering (see the fourth part of this chapter).

Filter

Fresh tap water can be cloudy and tinged green because of harmless algae, or rusty red because of iron in the water. The depth of the pool water will highlight the discolouration of the water and stain the pool finish. Then, even after the water has been chlorinated and flocculated, fresh contamination occurs. (Flocculation is the addition of a cleansing agent to

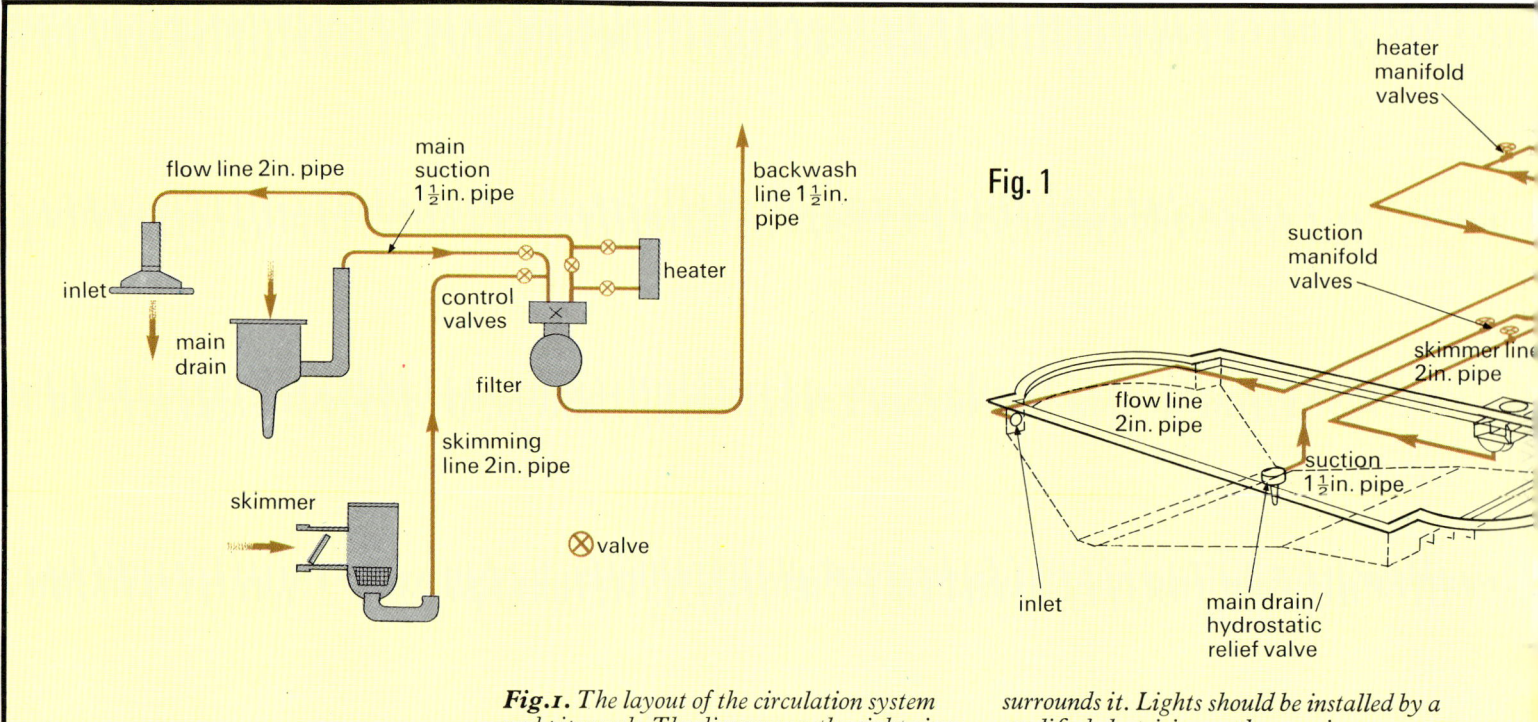

flow line 2in. pipe

main suction 1½in. pipe

inlet

main drain

backwash line 1½in. pipe

Fig. 1

control valves

heater

filter

skimming line 2in. pipe

skimmer

⊗ valve

heater manifold valves

suction manifold valves

skimmer line 2in. pipe

flow line 2in. pipe

suction 1½in. pipe

inlet

main drain/ hydrostatic relief valve

Fig.1. The layout of the circulation system and pipework. The diagram on the right gives a perspective view of the system.
Fig.2. A cross section showing the skimmer weir, a cup anchor and an underwater light. The skimmer weir is set at water level, in place of one hollow core concrete block. The cup anchor gives a fixing for a safety net between the shallow end and the deep end. The sealed light is cooled by the water that surrounds it. Lights should be installed by a qualified electrician as they are in a potentially dangerous situation.
Fig.3. A cutaway view of a pressure sand filter and the connecting pipework.
Fig.4. A typical pool heater. Heaters greatly lengthen the swimming season and are a valuable feature of the circulation system.
Right. A simpler filter than that shown on page 1924, mounted in the plant room.

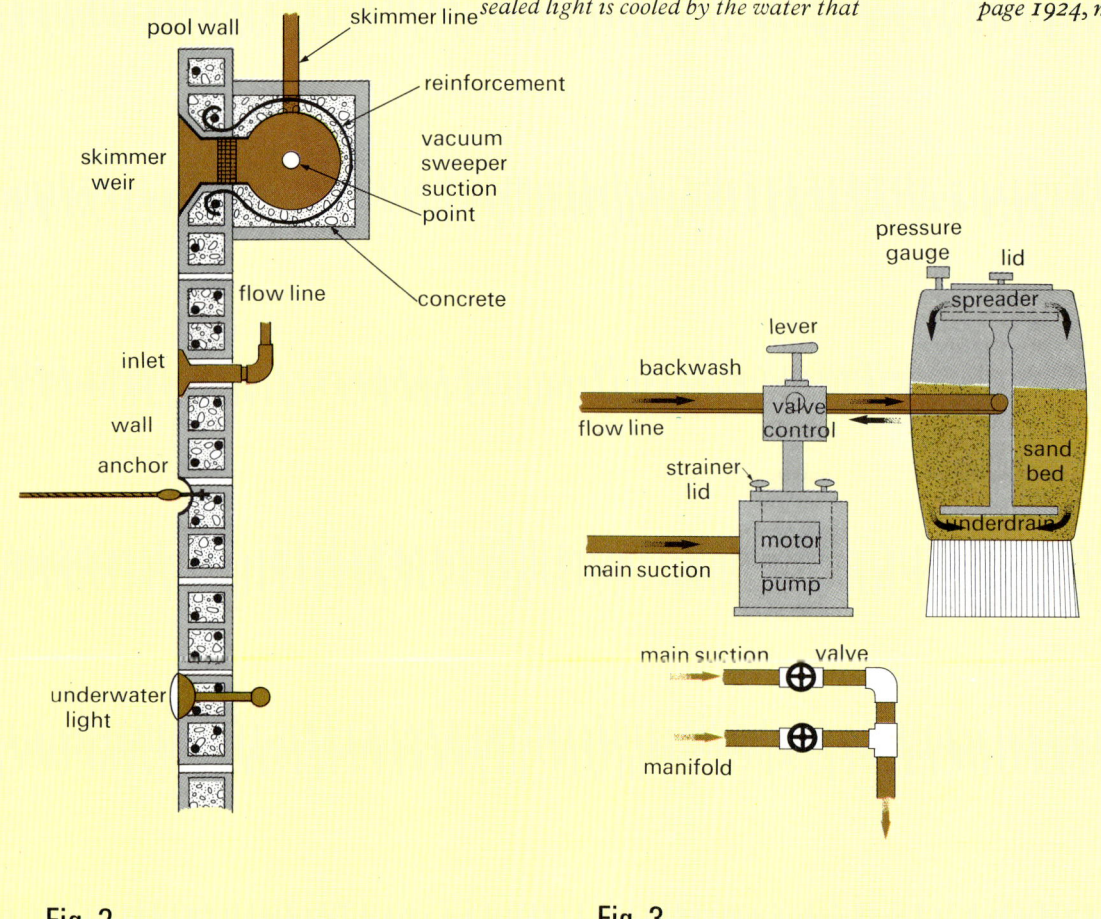

pool wall

skimmer line

reinforcement

skimmer weir

vacuum sweeper suction point

flow line

concrete

inlet

wall

anchor

underwater light

pressure gauge

lid

lever

spreader

backwash

flow line

valve control

sand bed

strainer lid

main suction

motor pump

underdrain

main suction   valve

manifold

Fig. 2

Fig. 3

Fig. 4

70

heater   filter

to waste

backwash
line 1½in. pipe

control valve
manifold

pump/motor/
strainer basket

skimmer/leaf
basket/vacuum
point

flow line   to inlet

heater manifold and bypass

when valve is closed
flow passes through
heater

OFF TEMP°C CONTROL
ON SUPPLY HEATER

element

electric water heater

TRI-ART

the pool water. This causes dissolved particles to come together, or 'coagulate', and fall to the bottom of the pool where they can be swept away when the pool is empty.) New impurities will enter the pool from the air—dust, insects and leaves—and from the pool users. The water quickly becomes polluted, so an effective filter is essential.

The filter consists of a pre-strainer, a pump, a motor, a flow valve and a filter valve. All the equipment connected with the filter should be non-corrosive. A self-priming pump is the best choice. This type of pump will operate even when placed above the water level and when the main suction pipe, from the main drain, is full of air. The other main type of pump, the non self-priming pump, will not work if any air is present in the main suction pipe.

There are two main types of filter, the pre-coat systems and the pressure sand filter. Of the pre-coat systems, the diatomaceous earth filter is the most common. It consists of a layer of diatoms, microscopic fossilised sea organisms which form a highly porous filter. The pump sucks water through layers of this material. Impurities are trapped in the tiny channels that run through these layers. Other pre-coat systems consist of very fine particles, formed into septums, or membranes.

Water filtered through these systems has a very fine 'polish'—that is, it is crystal clear. All these systems have to be recharged after backwashing (see below).

Pressure sand filters are cheaper than pre-coat systems and they do not have to be recharged. Water is filtered through a layer of special silica sands. These filters are probably the best choice for residential pools though they do not give quite such a good polish to the pool water as pre-coat systems.

Filters are rated by the manufacturer according to the number of gallons of water they can cope with in an hour. The rating should, however, take account of the resistance —from friction, for example—that the pump has to overcome when forcing water through the pipes. This resistance will reduce the amount of water that the pump can push through the filter and so the filter rating is reduced. Make sure than the rating given by the manufacturer takes this into account.

The pool circulation system collects matter which is deposited in the filter. In time the filter starts to block up and pressure inside the system builds up. At a certain point, the filter ceases to work properly and needs cleaning.

Cleaning the filter

Cleaning the filter is done by reversing the flow of water in the filter to 'backwash' collected dirt to waste. This process takes 2 to 5 minutes— 40 to 200 gallons can be pumped out in this time. Some filters have to be taken apart for cleaning or recharging (replacing the filter material) but the modern pressure sand filter simply reverses the flow of water to stir up small particles of dirt and carry them away to waste—some filters do this automatically.

The regularity of backwashes depends on how often the pool is used, its siting and the rating of the filter. In summer, once a week is a good average but the frequency also depends

on the filter turnover—this is the length of time it takes for the clean filter to draw through all the pool water. For residential pools this usually takes 8 hours but if you can install a filter that does this more quickly the pool will be easier to clean and maintain. Fig.3 shows a typical pressure sand filter and manufacturers provide detailed installation and operating instructions.

The pool described here has a capacity of 11,000 gallons and should have a filter with a rating of 1400 gallons per hour for an 8 hour turnover, or 2200 gallons per hour for a 5 hour turnover. The internal design of the filter should be as simple as possible to give maximum efficiency.

Pool heating

Warm water makes the swimming season longer and encourages greater use of the pool. If you don't install a heating system along with all the other pool fittings, make allowances for one to be added later. All you need to do is to make sure the plant room (see below) is large enough to take the extra equipment and to install a by-pass valve in the pipe line that carries water back to the pool from the heater. Water can then be channelled through the heater (see Fig.4).

There are several types of pool heater available. The solar heater uses the heat of the sun and transfers this to the water by 'heat exchange'. These systems are expensive to install but cost practically nothing to run. You must, of course, live in an area that receives enough sunlight to keep the solar heater functioning. Oil and gas heaters are also expensive to install but if well maintained the running costs are small. These heaters are quite bulky. Electric heaters are cheap to install and require little maintenance but running costs are high. They are quiet and clean to run though, and the units are compact. They can also take advantage of cheaper, 'off-peak' electricity, where such schemes apply.

Whatever the differences in installation and running costs between the different systems in the short term, the cost tends to equalize over five or six years. The cost of heating a pool in the summer is roughly the same as the cost of central heating in the home.

If you have central heating in your home you can choose another method of heating the pool. A heat exchange unit will tap heat from the domestic system to warm the pool water. This is the most economical form of pool heating. Unless your boiler has an extra capacity equivalent to 100,000 British Thermal Units (btu) per hour though, this system will reduce the amount of heating in the home. Also, if the house boiler is some way from the pool, heat loss will occur along the pipe length.

An electric pool heater should have a capacity of about 1 to 1½ kilowatts for each 1,000 gallons of water. An oil or gas boiler should have a capacity of 7 to 10 btu per hour. The 11,000 gallon pool described here needs either an 18kw electric heater or a 110,000 btu per hour oil or gas boiler. Makers of pool equipment and gas and electricity authorities will give more detailed advice on the size of heater you need, and give installation information.

The heater must give enough heat not only

BILL McLAUGHLIN

to heat up the pool in the first place, but also to compensate for heat loss. The initial heating of the water is best done during the spring and the pool will store most of the heat for the rest of the season. Most heat loss occurs at night from the water surface by evaporation and the smallest breeze considerably increases heat loss—one reason why a sheltered and sunny spot is best for a pool. The temperature of the pool water can fall by between 2° to 5°C (3.6°F to 9°F) at night and the heater will have to be switched on for about 4 to 10 hours to make this up. In Britain, a heater that raises pool water temperature by $\frac{1}{2}$°C per hour is usually sufficient to deal with nightly heat loss.

Surface heat loss can be reduced by as much as 50% if you cover the pool surface—thin plastic foam sandwiched between pvc sheeting is an excellent insulator. If there is a water table in your area, heat loss will also occur through the pool walls. This can be prevented by lining the walls with 2in. thick polystyrene insulation sheeting.

Circulation pipework

Pool fittings and pipe lines are arranged to form an enclosed circuit between the pool and the filter. An example layout is shown in Fig.1. The system must, of course, be perfectly watertight, durable and efficient.

Fittings and pipework can either be of stainless steel, chromed metal, gunmetal or plastic. All of these are rust proof. Some waters, though, are acidic or hard—these are harmless to the skin but they cause problems of corrosion to the pipework and fittings. The water, in these cases, must be neutralized. This is described in the final part of this chapter.

Circulation pipework is available in rigid or flexible plastic, copper or galvanized iron—the latter, though, corrodes and this can lead to damage of the pool equipment. Copper

Above. A pool design similar to the one described in this chapter. The setting is simple, with the plant tubs providing colour and the trees and fence giving shelter from wind.

pipework is expensive and can corrode as a result of electrolytic action (the chemical decomposition of the copper caused by its reaction with chemicals in the soil or in adjacent pipes of different metals). Plastic pipework is by far the best choice—it is easy to work with and does not corrode.

The plumbing for the pool is as straightforward as household pipework. The pipes used are 1$\frac{1}{2}$in. or 2in. (38mm or 51mm) rigid unplasticized pvc or flexible plastic pipes. Plastic pipes can be threaded for jointing but this is a long job and the amount of use you will get out of a die large enough to cut the thread is unlikely to pay for its cost. If you join threaded plastic pipes, the joint can be sealed with boss-white—a sort of putty made from whiting and linseed oil—but a better alternative is to use thin plastic tape called ptfe (polytetrafluraethylene). This helps make a really watertight joint.

Sound joints in plastic pipes can also be made with adhesive. Glueing pipes and alternative methods of jointing are relatively easy with plastic tubing.

Manufacturers of plastic pipes will supply full details of their products and directions on how to lay them. The setting out is straightforward (see Fig.1). Try a test joint before working head downwards in a trench. If you are glueing the pipes, wipe the ends with cleansing fluid before using plenty of adhesive —this will set in about a minute depending on the temperature.

Before fixing up the whole pipework system, remember to avoid sharp corners along the length of the pipework, and try to avoid very long runs of pipe. The filter may circulate between 20 and 40 gallons per minute and any restrictions in the pipes will reduce the efficiency of the pump. If the plant room (see below) is situated some distance from the pool, or if the pool is likely to be used by a lot of people, you will need a more powerful pump.

Fit the whole pipework system together dry in a test run, and then use plenty of adhesive to join the pipes. The joints must be sound. You can test the pipes for watertightness after you have allowed the adhesive to set for about 24 hours. Testing the pipes is done by sealing the ends of the pipework and then pumping air into the pipe. The pipe ends are sealed with rubber plugs, one of which has a central hole large enough to take the nozzle of a foot pump. You will need a pump that registers the amount of pressure it is exerting.

Fill the pipes partially full with water—this will reduce the amount of time you have to spend pumping air. Pump air into the pipes for about 5 minutes until the pressure inside the pipes reaches 15lbs per sq in. If the pressure stays at this level for 15 minutes the pipes are perfectly watertight.

The pipes should be laid in trenches in sand or soil—not in stones. The trenches should be deep enough to prevent ground frost affecting the pipes—about 12in. deep in Britain. Ensure that any slopes are even and that there is no air trapped inside the pipes. Avoid putting any pressure on the pipe joints while laying them. The trenches are filled with earth which is compacted carefully—but do not do this job until the mortar joints in the blockwork walls have set completely. If the soil under the pipes is likely to settle do not lay them yet. Lay paving slabs over the top of the trenches to accelerate settlement. Then lay the pipes.

Other fittings

When setting these fittings, be sure to compact the concrete in which they are set—this will prevent leaks. These fittings are shown in Fig.2 and you should follow the manufacturer's instructions carefully.

A *cup anchor* can be set into the wall to provide a fixing for a safety net between the shallow and deep ends.

Underwater lights can also be set into the wall. These operate safely on a low voltage, using a 12 to 24 volt transformer and a wattage of between 200w to 300w. You should get a qualified electrician to do this job, as the placing of the lamps, within water, is potentially dangerous.

The sealed lamp shown in Fig.2 is cooled by the water that surrounds it. A pool light should be positioned to shine away from sitting areas. Remember, when choosing your pool lamp, that one watt will illuminate about 1sq ft of surface water so select a lamp with the capacity to light the whole pool. But bear in mind that turbid water cuts illumination.

The plant room is simply a small shed that houses part of the circulation equipment and pool accessories. Most garden sheds will prove sufficient for this.

The final steps in the construction of the swimming pool are described in the next part of this chapter.

A swimming pool to make: 4

The major construction steps involved in building the swimming pool have now been completed, and all the equipment and pipework used in the circulation system has been installed. All that remains is to give a finish to the pool and its surround, and treat the water to give safe and healthy swimming.

The work described in this part of the chapter will always be on view, so good finishing is essential. Bad workmanship or poor quality materials will show at once.

Coping

The tops of the pool walls are finished with coping stones with a 'bull-nose' (rounded top edge) near the interior of the pool. The coping is higher at the edge with the bull-nose, so that surface water drains away from the pool. Reconstituted white Portland stone is used in this project. You should use the best coping you can buy for this job—it is the only part of the blockwork you can see in the finished pool —so it's worth buying the best.

The coping stones are usually 12in. (305mm) wide and between 18in. to 24in. (457mm to 610mm) in length. They are set to overlap the pool interior by 1in. (25mm) for terrazzo rendering or by ¾in. (19mm) for painted finishes (see below).

The coping is set on a ⅜in. to ½in. (9.5mm to 13mm) mortar course, laid on the top course of hollow core concrete blocks. To give a better key, coat the underside of the coping with a concrete sealant or adhesive such as Unibond.

Lay the corner stones first and make sure they are level—these stones act as a guide for the levels of the other stones. Check that the corner stones are level with a long spirit level. Lay the rest of the stones in a series of hops, missing out every alternate stone—this helps you line up and level all the stones. You may have to cut some of the stones. Do this with a rotary power saw with a suitable disc, or with a stonemason's saw. These produce far neater edges on the stones than a bolster chisel. Lastly, set the cut stones in place.

Fill the gaps between the stones with a 2:1 mix of white terrazzo dust and white cement. Smooth off the grouting. If you use coloured stones, mix a coloured admix to the grouting to match it to the stones.

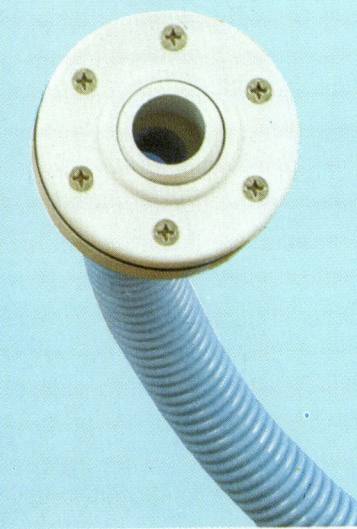

WATER LEVEL

A skimmer weir. Most pools need only one skimmer weir, set in place of one concrete wall block, for the pool described here. The circular disc on the right of the skimmer is for attaching a vacuum cleaner for sweeping the pool walls and floor. The inlet is shown in the top right of the photograph.

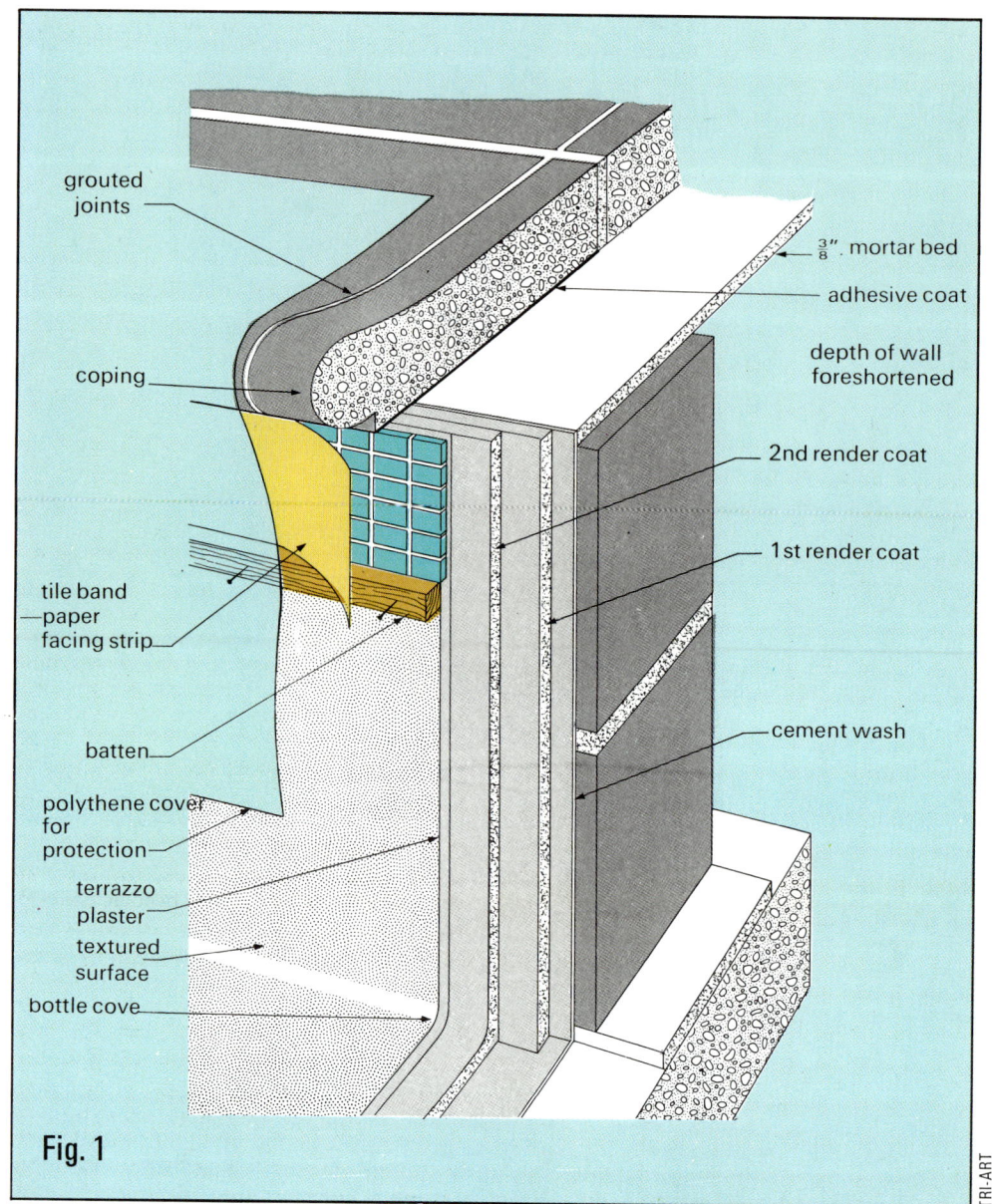

Labels on Fig. 1:
- grouted joints
- coping
- tile band
- paper facing strip
- batten
- polythene cover for protection
- terrazzo plaster
- textured surface
- bottle cove
- 3/8". mortar bed
- adhesive coat
- depth of wall foreshortened
- 2nd render coat
- 1st render coat
- cement wash

Fig. 1

TRI-ART

2

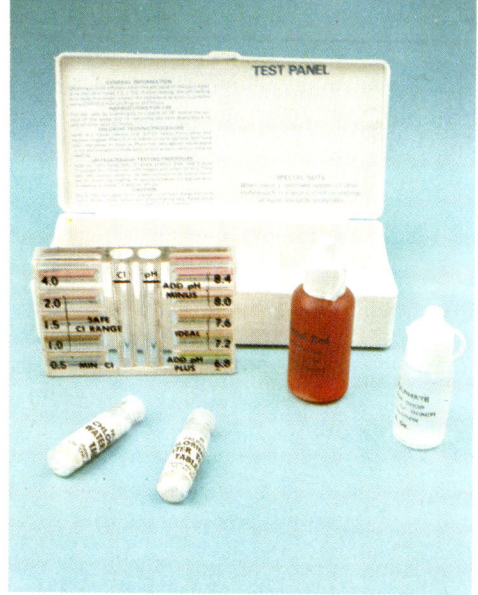

3

Cement rendering

The interior of the pool walls, for the pool described here, are covered with two coats of cement rendering, with a waterproof additive, and finished with a thin coat of terrazzo rendering.

Brush down the walls, floor, mortar joints and corners before you start to apply the pool finish. Cover up the fittings and brush a cement wash on to the walls—this is simply cement mixed with water. The cement wash gives a better key to the cement render coats that are applied now.

The next step is to cover the walls with a ⅜in. (9.5mm) thick layer of cement mixed 1:3 with sand. A non-staining waterproofing agent must be added to the cement, as the blocks used for the walls are porous. You can mix a special additive, such as Medusa, in with the cement or use a ready-mixed waterproof cement, such as Aquacrete, Hydracrete or Waterproofed Snowcrete. Apply the render to the walls and to the steps. Scratch the surface of the cement to provide a good key for the next coat.

Now apply a second coat of cement render, again with waterproofer included in the mix. Apply a ⅜in. (9.5mm) thick render coat to the

Fig.1. Details of the pool wall lining used in this project. The tops of the walls are finished with 'bull-nose' coping and the walls covered with two coats of cement render and a terrazzo plaster finish. The polythene sheets protect the finish while it cures.

walls and steps and a ½in. (13mm) thick coat to the floor. Then, with a bottle held almost vertically, cove the corners of the wall right down to the floor—do not do this at the steps. Score the surface of this coat with a pointed tool or a rake to provide a good key for the terrazzo render coat.

The floor of the pool is compacted concrete, so you need only apply one coat of waterproofed cement. Use a wooden float when smoothing the cement on to the surfaces—a steel float will produce too smooth a surface.

The tiling band

The next step is to apply the tiling band. This is a tiled surround, about 6in. (152mm) deep, set at water level around the pool walls. This makes for easier cleaning of the pool as the scum line, which forms around water level even in the

Fig.2. A recent development in pool cleaning, this device moves around the pool and sweeps debris and dirt from the walls and floor and from the water, towards the main drain.
Fig.3. A water test set tells you the acid/alkaline and the chlorine level of the water.

cleanest pools, can be wiped off easily.

You can either use 6in. (152mm) ceramic tiles for the tiling band, or mosaics—the type fronted with paper that can be peeled off when the mosaics are in place.

The first step is to nail wooden battens around the insides of the pool walls, at the level where the bottom edge of the tiling band will be. The top of the tiling band should be ⅝in. (16mm) down from the coping—do not cover the mortar on which the coping is set.

Mix a small amount of white render to a stiff paste, using a 2:1 mix of terrazzo dust to white cement. Add waterproofer. Don't use too wet a mix or the mosaics or tiles will 'float' and be very difficult to set smoothly. Use frost proof mosaics or tiles for the tiling band.

Apply the render to the wall blocks above the battens and to the back of the mosaics or

Above. Thoughtful landscaping of the pool area is essential if the pool is to be used to full advantage. A large paved area is necessary for sunbathing, and the honeycomb block wall will cast attractive shadows. Flowers and shrubs in brick planters add a splash of colour.

tiles. Press them in place and tap them with a wooden float to get them level. If you are using tiles, all you have to do is leave the render to set—this takes two to three hours.

If you are using mosaics, wait for the render to set and then dampen the paper covering the face of the mosaics. Peel off the paper and fill the crevices and joins with white render paste. The same procedure is used for tiles.

Terrazzo rendering

The next step is to apply the terrazzo rendering. This consists of $\frac{3}{16}$in. to $\frac{3}{8}$in. (5mm to 9.5mm) marble chips and terrazzo dust, mixed with white cement. It is sanded to a smooth surface when it has set.

If you are a good plasterer, the application of the cement render coats is straightforward, though time-consuming. You need to have a

lot of plastering experience, though, to apply a terrazzo render. If you feel unable to do the job, hire a professional plasterer or consider one of the alternative pool finishes described below.

To apply a terrazzo render, first mix the marble chips and terrazzo dust in a 2:1 proportion. Mix this with white cement, $2\frac{1}{2}$ parts marble chips to 3 parts cement. You do not need to add a waterproofer. Add water to the mix to produce a 'fatty' plaster—one which is workable but not too sloppy.

Apply a $\frac{1}{8}$in. to $\frac{1}{4}$in. (3mm to 6mm) coating of the terrazzo mix to the walls with a wooden float—don't use a steel float as this may leave marks that are difficult to remove. Make joints at the floor line and at corners—do not smooth the mix right round these corners. Do not overtrowel when applying the mix because cuts and marks may show up. If you have cleaned the pool wall properly the white terrazzo will not stain.

Allow the terrazzo coat to set—this takes about 24 hours. Don't leave the coat to set for any longer than this or the smoothing of the finish will take longer than necessary. With a heavy duty, flexible head power tool,

fitted with a tungsten carbide disc, clean off any high spots and marks. Do this until the surfaces of the walls are smooth. Do not smooth the floor surface too much as this may make it slippery.

Protect the finish from the weather while it cures. The best way to do this is to drape polythene sheets over the surfaces and then fill the pool. Good protection for the finish during curing prevents hairline cracks appearing.

Alternative interior finishes

Painted finish. Three types of paint can be used for this job—cement based paint, epoxy resins and chlorinated-rubber based paints.

These paints vary considerably in price. If you choose this finish, you will have to repaint the surfaces every year with one of the cheaper paints and apply a coat of the more expensive paint every four to five years. The success of painted walls and floor depends a lot on good preparation, the correct application of the paint and regular maintenance. You can get these paints in a variety of colours but remember that deep, clean water has a natural blueness.

Full instructions on the application of these paints are provided by the manufacturers. Paint is easy to apply to clean, dry and textured rendered surfaces. A painted surface does not stain as easily as white terrazzo and you have the choice of several attractive colours.

Liner membranes. PVC pool liners are popular since they are perfectly watertight and can easily be repaired if they become damaged. Manufacturers also guarantee their pool liners (usually for ten years), provide equipment for easy underwater repairs should they be necessary, produce liners with patterned and textured finishes and incorporate ultra violet inhibitors in the plastic to prevent such rays damaging the pvc. The main disadvantage, as far as the pool described here is concerned, is that liners are produced in standard sizes. You can have a liner custom made but this is more expensive.

If you wish to use a pool liner, you will have to re-design the pool excavation—for example, liners are laid on a compacted sand floor, not on concrete. Manufacturers will suggest structural designs for use with their liners, as well as give the precise dimensions to use.

Rigid glassfibre liners can also be installed, again following the manufacturers' instructions for the excavation. These liners, though, are made in large sections or in one piece, so they can be difficult to handle.

Hygiene and maintenance

The job of maintaining a swimming pool is not difficult or expensive. All the pool surround —the coping and the paving—should be washed down and swept periodically. The main task is to maintain the pool equipment and keep the water clean and safe. You should check the heater and filter periodically during the swimming season and once a year, at the end of the season, all minor repairs, reconditioning, painting and greasing should be checked again at the start of the next swimming season. Manufacturers of pool equipment will give plenty of advice on the maintenance of their products.

The real maintenance job is looking after the water. Firstly, the pool must be kept free of debris—if you don't do this regularly the cleaning up job will be considerable. Though the filter removes most of the debris, you should sweep the walls and the floor of the pool about once every two weeks. A vacuum sweeper is useful for this job. This is a suction sweeper that plugs into the skimmer weir (or a vacuum wall point installed in the walls during construction). You will also need a leaf net to scoop up leaves and a stainless steel brush for scrubbing algae from the pool walls. The photograph on page 73 shows a typical skimmer weir in operation.

You must also ensure that the pool water is pure. It has to be chemically treated for this. You can get devices that will do this automatically—these cost about as much as the filter—but the manual methods of pool treatment are straightforward.

The water must be chlorinated to kill bacteria in the pool. A water test set, shown in Fig.3, tells you how much chlorine there is in the water, and the alkaline/acid level, by comparing results of the test with a standard colour code. There should be a residual of about 0.5 parts per million of chlorine in the water. This registers as pink on the test set. The pool water, in this state, is a very mild disinfectant which kills germs. The water should be maintained at this chlorine level.

The measurement of the alkaline/acid level is expressed as pH. Untreated water is either acid or alkaline—for a pool the water must be just slightly alkaline. The job of achieving this is known as 'balancing' the water. The water should be alkaline to a pH level of 7.5 (7.0 is neutral). The water is balanced by adding appropriate chemicals.

If the water is too alkaline an acid is added to balance this. Public swimming pools are adjusted by adding hydrochloric acid but it is safer to use a dry acid mix for a residential pool. There are many proprietary brands available, Alkajust Minus being one of them. If the acid content of the water is too high an alkaline is added. Again there are many proprietary brands of alkaline solution, such as Protek, on the market.

The chlorine treatment kills most algae, but not all. An algicide is added to the pool water periodically to control the algae.

As long as you maintain the correct chlorine residual and pH balance, you will be able to swim in comfort, and there will be no ill-effects to the pool or the equipment. Pools which smell of chlorine and cause your eyes to smart are not properly maintained. Testing and treatment only takes about ten minutes a week.

Accessories around the pool

You can choose from a range of pool accessories. A non-corrosive ladder, anchored to the paving at the deep end, is useful. You could have a diving board—this should be installed over at least 6ft 6in. (1.83m) of water for a board at paving level. The water must be deeper if the board is higher. The board is set on stands fixed onto the paving, and overlapping this by about 18in. (457mm). A slide can be installed at either the deep end or the shallow end. One or two sockets for fitting sunshades can be set into the paving.

A safety net, fixed to cup anchors, and separating the shallow end from the deep end is valuable, especially if young children will be using the pool. You could also have a pool cover—some of these are designed to prevent heat loss from the pool, others to stop foreign matter getting into the water. A pool alarm will tell you if an unauthorized person is using your pool. One model floats on the water and shrieks when the water is disturbed. This is not a good idea, though, if your neighbour's cat should fall into the pool at 3 am!

Hydro devices, set into the pool, make water currents and streams of air bubbles. Underwater lighting can be attractive and you can even buy underwater music systems.

A final important consideration before you start to use your pool: a third party insurance policy will prevent you having to bear the cost of visitors to your home accidentally damaging the pool—or themselves.

Landscaping

Precise details of landscaping around the pool will depend on the size and shape of your garden and your personal taste. A few general points will help you to choose your landscaping.

The entrance to the pool area should be up or down wide steps. This helps focus attention on the pool. A gateway pool entrance—a rustic arch, perhaps—also does this.

Paving around the pool can be random slabs, crazy paving or bricks, or mixtures of these. A textured surface is best for safety. Cobbles look good in areas where you don't have to walk. Paving should slope away from the pool. If the ground around the pool is likely to settle, bed paving on sand for the first year and then set it on a 2in. concrete base.

A sun terrace is virtually a must and you could also install a stone seat. Honeycomb wall blocks will let light in to the paved area and provide attractive three dimensional shapes. Remember that stone absorbs the heat of the sun during the day and releases it during the evening. It is a good idea to use stone around the area where you will do most of your evening entertaining.

Flower beds add colour to a pool surround. Don't have fleshy fruiting plants around the pool though—these will stain the paving. Avoid thorny and prickly plants also, and keep sweet smelling flowers, which attract bees, away from the pool.

You could also consider a waterfall rockery, a pool inlet cascade, a pergola (for example one of the types outlined in PROJECT 11), a barbecue for pool parties (see PROJECT 2 for this). The possibilities, in fact, are endless and limited only by your own imagination.

Building a swimming pool takes a lot of time and effort. The effort—and the cost—is more than repaid though by the enormous increase in your leisure facilities that a pool provides.

Left. Colourful petunias and clematis add an exotic touch to this pool setting. The trellis work 'gateway' in the background help give the impression that the swimming pool is an 'extra room' of your home.

LESLIE JOHNS

The height of enjoyment

PROJECT
9

Combine all the most popular playground features—a climbing frame, a slide, and a sand pit, and you have a children's play area that will provide many years of active enjoyment for children of all ages.

This garden project is relatively easy to make and, by keeping the children otherwise engaged, will enable you to work on other projects, or relax in the sun with a cool drink, without interruption from the youngsters.

This play area has been designed so that it can be altered to suit the dimensions of any particular garden. It consists of a climbing frame, slide, and sand pit, any of which could be scaled down in size or omitted if you have not enough room.

The main feature is the climbing frame, and as this will be used by children of differing ages, platforms of varying heights have been incorporated. A slide has been included because it is one of the most popular playground items. And any timid types who do not wish to climb the rungs can make use of the stepped ladder which hooks on to one of the platforms.

The frame consists of towers made from 2½in. or 63mm square uprights in modules of 2ft 4in. or 700mm, the highest towers being 6ft or 1.9m, and the lowest platform 2ft or 600mm. The towers are joined by 2½in. x 1in. or 63mm x 25mm

cross members, and dowel rods $1\frac{1}{8}$in. or 29mm in diameter. These rods also provide the rungs for climbing.

Planning the project

It is not essential to follow the exact layout of the frame described here, as long as the structure is stable and strong. But various factors should be taken into account when planning the unit.

Safety is the main consideration. As the frame is likely to be used by several children together, a tower must be placed at the rear, and another at the front of the frame. These act as stabilizers, preventing the frame from toppling over if all the children happen to be playing on one section of it.

Your garden may not have enough level space for the design shown here. In this case you will have to limit your frame, or vary the tower legs to allow for irregularities or sloping ground.

Hardwood is an expensive item, and this too may well limit the size you decide on.

At the planning stage you should consider the placing of the feet of the frame. By placing them on concrete slabs you will be able to keep the grass from growing untidily against the uprights.

If you are altering the design of the structure, do not try to eliminate the dowelling that spans two modules. Dowelling that is inserted through three uprights makes for a stronger structure than dowelling through two uprights. Also, make sure the bottom rung is high enough to provide clearance for a lawnmower, as in the original frame described here. Otherwise you will have an untidy patch inside.

Materials required

The wood will have to be varied in length if you are adjusting the size of the frame. But the following materials are used for the frame and slide described.

Timber for uprights ($2\frac{1}{2}$in. or 63mm sq) :–

8 lengths of 6ft	or 2m
2 lengths of 5ft	or 1.5m
2 lengths of 4ft	or 1.25m
2 lengths of 2ft	or 600mm

Timber for cross members and bearers ($2\frac{1}{2}$in. x 1in. or 63mm x 25mm) :–

2 lengths of 6ft 3in.	or 2m
9 lengths of 2ft 4in.	or 700mm
2 lengths of 2ft 2in.	or 650mm

Timber for platform battens (2in. x 1in. or 50mm x 25mm) :–

37 lengths of 2ft 4in.	or 700mm

Timber dowelling for the rungs ($1\frac{1}{8}$in. or

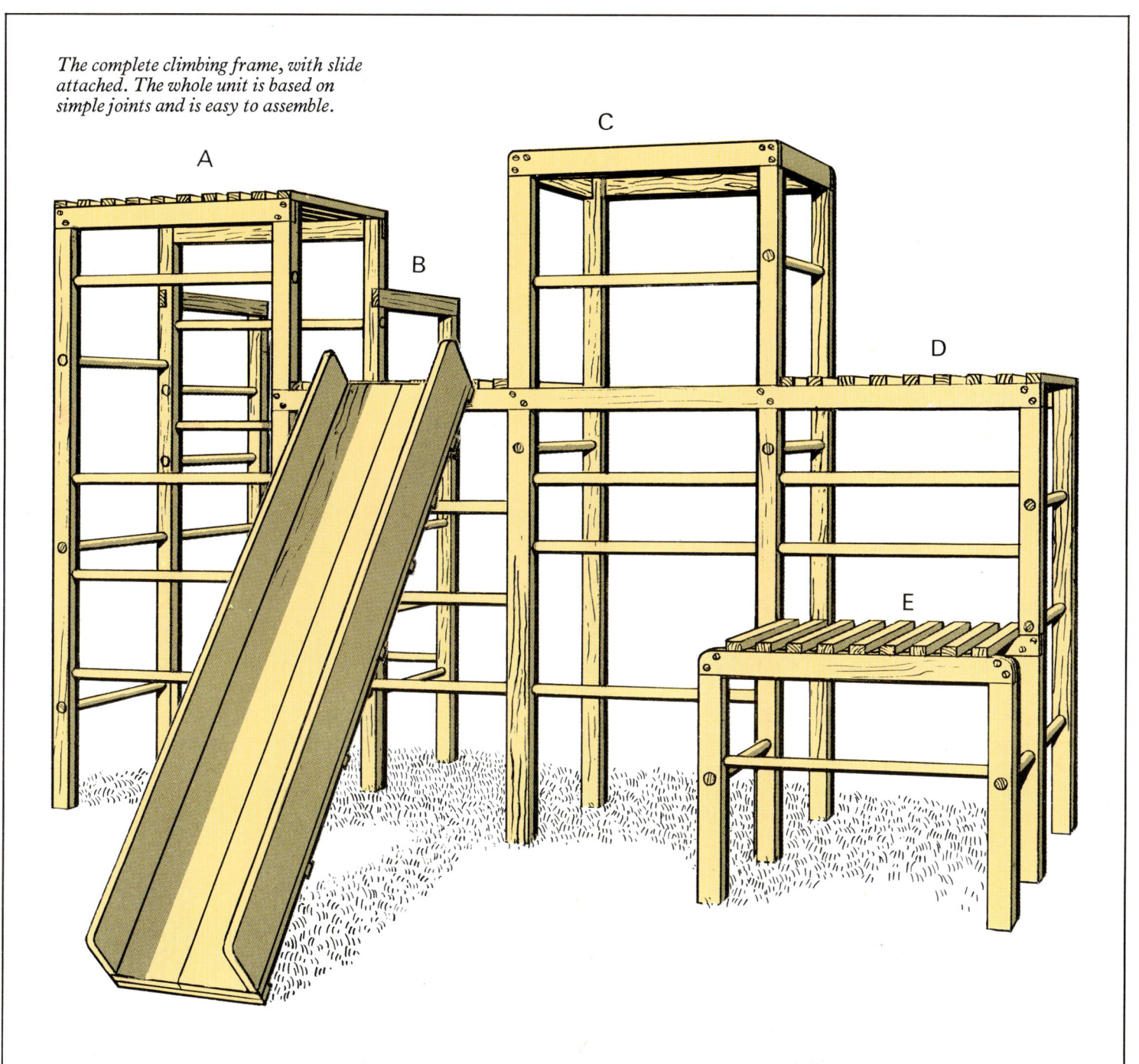

The complete climbing frame, with slide attached. The whole unit is based on simple joints and is easy to assemble.

28mm diameter) :—
11 lengths of 2ft 4½in.   or 730mm
23 lengths of 4ft 6in.   or 1.2m
Timber for the slide (parana pine planks) :—
2 lengths of 8ft x 7in.   or 2.5m x 180mm
x 1in.   x 25mm.
2 lengths of 4ft x 4in.   or 1.2m x 100mm
x 1in.   x 25mm.
*Battening, for the underside of the slide (2in.
x 1in. or 405mm x 50mm)* :—
8 lengths of 16in.   or 405mm.
Timber for the ladder:—
Planks for the sides (4½in. x 1in. or 115mm x
25mm) :—
2 lengths of 4ft 6in.   or 1.4m.
Short planks for the steps (3in. x ¾in. or
75mm x 19mm) :—
8 lengths of 1ft   or 300mm.

You will also require :—

A quantity of No.8 screws 2in. or 50mm long,
some of 1½in. or 35mm, and a few ¾in. or 19m.

Nails to secure sand-pit boarding.

Six steel L brackets for reinforcing the side
planks to the bottom of the slide. The brackets
should be no more than 3in. or 75mm along
each angle.

Steel strips or hooks for attaching slide and
ladder to frame.

Wood adhesive.

In addition to standard tools, the following
would be helpful :

Dowelling jig. To ensure that dowel or rung
holes are precisely located.

Tubular Surform plane. For cleaning out the
rung holes after drilling. You could use a
curved wood rasp, but the Surform is better.

Select the uprights from the straightest wood,
dowelling is difficult with bowed timber.

The eight 6ft lengths are for towers A and C,
and the two 5ft lengths are for tower B, which is
a stabilizing structure. This is joined to tower A
by bearers. The two 4ft lengths are for the two
legs at the right end (d) of the frame, and the
shortest lengths are for the lowest jumping
platform, E, which acts as a front stabilizer.

Tower B is a stabilizing structure at the rear
of the frame. The two 5ft uprights have joints
cut at the top of each, to take the bearers which
connect it to tower A. Additional joints 9in.
down are cut to take a cross member.

Tower C is a hollow climbing frame (it has
no platform on the top). It consists of four
uprights, 6ft in length, held together at the top
by bearers.

The addition of tower D is made by two 4ft
uprights, which join to the main cross members
linking towers A and C. These members also
act as bearers for the platform battening on the
top of tower D.

The front of the structure is stabilized by
tower E, the low level jumping platform. This
consists of two 2ft lengths which act as uprights,
joined by a bearer on the front, and at the back
to the bearer on the front of tower D..

Cross members and bearers

These are used to connect the three main
towers as well as to strengthen the tower tops.
(Cross members are horizontal timbers used to
strengthen a structure : bearers both strengthen
and support a load—in this case, the platform
battens.)

For safety alone it is important that all cross
members and bearers fit snugly at the joints and
are securely screwed and glued. Several children
weigh a considerable amount.

Constructing the frame

Plane all timbers to a smooth finish to prevent
splinters from forming. Sand, then mark out the
joints as indicated in the diagrams. Each upright
is described as though looking at the front of the
frame—that is, the face to which the slide is
attached.

The joints are all of the simple halving type,
which makes the unit particularly easy to
assemble. But take care to mark the joints on the
correct faces. It will be a great help if you pencil
an identification on each upright, as shown in
the illustrations.

Countersink all screws.

The two main bearers are the 6ft 3in. lengths
at the front and rear. Tap these into the joints of
the uprights, drill holes for screws, then screw
and glue to the front uprights. Assemble the
rear uprights and tower B in the same manner.
This allows the top bearers to be screwed and
glued into place, and the battens to be screwed
in place between towers A and C to form the
platform access between ladder and slide.
Allow a gap of 1in. or 25mm between the
battens. Then screw the battens for towers D and
E in place, and fix the top of tower C with the
four bearers (two of 2ft 4in., two of 2 ft 2in.).

Fitting the rungs

Once the main frame is screwed together, the
next step is to mark out the centres for boring
the holes for the dowelling.

It is essential to work out with care the
spacing of the dowelling. The rungs should not
be too close to one another, as this takes the fun
out of climbing. Also, where two dowels are to
be inserted through an upright in different
directions (at right angles) the holes should

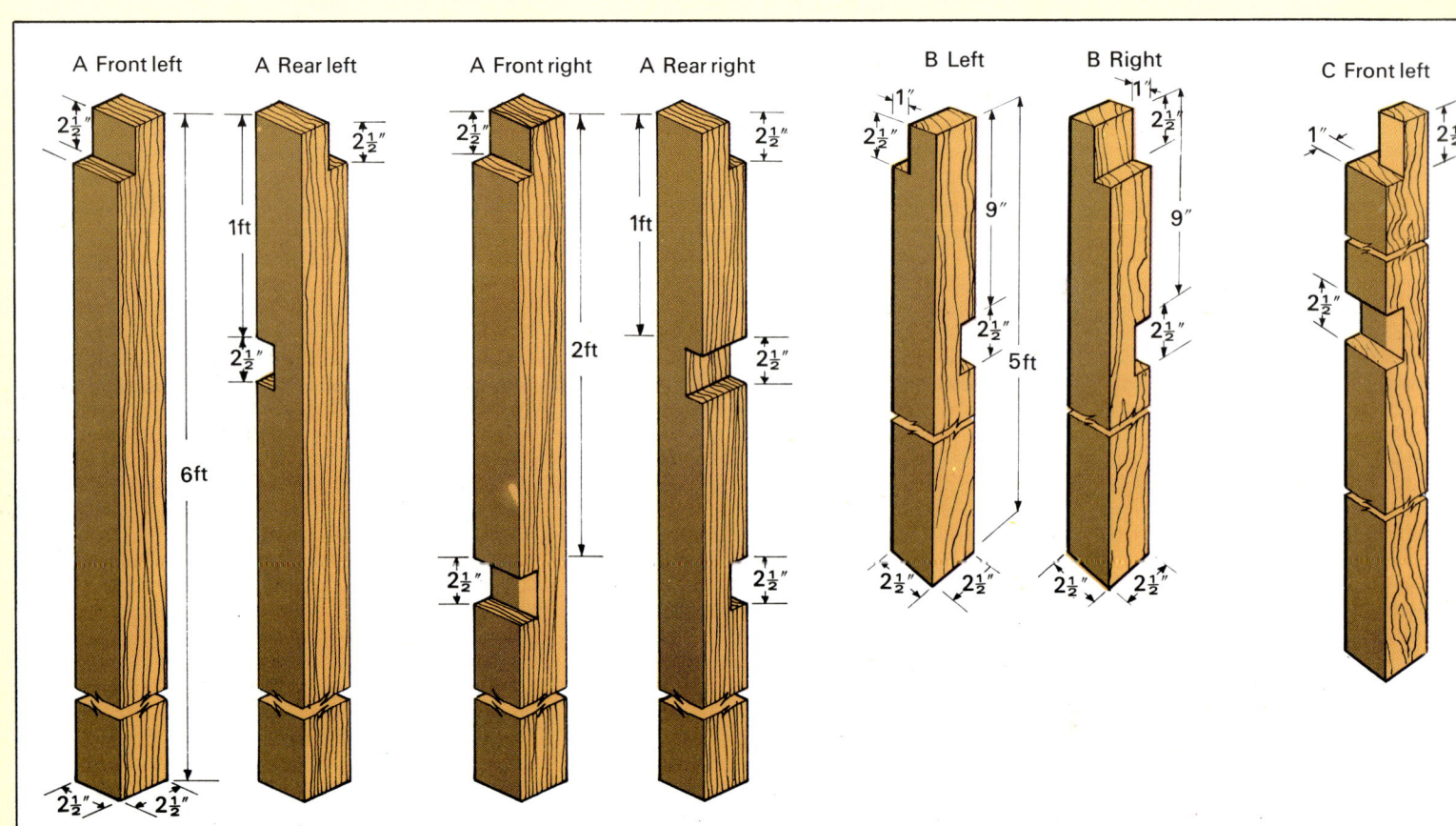

A Front left   A Rear left   A Front right   A Rear right   B Left   B Right   C Front left

not be bored too close to each other as the upright will be weakened and might split.

First, mark out the centre line on the uprights with a try square. Then mark a line half way at right angles to produce a cross, the middle of which will be drilled for the dowel.

Secure the dowelling jig so that the guide hole is right over the mark, then drill the holes with a No. 8 bit on the power drill.

When you have drilled all the small No. 8 holes, thread a string line through them. This will indicate whether the line is running correctly, at right angles to the uprights.

Now insert in the brace, a bit the same size as the dowelling, and bore out the holes. Do this fairly slowly. As soon as the point of the bit shows through the pilot hole, stop and drill from the opposite direction, using the pilot hole for centring. This will prevent the edges of the hole from splintering.

Now clean up around the inside of each hole with the Surform or curved wood rasp.

You are now ready to tap the dowels through with the mallet. It helps to have someone to give some support to the uprights when knocking in the first few dowels. Any spare dowelling which sticks out should be left until the frame is well and truly squared up. Then the spare bits can be cut away.

Making the slide

Place the two 7in. planks side by side and secure them with the eight battens (Fig.F). Allow the battens to overlap the edges of the planks by 1in. on both sides.

To form the sides of the slide, place the 4in. planks on the overlapping battens so that they are at right angles with the slide planks. First screw the sides on to the edges of the slide, then screw the battens to the bottom of the side planks.

Secure the three steel L brackets down each side for additional support.

Plane any corner edges—the top of the sides and the top and bottom of the slide itself—to half round, so that no nasty angles protrude.

The method of attaching the slide to the frame depends on whether you want it to be screwed in a semi-permanent manner, or hooked on so that it can be detached quickly. An L bracket could easily be bent to fit, and screwed to the underside of the slide, while a simple hook-and-eye provides an easy slip-on fitting.

Cutting the ladder steps

The ladder is secured to the side of the tower opposite the slide. It is made out of two 4ft 6in. lengths of timber, with shorter planks providing the steps.

Recesses for the steps are cut out by sawing uniform V sections along one side of each plank. This requires nothing more than a measuring rule, a pencil, and a panel saw.

To mark out the step positions, begin by fixing one side of the ladder temporarily in place to establish the correct slope. Next, use a builder's level and pencil to mark one horizontal guide line across the board. (This is to ensure that the steps are level). Remove the ladder side and lay it flat while you do the rest of the marking out. For this, you will need a cardboard or hardboard triangle, whose shortest side is 3in. and whose longest side matches the slope of the steps. Simply by sliding the triangle along the board you can mark each successive step on the face side. Use the try-square to carry the marks across the edge of the board, and the cardboard triangle to mark the other side. Finally, mark out the second board so that it matches the first.

Saw along the zig-zag lines to cut out the outline as in Fig.F.

Screw the steps in position and round the edges with the plane.

The ladder may be attached to the frame in the same way as the slide.

Polyurethane varnish should now be applied to all woodwork. In view of the fact that this unit will spend its life outdoors, two coats are recommended.

The sand-pit

The area of this sand-pit is approximately 6ft by 4ft or 1m by 1.3m.

Dig the pit to a depth of 2ft 6in. or 770mm, and line it with any old planking that you can get. Cresote the planking well. Secure the planks at the corners by simple square stakes driven into the ground, and then back, fill them. When the top edge of the planking is level—a visual sighting is sufficient for this—nail through the stakes into the planks.

For this pit, ornamental square concrete slabs are laid round the edge, giving a slight overhang which provides an on-site seating arrangement, and a firm base for building sandcastles. The slabs also make it easier to sweep the surround free of excavated sand. If possible, obtain slabs with rounded edges—these are kinder to children's legs.

To assist drainage, line the bottom 6in. of the pit with gravel and ram it down well. Finally, fill the pit with sand (of the non-staining variety if possible).

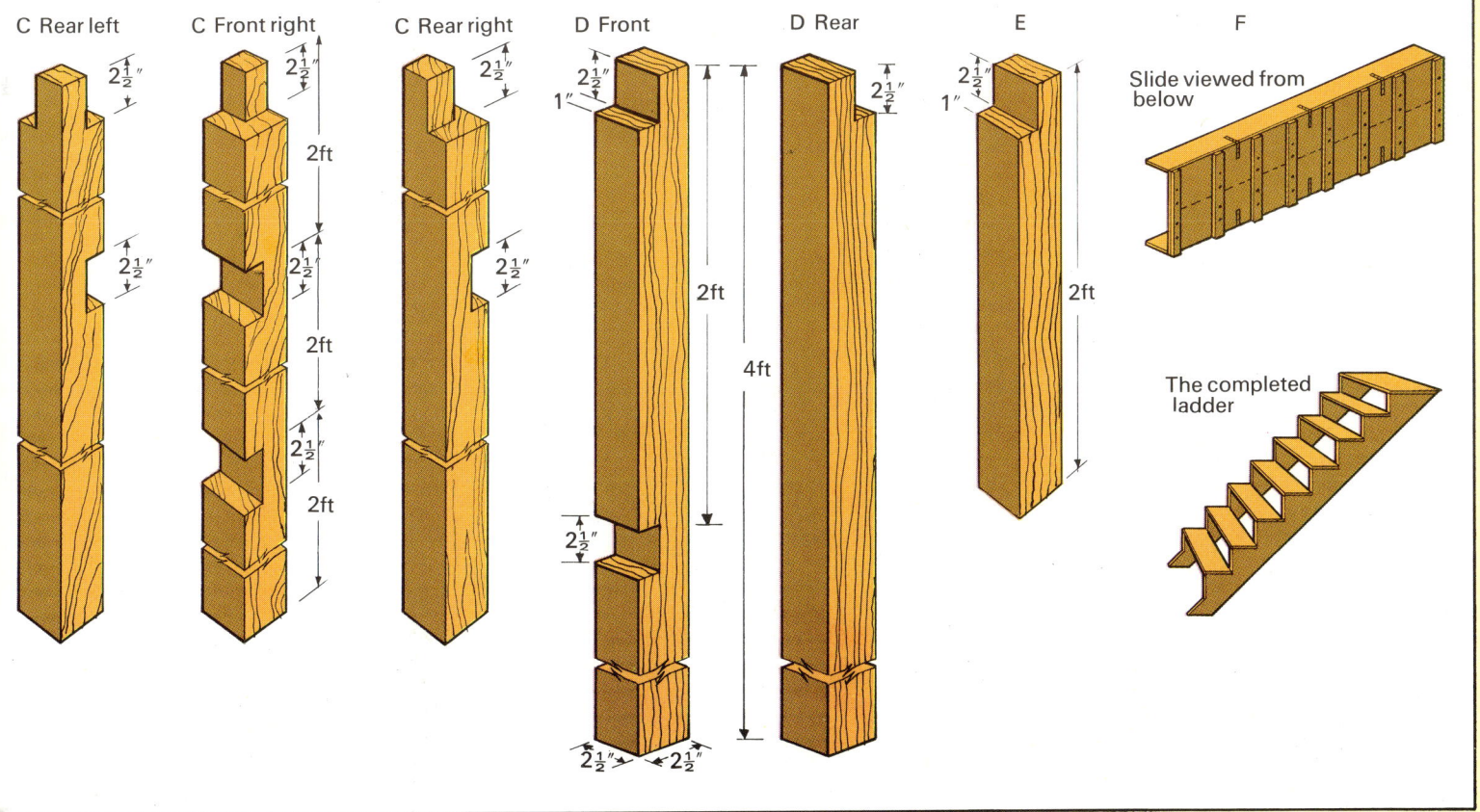

C Rear left   C Front right   C Rear right   D Front   D Rear   E   F

Slide viewed from below

The completed ladder

Fig.1. *This attractive shed is clad with an exterior grade hardboard, which makes it easier—and more economical—to construct.*

A garden shed to make

PROJECT
10

It is difficult to appreciate the versatility of a garden shed unless you've actually possessed one. Not only is it a building to house muddy garden tools; it also acts as a potting shed for raising plants, a workshop, and storage space for cycles and prams—facilities that are difficult to find room for in most modern houses.

There are two methods of obtaining a garden shed. You can build one from scratch, or you can buy one of the prefabricated kits on the market and fit this together. This article deals mainly with the former method.

Garden sheds usually consist of a timber framework clad with boarding such as weatherboard or shiplap. This is an excellent form of cladding, but it does require considerable care in fitting. In this project, the timber frame is clad with an exterior grade hardboard such as Tempered Royal Board. This is a material that will last for years if painted, and is both quicker and more economical than solid wood boarding.

Construction

The floor of the shed is a conventional concrete raft base.

The wall sections consist of four softwood frames. All frame members are jointed with glued and screwed halving joints, and the frames are erected by securing all butting surfaces with carriage bolts.

Fig.4 shows a side frame (with window spaces) joined to an end frame. The side wall

Fig.2. *If you prefer, the shed can be constructed with a flat roof. This is easier to make, but provides less headroom.*

is about 8ft long and 6ft high (2.4m x 1.8m). The end or corner studs are of 2in. x 1½in. timbers, as are the top and bottom plates. All other framing is of 2in. x 1in. timber. All members are placed so that the 2in. dimension is across the thickness of the frame to give a 2in. thick wall throughout. Studs are at 14-16in. (about 380mm) centres.

The remaining frames are made in the same way, except that 2in. x 1in. timbers are used for the corner or end studs. Thicker timber is not needed here because the end frames are fitted inside the side frames.

The roof, as shown in Fig.5, comprises a ridge board and six joists, all of 3in. x 1in. timbers and four purlins four barge boards, and two fascias, all of 2in. x 1in. timbers. Joints are all glued and either half lapped and screwed, or butted and nailed.

When the door and window frames have been fixed in position, weatherproof hardboard is used to clad or cover the exterior framing of walls and roof, and the roof is finished with a couple of layers of roofing felt.

Foundations

This is a concrete platform into which rag bolts are set to provide anchors for the bottom plates. It is essential that the rag bolts are set in their exact positions at the outset. And these positions depend on the dimensions of the

platform. For instance, if you intend building the shed so that the bottom plates overlap the edges of the platform, as in Fig.4C, then the rag bolts will be near the edges. But if the platform is to be extended beyond the outside edges of the shed, as in Fig.2, then the bolts will be set farther back. Bear this in mind when marking out.

The method is the same as that used for the foundation shown on page 24, except that these foundations are not so deep, being a slab of concrete 3in. or 73mm thick over a 3in. layer of hard core, and 6in. or 150mm thick at the edges.

Clear the area, lay out profile boards, and mark out the excavation area.

Excavate the ground down to a depth of 6in.

Scaffold boards must now be firmly fixed round the perimeter of the base to provide a mould into which the concrete will be poured. Arrange the levels and fix the boarding so that the finished floor level will be a few inches above ground level.

For economy, hardcore is spread over and rammed into the shallow part of the foundation pit, but ensure that there is no hardcore round the edges, as shown in Fig.3.

The concrete for a small area like this can be laid in one section, using the technique shown on page 24.

While the concrete is setting the rag bolts are placed in position. The bolts are held in place

with strips of timber. These are removed when the concrete hardens.

The wall frames

Start with the side frame shown in Fig.4. This one has two windows, placed side by side. You could leave out one window if you wish, or place one large frame over the two openings, but whatever you do you must not eliminate the top half of the *middle* stud, otherwise you weaken the structure.

Use a flat surface for the construction of each frame.

Cut the top and bottom plates to the same length, and place them on the flat surface about 6ft apart. Cut the end or corner studs into 6ft lengths, then place each one in position between the ends of the plates, check that the rectangle they form has squared corners, and cut the halving joints as shown in Fig.4A. Dry assemble, check for squareness again, then glue and screw in position.

Add the nogging or horizontal member, by direct marking, in the same way.

Mark off the positions of the remaining studs at approximate 15in. intervals along both plates, cut and fit these, then glue and screw in position, check for squareness again, then leave for the glue to set.

Repeat this procedure for all four frames. The main variation will be with the end frame

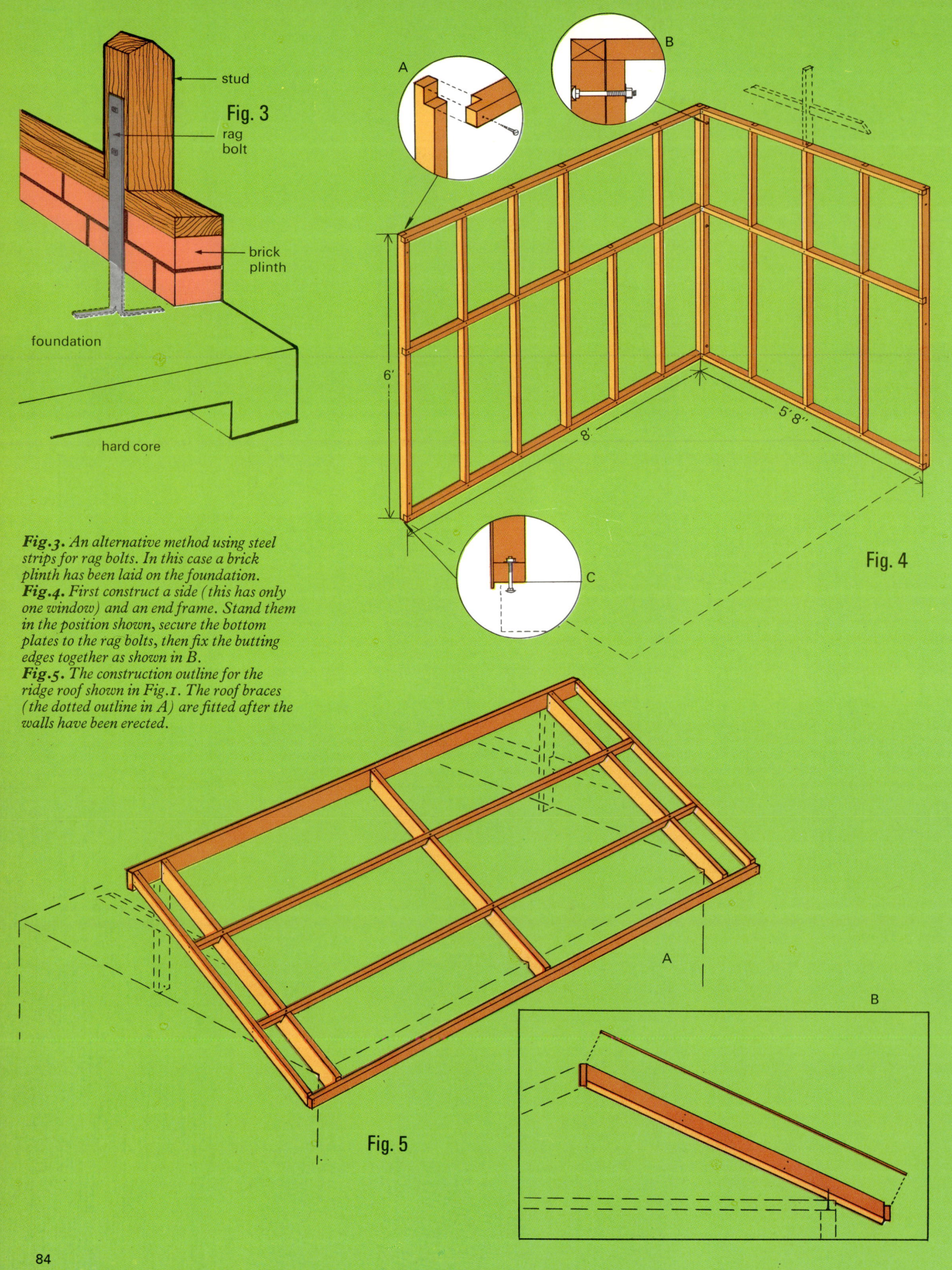

stud

Fig. 3

rag
bolt

brick
plinth

foundation

hard core

A

B

C

6'

8'

5'8"

Fig. 4

Fig.3. An alternative method using steel strips for rag bolts. In this case a brick plinth has been laid on the foundation.
Fig.4. First construct a side (this has only one window) and an end frame. Stand them in the position shown, secure the bottom plates to the rag bolts, then fix the butting edges together as shown in B.
Fig.5. The construction outline for the ridge roof shown in Fig.1. The roof braces (the dotted outline in A) are fitted after the walls have been erected.

A

B

Fig. 5

that holds the door. The opening for the door is created by omitting the middle stud and replacing it with two studs, one on either side of the door. The bottom plate is left complete until the frame has been assembled, then the portion at the foot of the door is cut away.

Assembling the walls

Construct a side and end frame first. Lay each frame down so that the bottoms of the end plates can be marked off against the rag bolts, and drill the bolt holes in the plates. You will probably need assistance for the next step.

Place the side frame in position over the bolts, get someone to hold it, or prop it in place, then lift the end frame into position over the respective bolt holes and butting against the side frame. With cord, tie the butting studs together at top, bottom and middle. This will hold the two frames in the correct positions while you check for square and plumb, fix the rag bolt securing nuts, and drill holes for, and fit, the three carriage bolts as shown in Fig.4B.

The two remaining frames can be constructed and fitted, one at a time, in the same way.

The roof

The roof described here is of the gable type, as shown in Fig.5. First cut and fit the cross bracing at each end as shown in Fig.5. Next lay the ridge board across the tops of the bracing and nail it in position. Trim three joists to size. Using direct marking, cut each joist to butt neatly against the ridge board at the top end, and mark out the positions of the birdsmouth butting against the plate and the two recesses for the halving joints for the purlins. Remove the joist and cut these out.

Nail each rafter in position at each end, then place the purlins across and glue and screw these in place. The barge boards, as shown in Fig.5, are fixed by nailing to the ridge and fascia boards at each end, and to the end grain of the purlins along the length. The fascia is nailed direct to the ends of the joists and barge boards.

You may prefer a flat roof, as shown in Fig.2. This is probably simpler to construct, but it lessens the head room. This is particularly important in a structure such as a shed, because the extra room created by a ridge allows you to fit screws along the roof joists for hanging certain items on. Details of the construction of flat roofs are shown on page 24.

Doors and windows

As mentioned in the Cutting List, the doors and windows are purchased ready made, although there is nothing to stop you from making your own if you feel up to it.

Fit the door and windows in position. If the windows are not glazed, then leave this chore until the shed has been completed, otherwise you might break a pane during construction.

Fitting the hardboard

Ordinary grade hardboard can be used for exterior purposes, but it does require looking after, with regular applications of paint. The best material to use is an exterior grade such as Tempered Royal Board.

Using direct marking, mark and cut the various panels according to the patterns shown in Fig.6. This is quite straightforward, and is simply glued, then pinned to the frame at 2in. or 50mm intervals. But there are some pointers about the fitting of hardboard.

Condition the hardboard to ensure that it is fully expanded, before nailing it in position.

This consists of scrubbing cold water, using about 2 pints for each 8ft x 4ft sheet, into the reverse of the dimpled side of the board. When this has been done, lay the boards down, back to back, for at least 48 hours so that the water is fully absorbed. This is done so that the hardboard will shrink after fixing, and will remain flat and taut. If you don't do this, the hardboard will invariably buckle.

Before you nail any of the hardboard spread a liberal coat of waterproof sealer, such as Aquaseal, along the underside around the back edges, to provide waterproof joints.

Weather proofing

The roof must be covered with at least two layers of roofing felt to provide a sufficient waterproofing layer.

To ensure a long life for your shed, it must be finished off with at least two coats of waterproof paint, making sure to spread the paint liberally along all joints.

The exterior colour scheme is up to you. It can merge quietly into the overall garden design, or stand out in a blast of psychedelic colours. But whatever scheme you choose, you will soon be wondering how on earth you ever managed without a garden shed.

Fig.6. The cladding for this garden shed can be cut from 10 large sheets of hardboard. The various outlines for specific sections are shown, but no dimensions are given because these are bound to differ slightly for each shed. Use the outlines as a guide, taking the measurements by direct marking.
Over the page. *If you fancy solid wood cladding, you should seriously consider the excellent prefabricated kits on the market.*

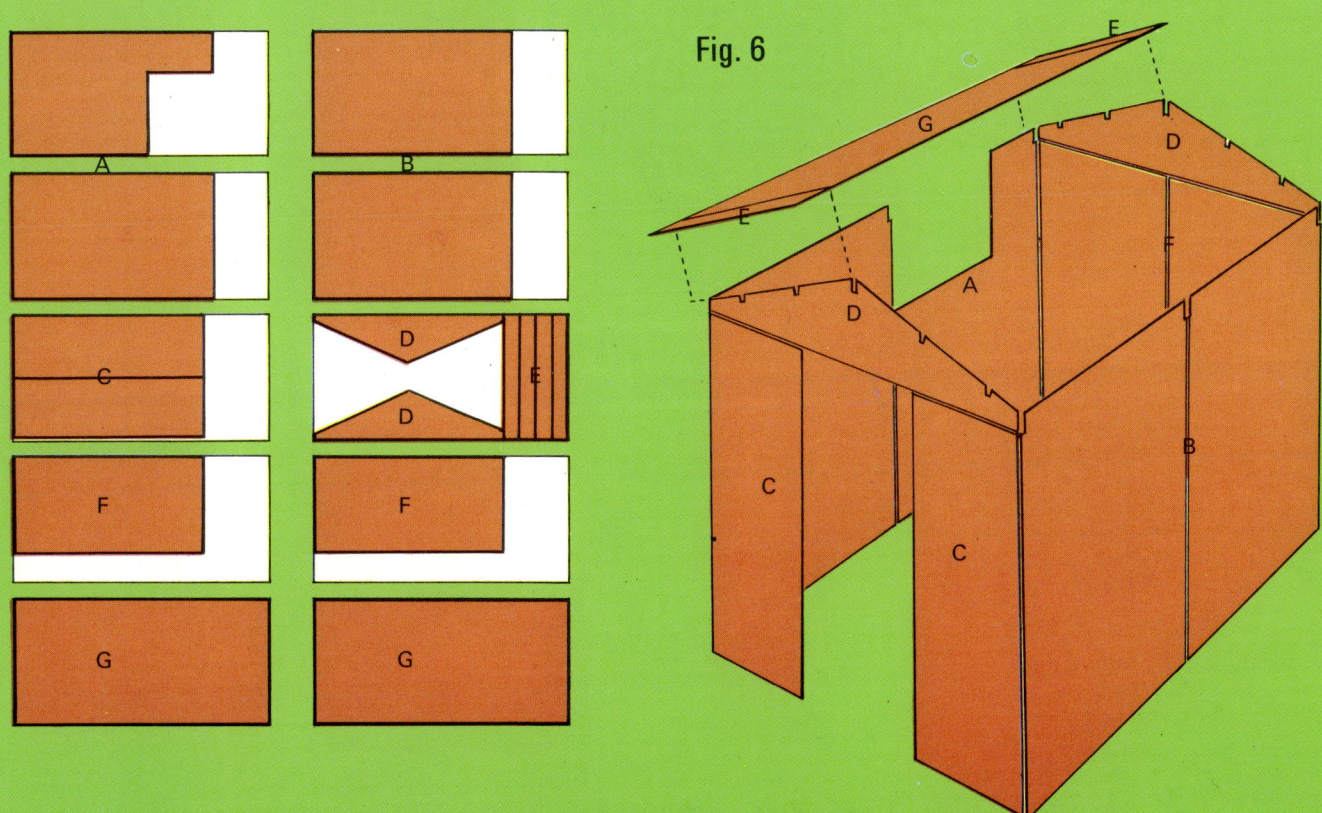

Fig. 6

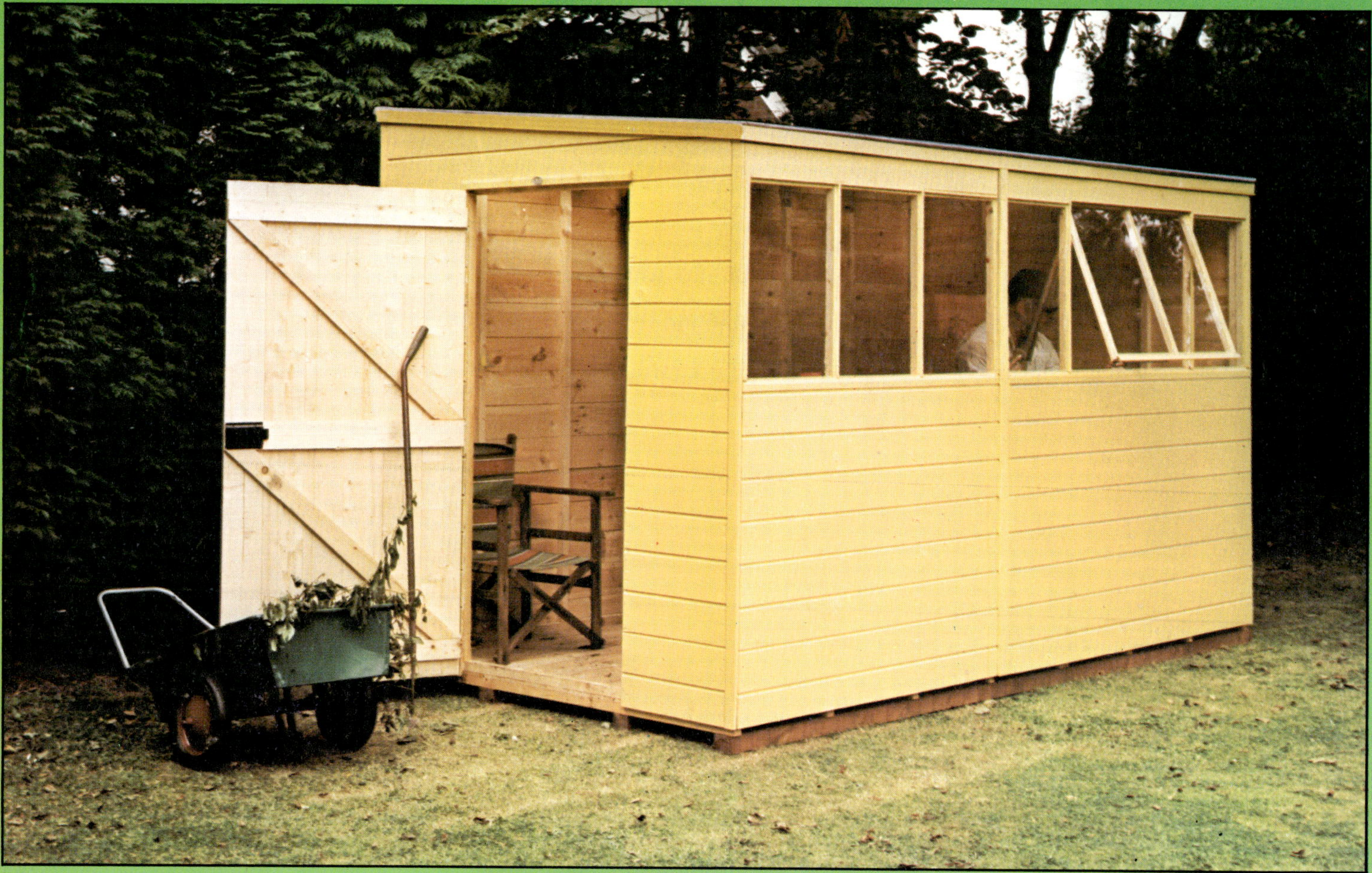

CASES OF TAFFS WELL

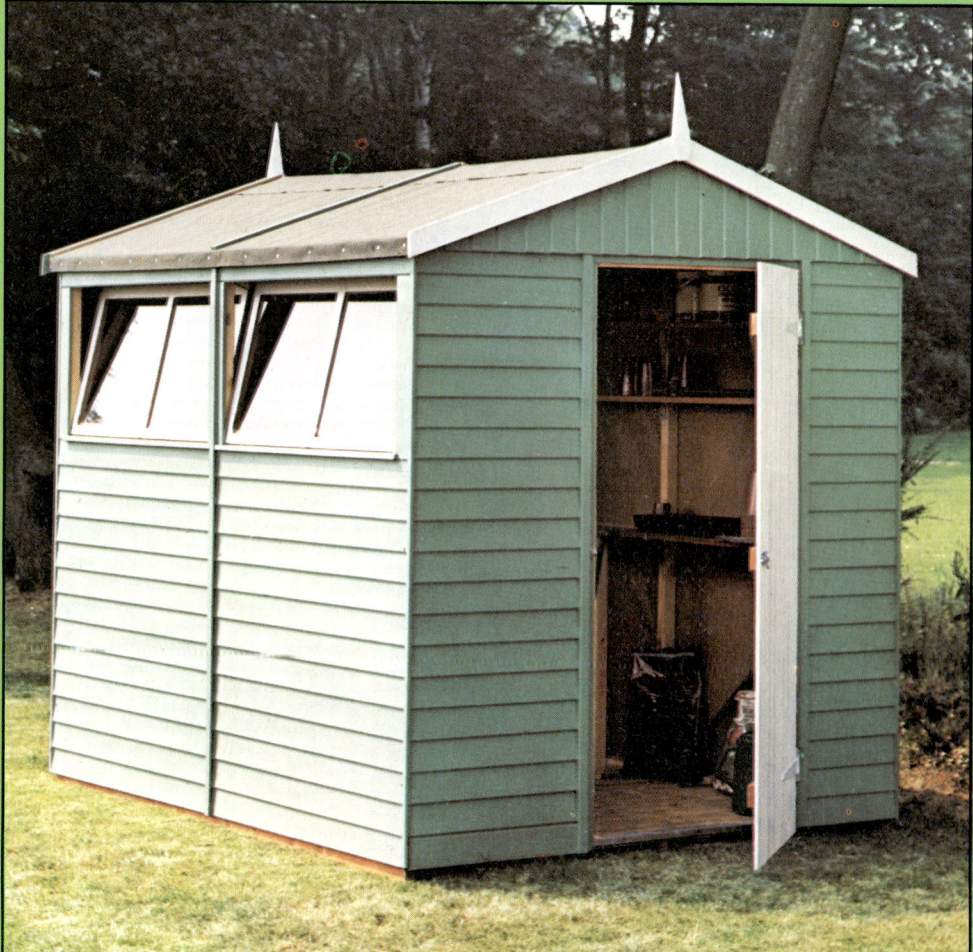

***Above.** The PC7, a prefabricated kit produced by Cases; and **(right)**, the 'Bewdley', one of a range by Banbury.*

BANBURY BUILDINGS LTD

CUTTING LIST

Solid wood	imperial	metric
Wall frames		
6 lengths	8ftx2x1$\frac{1}{2}$	2.44mx50x38
15 lengths	6ftx2x1$\frac{1}{2}$	1.83mx50x38
Wall frames and roof		
14 lengths	6ftx2x1	1.83mx50x25
4 lengths	4ftx2x1	1.22mx50x25
7 lengths	9ftx2x1	2.74mx50x25
Roof joists		
1 length	9ftx3x1	2.74mx75x25
6 lengths	4ftx3x1	1.22mx75x25
Hardboard cladding		
10 sheets	8ftx4ftx$\frac{1}{8}$	2.44mx1.22mx4
Ready made door and windows		
Door (ledged and braced)	72x30	1.83mx762
2 windows	32x24	813x610

You will also require: Roofing felt; paint; 20 $\frac{3}{8}$in. or 4mm carriage bolts; screws and nails. The above are lengths from which the final members are cut. Imperial dimensions are in inches unless stated, and metric dimensions are in millimetres unless stated. When ordering, allow 10% extra for wastage.

Pergolas and rustic fencing

PROJECT 11

A pergola draped with flowering plants will enhance any garden and not only is it attractive, it can be placed to give seclusion to a favourite spot or cut off an unwanted view. When pergolas and fences are carefully planned they make a garden a more beautiful and intimate place.

There is no strict definition of what a pergola is and the variety of designs, some of which are shown in Figs.1-6, is endless. At its most basic, the pergola consists simply of a single line of upright posts which are linked at their tops by thinner horizontal sections. Various patterns can be created by adding more poles between the uprights, or by combining conventional trellis work, so that even this simple structure is capable of great variation. By bridging two parallel lines of uprights a simple arch is created which can be built over a path to provide an attractive covered walk.

Really, the only limitations on pergola design are provided by your imagination. As the designs become more complex, the finished structures should perhaps be more properly

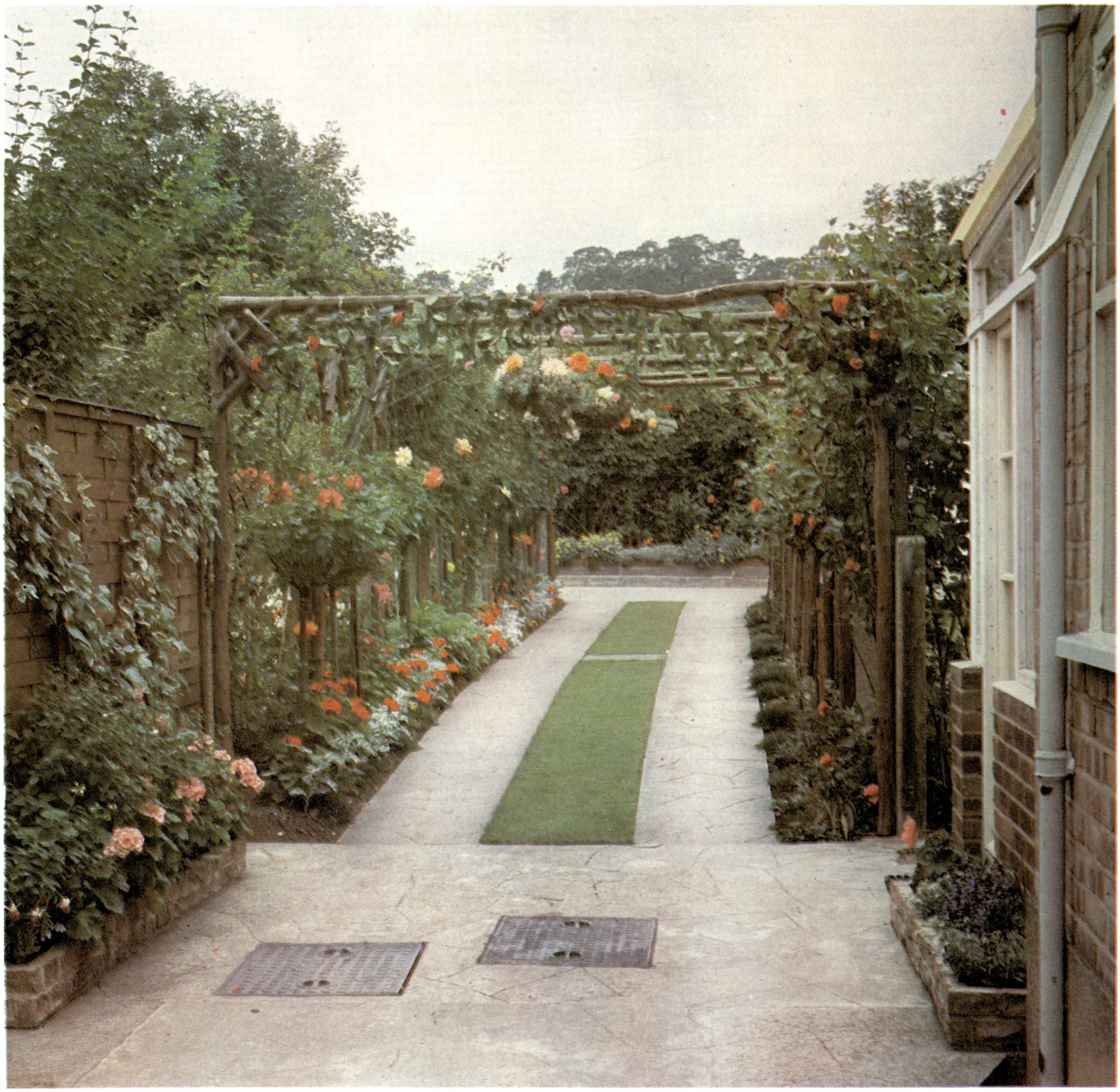

SYNDICATION INTERNATIONAL

SYNDICATION INTERNATIONAL

called arbors, but the construction techniques and materials remain the same.

The well designed pergola is an attractive feature in itself, but it is seen at its best when clothed in climbing or trailing plants. Because it will be a prominent feature of the garden a lot of thought should go into its location. A simple design can be set in the middle of a lawn to provide a feature of interest; or it can act as a divider between, say, a flower and vegetable garden. A pergola may also be used to hide an unsightly view. The arch type structure is best situated over a path or gate, and will give added emphasis to these features as well as providing an attractive covered walk.

Materials

Traditionally, a pergola is made of rustic posts which have the bark left on. This rather limits the type of wood which can be used, as few woods combine the ideal qualities of durability, tight bark, and workability with an attractive appearance. Larch and birch poles are probably the most suitable timbers for the rustic pergola and easily obtained. However, if you do not insist on undressed timber, the range of materials is much wider. Dressed pine poles which have been suitably treated are ideal.

All the timber mentioned so far is left in the round, but a more contemporary design can be created using squared and planed timber. Cedar is a good choice, not only because of its attractive colour, but because its high resin content makes it naturally rot resistant. Squared deal is suitable, but oak, while very durable, is difficult to work.

Your choice of materials should be dictated by the style of your garden and for this reason brick and stonework can be used for the uprights in a garden which is both formal and modern. The rustic pergola is obviously suited to a traditional flower garden.

Whatever materials you choose they must be thoroughly weather proofed with a horticultural grade preservative and should be strong enough to support fairly heavy weights. The length of the horizontal sections is not vitally important, but the uprights should be cut long enough to insert 2ft (610mm) into the ground and provide 6ft clearance overhead.

In addition, you must ensure that the horizontal members do not have too long a run between uprights, or they will sag in the middle. Provide an upright every 6ft or so.

Fig.2. A most attractive pergola, with piers of natural stone, and trellis work along the sides for the plants to climb.
Fig.3. This is just one example of the many different designs you could use or adapt for your garden.

Treating the timber

Where bark covers the posts it provides its own protection against damp and most fungal attacks. The only parts which require treatment are all the cut ends. These may be coated in hot pitch, burnt with a blowlamp, or dressed with a proprietary horticultural grade preservative such as a copper naphthenate solution. Special attention should be given to the base and this must be treated to a height of 6in. (152mm) above its proposed ground level.

Dressed and squared timber is not only sealed at the cut ends but must be painted all over with a resistant varnish.

If creosote is used, the wood must be left to dry for several days, otherwise the creosote will damage plants.

Joining timber

One of the attractions of rustic posts is their natural appearance, so that there is no need to fix the sections together with elaborate joints. The simplest method is nailing or tying the timber with strong coated wire. However, a more attractive method for joining rustic posts which also gives greater strength, is to use simple joints as shown in Figs.7-8. These can be cut roughly with a bill-hook or axe as well as with a saw. The bridging sections of a covered walk do not bear any weight and can be nailed to the horizontal sections as shown in Fig.9.

Squared timber presents a more formal appearance, and is best jointed together with very simple joints – butted or halved – glued and screwed. Non load-bearing sections can be slotted together as shown in Fig. 4.

Erecting a pergola

The main uprights should be inserted 2ft (610mm) into the ground; more if the soil is very loose and sandy. In heavy soils the excavation hole must be kept as small as possible and when the post is inserted the surrounding soil should be well compacted. To allow water to drain away from the base of the uprights place a layer of stone at the bottom of each hole. A stronger foundation, which reduces timber rot, is made

by setting the upright in cement. If brick or stone uprights are used they must be set on proper concrete foundations. The size of these will depend on the type of surrounding soil; in a compact soil they should be twice as wide as the piers they support, in a light, sandy soil a larger foundation is necessary. Where timber sections join the piers they are fixed to the brickwork by bolts cemented into the top of each upright.

Pergolas are assembled in situ and the construction is easy if all joints have been cut correctly. Care should be taken when spacing all the sections to ensure that a uniform pattern is maintained.

Circular pergolas

It is possible to build a pergola which is completely round, but a lot of difficulty will be encountered in cutting the rim sections to the correct size and shape. However, an attractive alternative is the polygonal pergola shown in Fig.5. This structure has six sides, but the number can be varied. The uprights and rim sections would need to be 4in. (100mm) thick and though rounded timber could be used, squared dressed timber would be easier to assemble neatly.

The top of this structure can be bridged with thinner sections, or a spoke pattern can be created with timber sections radiating from a centre post as in Fig.5. The rim sections are mitred and the angle of this mitre is calculated by dividing the number of sides into 360°. The roof sections are housed in slots cut into the centre post and are notched where they meet the rim sections.

An ingenious handyman gardener will be able to devise variations of the polygonal design but should bear in mind that the spaces between sections should be large enough to allow climbing plants to grow unobstructed and in good light. Too much elaboration is unnecessary, because when the finished pergola is clothed with climbing plants the details of the patterns are obscured.

Rustic fences

The overall appearance of your garden owes a lot to the type of fencing which surrounds it. Not only are fences decorative, there are styles which lend seclusion to a garden, or provide protection from wind and rain. Before choosing a fence, look at your own garden and decide whether it is too exposed or too enclosed and

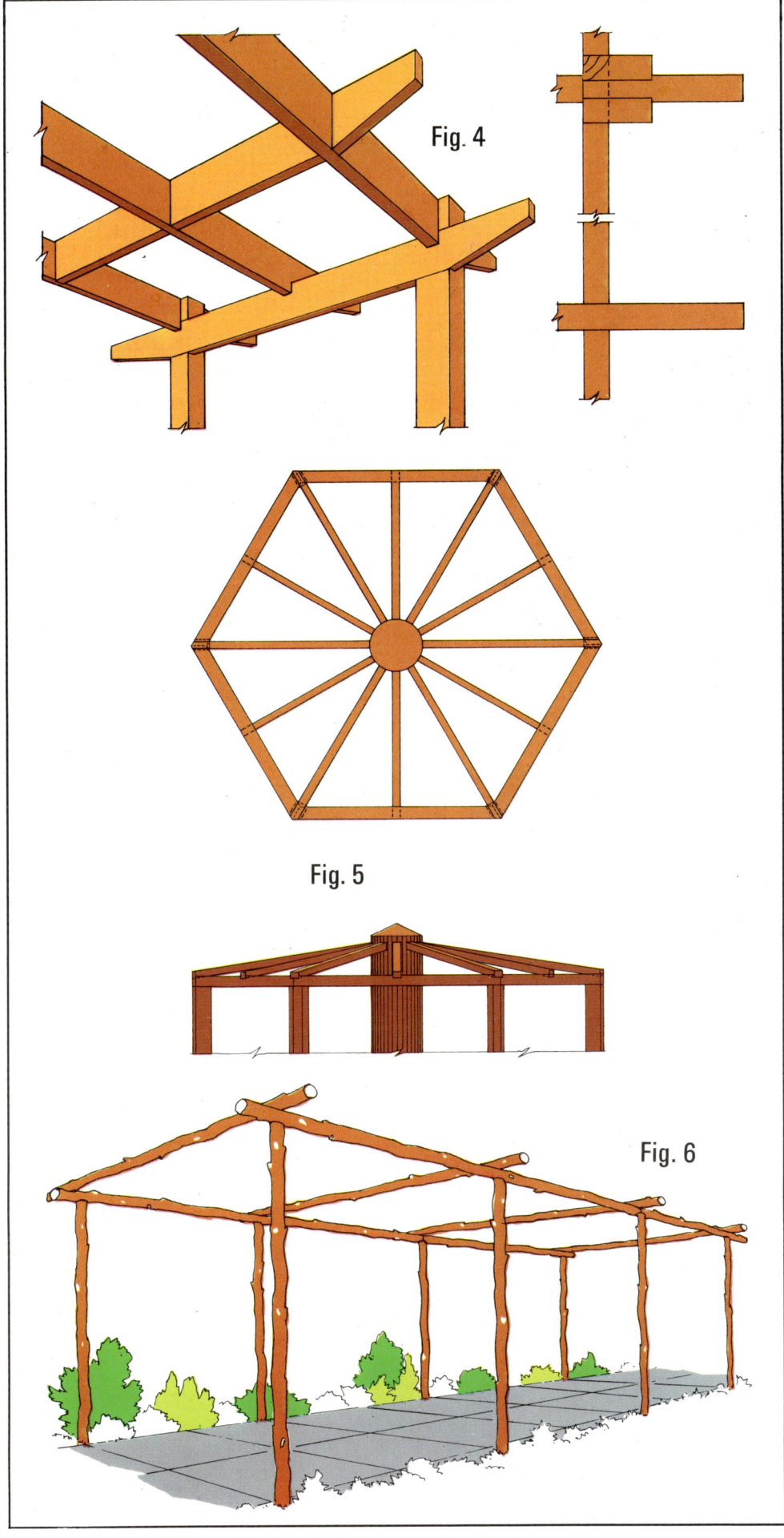

cramped looking. Then choose a design of fence which not only looks good but which is suited to your particular garden. This section concentrates on helping you choose rustic fencing that best complements the traditional garden; it is best to follow this avenue of design – that of selecting fencing to suit the overall garden design. Nothing looks worse than, say, rustic fencing in an ultra-modern garden with plastic or concrete furniture.

Perhaps the simplest type of rustic fencing is that shown in Fig.13, which is made of hazel branches woven between and nailed to 6ft horizontal sections. The drawback of this type is that it is not very strong and is best situated against a well-planted hedge. Wattle fences, which have a basket weave construction, are sturdy and rustic in appearance. They can be purchased in sections which are fixed to oak stakes driven into the ground.

Another simple rustic fence, shown in Fig.10, is easily made using many of the techniques used in the construction of rustic pergolas—it can also be bought through some garden suppliers. It is generally constructed from undressed larch or pine fixed in a repeated diamond pattern. The uprights should be 3-4in. (76-102mm) thick while the design work between them is of thinner section—about $1\frac{1}{2}$-2in. (38-51mm).

Of course this type is almost wholly decorative, giving no protection against the weather or stray animals. A rustic fence which retains the natural look yet provides seclusion and weather protection is the interwoven type. Fig.12 illustrates a larch weave fence which is sturdy, attractive, and virtually wind-proof. A more sophisticated design which meets the same needs is double-ranch. This is constructed from chestnut boards which overlap to prevent casual passers-by looking into the garden. It is sold commercially, but it is relatively simple to build your own, using very elementary carpentry techniques.

Where privacy and shelter are not the most important considerations a more open fence can be erected. The palisade type is popular and lends itself to both traditional and contemporary styles. This can be a very sturdy construction which has a neat and formal pattern but which retains its natural look by the use of split larch poles with the bark left on.

There is no reason why more than one type of fencing should not be used in gardens. For weather protection and seclusion a high solid fence can be erected round the garden, while different areas inside the garden can be fenced off with more open designs. In this way a garden takes on a well planned aspect, and if fences and pergolas are planned carefully with your own garden in mind, even a smallish garden becomes a more interesting and intimate place.

Fig.4. *Squared timber can be jointed at the tops in the same way as bottle partitions in wooden crates. The joints used here are cross-halving joints.*
Fig.5. *Construction outlines of a polygonal pergola. There is no need for a centre pole if you run the top members straight across.*
Fig.6. *A simple, popular, and very effective pergola design—similar to the one in Fig.1.*

Fig. 4

Fig. 5

Fig. 6

Fig. 7. *A simple lapped or halved joint will suffice for rustic woodwork joints. These are just pinned and glued, using a waterproof adhesive such as a urea formaldehyde.*
Fig. 8. *Verticals are housed into the horizontal members, then pinned and glued.*
Fig. 9. *Bracing members are just pinned and glued—no joints need to be cut.*
Fig. 10. *A simple rustic fence.*
Fig. 11. *A modern design of pergola, showing many interesting features, and incorporating a screen wall and a barbecue.*
Fig. 12. *Interwoven wood strips provide a peep- and wind-proof screen.*
Fig. 13. *A fence with 'woven' timbers.*

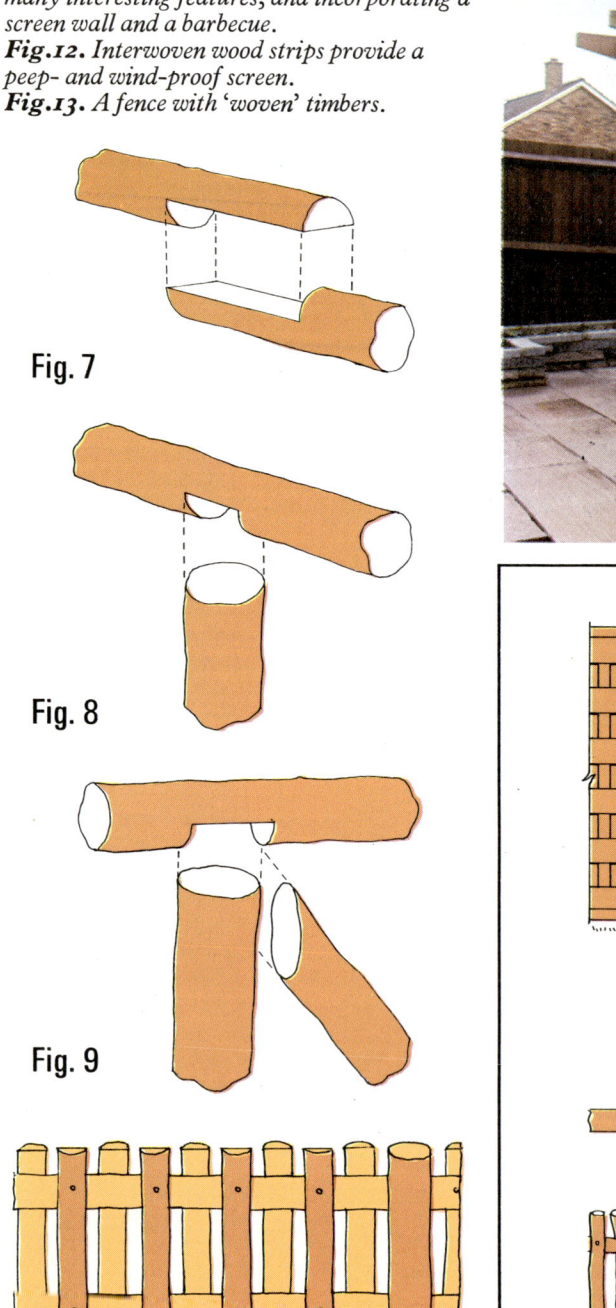

Fig. 7

Fig. 8

Fig. 9

Fig. 10

11

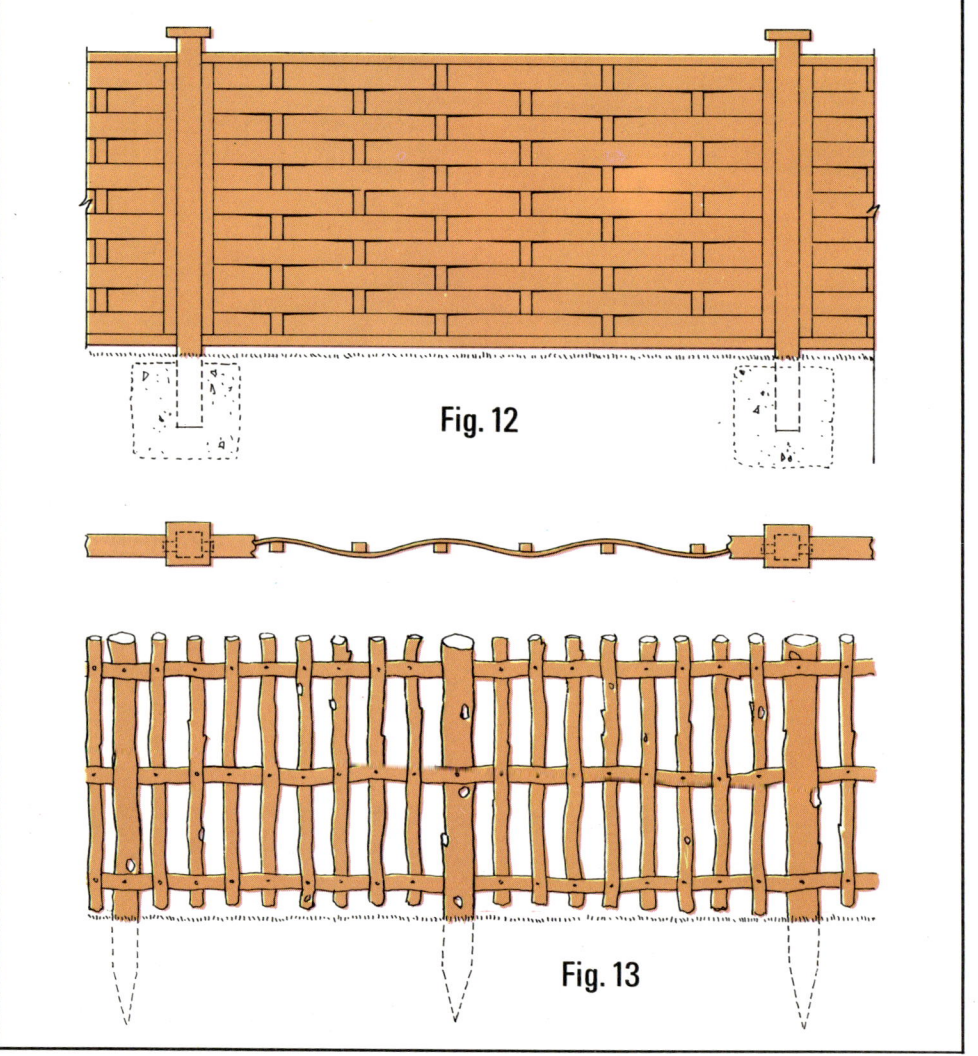

Fig. 12

Fig. 13

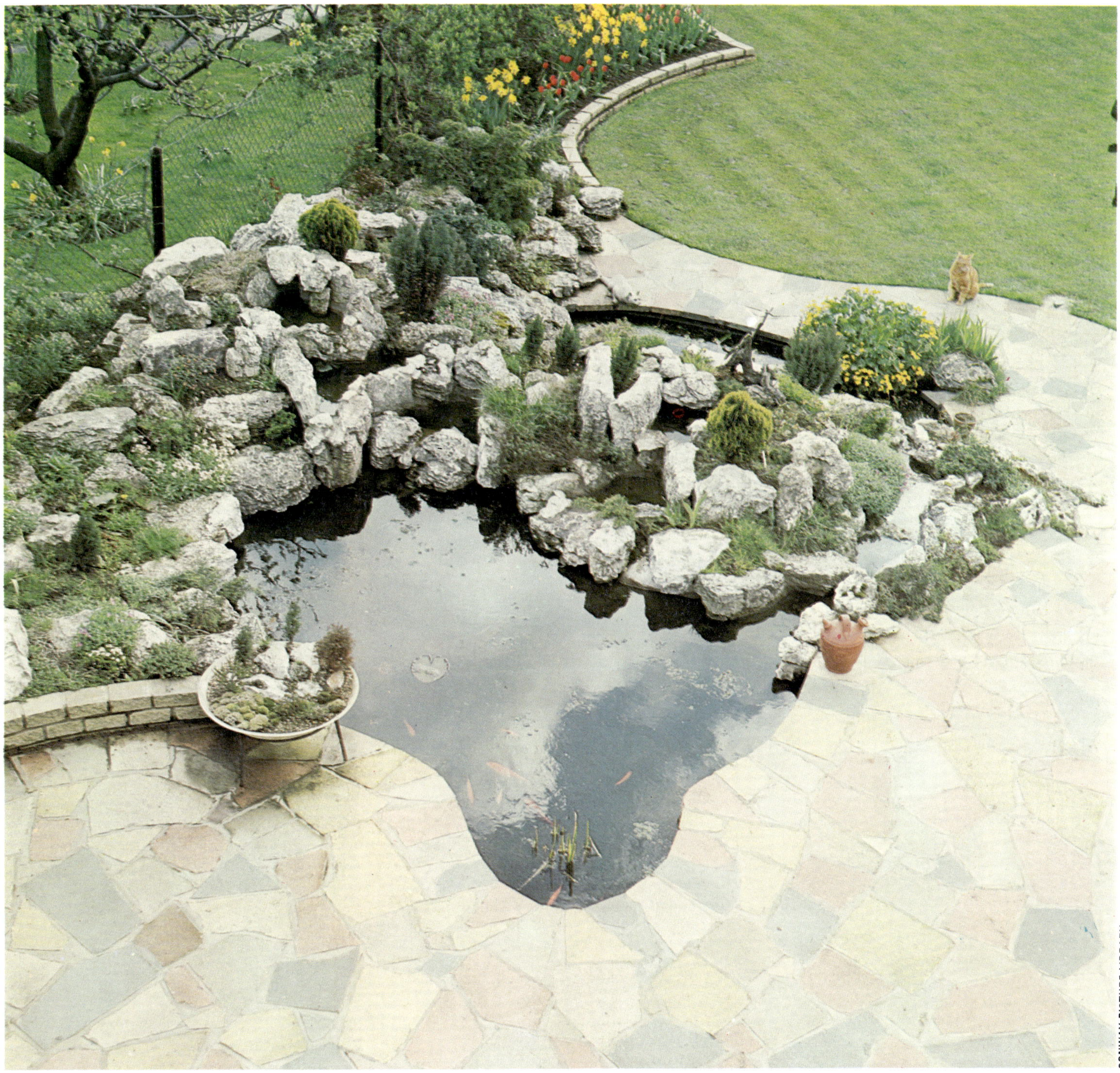

CONWAY PICTURE LIBRARY

Garden pools – from easy to elegant

PROJECT 12

A garden pool will transform the most ordinary garden—or make even more attractive a garden which is already beautiful. And just how easy the installation is depends entirely on you.

A garden pool can completely change the character of your garden. The use of water as a garden feature is one of the most important and far-reaching of home improvements and, to be most effective, requires careful pre-planning.

***Above.** An attractive pool into which the adjacent rock garden has cleverly been led. This creates a more natural effect and combines the best of both designs.*

The installation of a garden pool will necessitate the removal of a considerable quantity of earth. This may be disposed of or used as the base of a rock garden. In any case, it will require some effort and expense to return the garden to its original condition. So, before you reach for a spade, map out a course of action and make sure you really want a pool and that it is sited in the right place.

Siting the pool

The most successful water gardens are situated out in the open, in full sunlight. Most

aquatic plants thrive in warmer water, and an open site will extend the flowering period in both autumn and spring. For the same reason, it is advantageous to give protection from cold winds. A belt of trees, a hedge, or buildings can all provide suitable cover. Shade, on the other hand, will promote leafy growth, but hinder flowering.

Pools should not be placed beneath overhanging trees as leaves will fall in during autumn. As they rot, the decomposing leaves can destroy plant and fish life in the pool.

An important consideration is the water supply. Generally, large quantities of water are not required after the initial filling. Even in a discoloured pond you should not continuously run in fresh water, or make frequent changes, as this tends to stir up the sediment.

Finally, to look right, an artificial pool needs to be in the sort of position where a natural pool might occur. On a low-lying area of your garden it will look natural; on a high spot it might easily look ridiculous.

When you have decided where to site the pool, place a line of paving slabs, bricks, or even a garden hose, round the outline where the pool will be built. Then, if possible, 'live' with this shape for a few weeks. You may decide, after a while, that you prefer a different location, in which case you will have saved yourself from a disappointing venture.

Choosing the right pool

The type of pool you build is almost as important as the location. It is pointless building an ornate, solid pool in concrete, when you only require a temporary, shallow pool. On the other hand a pool several feet deep, and lined with a flimsy polythene lining, would be a waste, as it could collapse in time. It pays to know exactly what types of pool are available for the home handyman, and what their respective advantages and disadvantages are.

Concrete is a widely used lining and, for deep pools, is virtually essential. It can be contoured to suit almost any shape, and so is an excellent material if you wish to build a pool to your own design. And it can be coloured to blend in with a rock surround or rock garden. It is, however, relatively expensive compared with plastic sheeting, requires a considerable amount of heavy labour to lay, needs proofing to make it watertight and—should you ever change your mind—is rather difficult to dispose of.

Prefabricated containers, and these include modern fibreglass mouldings as well as wooden tubs, discarded baths, or any other receptacle that will hold water, are a better bet if you want to save some hard work. Some of the commercial fibreglass mouldings are extremely attractive and have stepped sides and varying depths which can accommodate a variety of plant life.

Plastic lining can be used for building the simplest kind of pool. You just dig a hole, cover the inside with a plastic sheet, and fill with water. It is the cheapest method by far, but not necessarily the best. The main disadvantage is that the lining can be easily punctured. Also, the sheeting along the water/air demarcation line is liable to deteriorate in a few years. It is, however, cheap and uncomplicated to replace.

General construction details

The method of construction varies with each type of pool, but there are construction details that apply to all types. One of the most important—and the one most frequently overlooked—is that the area from which you dig must be level. It is all too easy to dig a hole, line it and fill it with water, only to find that it is half full at one end, and overflowing at the other.

Walls should never be vertical. If they are, there will be a terrific strain on them when the water freezes in winter. Pool walls should have a slope of approximately 20 degrees, so that if ice does form it will tend to push up and out, rather than against the side of the structure, causing the concrete to crack.

Pools are often built not deep enough. If they are too shallow the water will freeze solid in winter, and become excessively warm in summer. The minimum depth for even the smallest pool is about 15in. or 380mm. There is no reason for a pool, whatever the size, to be deeper than 30in. or 760mm, despite what you may hear about greater depths providing adequate protection for fish in winter.

An important consideration is the positioning of plants. Most aquatic plants grow best at specific depths. Marginal or shallow water plants, for example, need a soil depth of 6in. or 150mm, with a water depth over the soil of 4in. or 100mm, while water lilies need a soil depth of 8in. or 200mm and will reach the surface from a depth of 15in. or 375mm. This means that the bottom of your pool must be 'stepped' with a series of ledges, so that you can place each plant where it will thrive. Moulded fibreglass containers are all stepped, but with any other kind of pool you will have to build in this feature. Each ledge can be built in the form of a trough in order to contain the soil at that particular level. A better method is to build flat ledges, and place each plant in a pot or container. This has the additional advantage of ensuring that the plants will not spread and choke the pool.

It is undesirable to fit a pool with a drain plug. Water draining away underneath can lead to erosion and subsidence. On the rare occasions when it is necessary to empty part of a pool, this can be done with a bucket. With a large pool it will be necessary to install a pump, which can also be used to operate a fountain or waterfall.

Making a concrete pool

Before starting work, draw a plan on paper to ascertain the exact design and amount of concrete required. Consult your local builders merchant to estimate the correct amount – you don't want to be left with a load of waste. But a pool is not a flat surface, and you will need to know the area you have to cover. This is worked out by measuring the length and width of the pool across the surface, then adding twice the maximum depth to both the length and the

Fig. 1 (top right). *Marking out, the first stage in building any pool.*
Fig. 2 (second top). *The container is placed in the excavated pit.*
Fig. 3 (third top). *Levelling off. Depressions are filled with compacted sand.*
Fig. 4 (bottom). *A surround of paving slabs or crazing paving finishes the job.*

R. J. CORBIN

A cut-away view of a typical garden pool. The ledges afford different depths so that a wider variety of plants can be grown.

width. For example, a pool with dimensions of 12ft x 7ft, and 1½ft deep, will contain concrete whose surface area is approximately 15ft x 10ft. The thickness of the concrete should be 6in. or 150mm. Do not forget to allow for this when digging out the pool.

You will need the following materials for making the pool: Best quality ¾in. or 18mm ballast; Portland cement; sharp sand; builders' soft sand; proprietary compound such as Silglaze, for sealing off the cement and preventing the harmful effects of lime from contaminating the water; waterproofing powder; expanded metal laths; 1in. or 25mm mesh galvanized wire.

Mark out the outline of the pool, and excavate the whole area down to the depth of the first ledge. This must take into account the eventual thickness of the concrete. For instance a ledge 6in. or 150mm deep will have to be excavated to a depth of 12in. to take into account the 6in. thickness of the concrete. The soil can now be marked to outline the deeper area, and the inside excavated down to the final depth required (plus 6in.). Tamp the soil hard with a heavy piece of timber to ensure that the bed is firm.

Press down the galvanized wire so that it moulds to the shape of the excavation. Make sure the wire covers the whole area, with 6in. overlaps where there are joins.

Prepare the concrete mix, using 4 parts of ¾in. ballast to 2 parts of sharp sand and 1 part of cement. The mix must be firm, not runny, so that it can easily be worked up the sides of the pool.

Spread a 3in. or 75mm layer of concrete uniformly over the wire mesh. As soon as you have finished this, lay the metal laths on top and press them into the moist concrete.

Now spread a second layer of concrete, about 2½in. thick, over the laths, working over the surface with a float trowel. Leave the concrete to dry for two days.

For the final rendering, prepare a mix of 3 parts soft sand to 1 part cement into which the waterproofing powder is introduced in accordance with the instructions on the packet. Float a half inch thick layer of this mix over the concrete shell. Be sure to smooth out all air bubbles as they appear, otherwise leaks might occur. In dry weather, damp the concrete before applying the rendering, to ensure good adhesion between the surfaces.

Leave the rendering to dry for four days, then apply the Silglaze compound to seal off the cement. After two or three days the pool will be ready for filling.

Installing a container pool

These pools include moulded fibreglass shells which are sold in a variety of shapes, or any other suitable waterproof container.

Containers do have one enormous advantage if you like to take your toil in easy doses—the pool can be installed on the surface, without digging. This can be quite attractive if your garden is flat and featureless. It also makes for easier draining.

If you want an 'upright' pool, place the container on an even, firm surface. If the ground is not level, fill any depressions with soft sand. Bank up soil against the sides, and tamp it down well. The soil can then be sown with grass seed or made into a rock garden surround.

If the container is to be sunk into the ground, make the excavation slightly larger than the pool itself. Consolidate the bottom by ramming or treading, and make sure that it is absolutely level. If necessary, level it with soft sand.

Place the container in the excavation and back-fill the sides with stone-free soil or soft sand, ramming it well in so that the pool is supported firmly on all sides.

Pool liners

Constructing a pool with a waterproof liner is the least arduous way of making a sunken garden pool, but it is not nearly as permanent as other methods.

There are three main types of pool liner. The best is a thick pvc sheeting reinforced with nylon mesh. The same sheeting is also made without the nylon reinforcement, which reduces both the cost and the expectation of useful life. Sheet polythene is sometimes used, but this is a relatively fragile material and can be recommended only when a temporary pool is required, or where maximum economy is the prime consideration.

The size of liner required for a pool is calculated in the same way as the surface area of the pool, but to provide for the overlap around the edges, 2ft or 600mm must be added to both the length and width.

The excavation must be carefully prepared if you are lining a pool with plastic sheeting. All sharp stones must first be removed before spreading a two inch layer of soft sand on the pool bed and ledges.

Lay the liner over the excavation, making sure that it overlaps the edges evenly. Stretch it fairly taut and hold it in position by placing bricks or slabs on the overlap at regular intervals all round.

Fill the pool slowly from the garden hose. The liner will sink into the excavation, and the weight of water will mould it to the sides. Leave the bricks or slabs in position, holding the overlap in place until you have laid in a more permanent surround of stone or brick.

Stocking the pool

After the pool has been filled with water, it should be left for a week before plants and fish are put in.

Floating aquatic plants are simply placed on the water's surface, but all others need a sufficient quantity of soil to grow in. Use a plain, heavy, fibreless loam but avoid adding organic materials such as manure and leafmould which are normally used for potting composts. These will give off poisonous gases as they decompose and suffocate any fish.

Place an 8in. or 200mm thick layer of soil on the bed of the pool, then cover it with a layer of gravel to prevent bits of loam rising and clouding the water. A better alternative is to introduce the soil in pots or containers which have holes in the sides to allow the water to circulate. Plastic baskets, lined with sacking to prevent the soil from filtering through, are ideal. Or you can buy pots ready made for this purpose in most gardening shops.

The most suitable fish for pools are those which stay near the surface and are easily seen, such as goldfish and golden orfe. Avoid mirror carp, or tench which are bottom dwellers and constantly stir up the mud. Use any recommended proprietary compound for feeding.

Maintenance

If your pool is to remain attractive it will require regular attention. Never let scum accumulate on the surface. Remove it either by flooding the pool over, or by drawing a newspaper across the surface. Dead leaves and similar debris should be removed immediately. Never over-feed fish, as this can cause the water to discolour, and always feed in the same place, giving only as much as can be consumed in five minutes. Do not spray insecticides near the pond as even minute quantities can kill fish.

Fig. 5 (*top left*). *A charming pool set in a natural surrounding. The effect is superb—but remember that the nearby trees will deposit leaves in the water.*
Fig. 6 (*above*). *This concrete pool adds great charm and character to the extensive stonework terrace around it.*
Fig. 7 (*below left*). *This pool, surrounded by rockwork, has been naturally and imaginatively designed.*
Fig. 8 (*top right*). *Excavating a pit for a plastic sheet lined pool.*
Fig. 9 (*second top, right*). *Filling the pool with water to mould the sheet to the sides.*
Fig. 10 (*third top, right*). *A surround of paving slabs is placed round the edges.*
Fig. 11 (*bottom right*). *The finished pool, ready for stocking with fish.*

Brick trick: a garden planter in five easy courses

A hollow brick planter is an attractive feature that will visually improve any garden. It consists of low walls filled with soil in which flowers, shrubs, or trees are planted.

The planter has many applications in landscaping a garden. If the garden is flat and monotonous, the planter will create raised levels, 'breaking' the area. It can also be used as a decorative partition, for example, to divide a long garden by forming a 'fence' in which flowers are grown.

Another use is to fill the planter with soil of a different type from that in the surrounding area, and grow plants that would not ordinarily thrive there, giving you greater variety.

If you decide to grow a tree in a planter, make sure you buy a deep rooting one. Trees with spreading roots could undermine the walls; or have their growth stunted because their roots were confined; or both.

Tools required

Bricklayer's trowel. The main tool, used for lifting and spreading mortar, forming joints and, if you are practised, cutting bricks.

Pointing trowel. Sometimes called a 'dotter'. For finishing the joints.

Below. *A planter need not be a long trough; this is an attractive 'L' shaped variation.*

LESLIE JOHNS ●

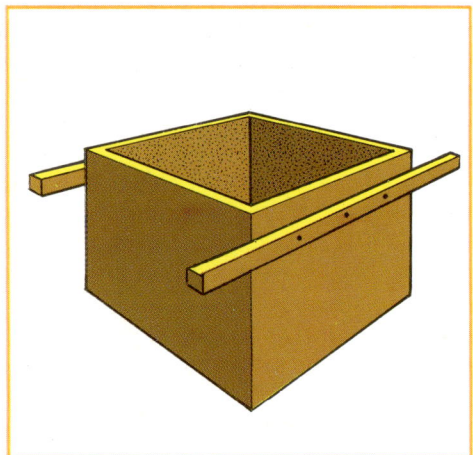

Fig. 1 (above). A gauge box is essential if accurate proportions of sand and cement are to be measured.

Fig. 2 (above). Picking up a pear of mortar from the spotboard. Draw the mortar towards you with a slicing action.

Fig. 3 (above). Laying a bedding course. This is spread slightly thicker than the jointing layers that will follow.

Fig. 4 (above). 'Buttering' the end of a brick. The buttered end provides the vertical joint with the previous brick.

Fig. 5 (above). Laying a brick in position. Make sure that it is pressed firmly down into the mortar.

Fig. 6 (above). Tapping the brick down after it has been laid in position. There is no need to do more than tap gently.

Medium-sized shovel. For mixing the mortar.
Water bucket. Heavy duty.
Broad cold chisel or bolster, and heavy hammer. For cutting bricks.
Two bricklayer's pins, four stakes and a ball of string. For keeping the courses (lines of brick) straight, and for pegging outlines.
Spirit level. A 3ft or 1m builder's level.
Straight edge. An absolutely straight length of wood, at least 3ft or 1m long and ½in. by 3in. (or 13mm by 75mm) thick. This is for checking that brick faces are in alignment, and for levelling the finished foundation concrete.
Spotboard. Approximately 12in. or 300mm square, for handling small quantities of mortar.
Gauge box. For accurately measuring amounts of cement and aggregate.

The gauge box

When mixing concrete and mortar, it is difficult to gauge accurate proportions if you are measuring by the shovelful (how much *is* a shovelful?). And buckets, especially plastic ones, are not made to take the pounding this job would give them.

One answer is to be over-generous with the cement. A more economical one, in the long run, is to make yourself a gauge box, which is

simply a strong box of known volume, with an open top. When filled with sand or coarse aggregate it will hold the same quantity every time. Handles are usually fitted to make carrying and tipping easier.

In use, the gauge box is slightly overfilled, then a straight edge is run across the top to level off.

Before making a gauge box, you must first decide whether you will be using imperial or metric volumes. A box whose internal dimensions are all 12in. will have a capacity of one cubic foot, but in the building trade in Britain most boxes are now metric, with the smallest recommended dimensions being 315mm deep, and 315mm by 350mm across, giving a capacity of 35 litres.

When measuring sand, bear in mind that it increases in volume when damp. To correct for this, use 25% more when sand is damp than you would if it were dry.

Planning and preparation

It sounds silly, but planning and preparation is probably the most neglected aspect of home building work, despite the fact that a few moments' thought could have averted many 'disasters'.

First, consider carefully where the planter should be sited, how well it will blend with its surroundings, and so on. Don't rush this part of planning, because while it is quite hard work building a planter it is much harder to shift it.

Note that no individual wall in a planter should be more than 6ft or 2m in length unless the brickwork has an intersecting wall, or piers, pillars or metal ties for support. The height is a matter of preference, but five courses is about as high as you can safely take a single-skin wall.

Next, check tools and equipment you require —not only whether they are available, but whether they have remained in good order since you last used them! When you have the complete 'set', put everything in one place so that you don't have to repeat the procedure when you start work.

Calculating quantities

To estimate the number of bricks required, measure the length of a brick you will be using, and add half an inch or 10mm for the thickness of the joint (the mortar between the bricks). Next measure the perimeter of the wall—for instance, a planter measuring 6ft by 3ft would be 18ft round the outside. Now divide the perimeter by the length of a brick, plus the

about 4in. or 100mm bigger all round than your proposed planter. This establishes the outside perimeter of the foundations. Inside these lines, peg out four more to establish the inside perimeter; remember to allow for the thickness of the bricks, plus 2in. or 50mm extra 'footing' on each side of each wall.

When you have marked out the foundation area, whether on existing concrete or on new ground, make sure that it is square either by measuring the diagonals or by using the 3:4:5 rule (outlined in PROJECT 2, 'Setting out the site').

Laying the foundation

The foundation concrete should be 2½in. or 65mm thick (deep). If the soil is reasonably solid, this can be laid directly into the foundation trench provided the bottom of the trench has been levelled and tamped firmly.

Dig a trench between the marked foundation lines, making sure that the bottom of the trench is as level as you can get it. The trench should be as deep as the foundation, plus half an inch or 15mm. This is so that the 'footing', or edge of the foundation that extends beyond the brickwork, can be covered with earth once the planter has been completed.

With a hefty piece of timber, or the end of a brick, ram the bottom of the trench firmly so that the earth is well compacted.

Mix the concrete and pour it into the trench just level with the surface of the soil. With the piece of timber or brick you used for ramming the bottom of the trench, tamp or compact the concrete all over. When you have finished compacting, the surface of the mix should lie just below the surface of the soil.

Brickwork

Bricks, as you may have noticed, are not always laid in the same pattern. Sometimes bricks are laid only end-to-end, and in the same fashion in each course. Others are laid longways in one course and endways, in half bricks, in the next course. There is a wide variety of these styles, or *bonds*.

Perhaps the most common bond is *stretching bond,* which consists of bricks laid longways in each course, with each brick overlapping the joint of the two bricks immediately below. (Bricks are nearly always overlapped in some way, to ensure maximum strength of the wall. An unbonded wall, with continuous vertical joints running up the height of the brickwork, would crack under a heavy load; such walls are used only for decorative work.)

The layer of mortar on the top or bottom of each brick, that is, running parallel to the courses, is called a *bed joint,* and the upright layer between the ends of two bricks is called a *vertical joint.*

If you plan the planter correctly, you will probably be able to run a stretching bond round the wall using whole bricks throughout. But if the bricks do not match the overall dimensions you want, you might need some half, or quarter, bricks to complete the corners properly. In this case you will have to cut a *bat.* A bat is a portion of any brick that has been cut across the width of the brick; thus you can make half bats, quarter bats or any other fraction you need.

An imaginative group of planters. The two at the rear are planted out, while the other one is being used as a sunken pool.

thickness of a joint, and you have the number of base bricks you require. The number you arrive at will have to be multiplied by the number of courses (a course is a line or layer of bricks) in the wall. If you are using five courses of 9½in. bricks, for example, you will need 22 bricks to form a 16ft perimeter, and 110 for all five courses. You should allow about 5% extra for breakages.

Low brickwork—up to five courses—can be laid on an existing solid surface, such as a path or patio, if it is reasonably level. Otherwise, you will need a shallow concrete foundation beneath the walls. For the concrete, use a mix of cement, sharp sand and coarse aggregate in the proportions of 1:2:4 by volume. Ask your local builders merchant to estimate the quantities—you don't want to be left with a lot over.

For the bricklaying mortar, you will need cement, soft sand and a proprietary plasticizer. Quantities are difficult to estimate, but if you buy a 1 cwt or 50kg bag of mortar mix, which includes the plasticizer, it will give you at least a good start.

Marking out

If an existing solid area is being used for the foundation, mark out the outline by tying one end of a length of string round a brick, running out the string a couple of feet longer than the length of the planter, and tying the other end to another brick. The two bricks can now be edged apart until the line is taut. The principle is exactly the same as when working with pegs and line, except that as it is impossible to drive pegs into concrete, a surface weight is used instead. When you have four such lines stretched out in position, one for each wall, run a chalk mark on the ground round the base of each brick. This way you will be able to see at a glance whether a brick has been knocked out of position while you are working.

If the foundations are to be laid on new ground, they are set out in 'strip fashion. This means that the foundation does not cover the whole area of the planter, but that each side of it is a strip directly under one brick wall. You make each strip about 2in. or 50mm wider, on each side, than the thickness of the wall you intend to build.

First, clear and level the whole site of the planter, removing all grass, loamy topsoil, tree roots and so on. If the area is not properly levelled, you will have difficulty in keeping your marking-out lines 'square'. For a big job it is usual to build profile boards to correct any inaccuracies, but here it is simpler to level the whole area. Check that you have done so by using the straight edge and builder's level.

Next, mark out with pegs and lines an area

NELSON HARGREAVES

Fig. 7 (top). As each brick is laid, the excess mortar is sliced off flush with the surface of the brickwork.
Fig. 8 (middle). Racking back—laying one brick fewer each successive course. The laying line helps keep the wall straight.
Fig. 9 (bottom). Weather pointing, one of the simplest kinds of pointing. On horizontal joints, the trowel is held point upwards, and sideways on vertical joints.

Bricklaying procedure

The first bricks you will lay will be those at each corner, or *quoin.* Two bricks are laid, one running along the longer wall, and the other at right angles, running along the narrower wall. The two bricks will thus form a 'V' in the corner. This will be repeated at each corner.

Before you start the actual laying, however, it will pay you to set out one course of bricks 'dry' to ensure that the corner bricks fall correctly, and that you do not finish needing half bats in two places instead of a whole brick in one.

The first course of bricks, including those for the quoins, is laid on a *bedding course.* This is a layer of mortar, slightly thicker than the jointing layers that will follow (to allow for irregularities in the foundation) and spread directly on the foundation strip.

Once the quoins have been started, a line must be run along the outside face of the base course (Fig. 8). Bricklayers usually do this by scratching a *course line* on the bedding mortar. In this case, since you have no profile lines from which to project such a course line, you could use bricks and string in the same manner as detailed above for marking out on a solid area. Bricks, with a line stretched between them, are placed outside the bricks forming the quoin. Make sure the line is firmly and accurately in position; it is virtually the only means you have of ensuring that your brickwork is laid in a straight line.

Once the quoins have been started, and the course lines marked out, each quoin is built up to its full height before the intermediate bricks are laid. This is done by *racking back*—that is, extending each quoin, by laying one brick fewer in each successive course, until it looks like a flight of stairs (Fig. 8).

Then the intermediate bricks are kept level, course by course, by running a line from one quoin to the next (Fig. 8). The line is fastened around bricklayer's pins, driven into the mortar 'around the corner' from where the line is to run, and then 'snagged' over the top edge of a quoin brick to keep it in the right plane.

Bricklaying technique

Laying bricks is easier if you 'get the feel of it' first by laying a few trial bricks somewhere. The bricks, but not the mortar, can be used again.

Start by mixing a small quantity of mortar, then transferring it to the spotboard; placed handily to where you will work.

A bricklayer's trowel has one curved edge, and one straight edge for 'drawing off' the mortar from the board. When drawing off, keep the trowel at right angles to the board, with the straight edge down. 'Cut' off some mortar from the spotboard and draw it towards you with a slicing action. This turns the mortar into a pear-shaped roll. Draw the trowel towards you, with the leading edge scraping the board clean and the trailing edge raised slightly to trap the mortar.

Pick up your first pear of mortar and spread it thickly on the foundation, 'joggling' the trowel through the centre to make a furrow (Fig. 3). Lay the brick carefully up to the marking line; make sure that your line of vision is directly over the brick so that its position can be gauged accurately. Now tap the brick on to the mortar, using the handle of the trowel.

Take up the next brick and spread mortar on one end for the vertical joint (this is known as 'buttering'). Spread mortar on the foundation as before, lay the brick in position next to the one just laid, and tap it into position.

The mortar jointing between bricks should be

about a half inch or 10mm thick; in any event it should be uniform.

As work proceeds, use the line and the spirit level to check horizontal and vertical alignments.

An experienced bricklayer will lay sufficient mortar to 'bed' several bricks at a time, but until you have had a little practice, lay only enough for two or three bricks at a time.

Cutting bricks

A skilled tradesman can cut a brick neatly in half with a single stroke of his trowel, like a karate chop. But until you reach this stage, it is better to use a cold chisel and hammer.

Mark the brick, with the tip of a nail or similar implement, round the section to be parted. Lay the brick on a solid surface and run a groove round the marked line with the chisel, tapping gently with the hammer. When you have cut the groove about half an inch or 12mm deep, place the chisel blade firmly into the groove and hit the chisel head hard with the hammer.

Pointing

Mortar joints are trimmed flush as each brick is laid, but unless the brickwork is going to be painted or covered in some way, flush finishing is not particularly attractive.

A neater finish can be made by running a 'V' into the jointing with the point of the pointing trowel. Alternatively, the trowel blade can be inserted into the bed joint at the base of the joint and pushed upwards and inwards at an angle of 45 degrees. This will slice off a sliver of mortar that will leave the jointing mortar sloping downwards. The vertical joints, of course, cannot be angled from the bottom, and must be sloped from right to left, or vice-versa. Whichever way you do this, make sure you keep to the same pattern; otherwise, you will have the vertical joints sloping in different directions.

Pointing is best carried out when the mortar has become stiff but (obviously) before it sets. In some building, the mortar is recessed by about half inch or 12mm during laying, and the actual pointing is laid in with a mortar of higher cement content after the first joints are thoroughly dry. But this is done mainly on the outside walls of buildings, to minimize rain penetration. It is not necessary on garden walling.

Finishing

All joints must be cleaned out as much as possible during pointing, by ensuring that no lumps of mortar adhere to the edges of the bricks. However, it is impossible to achieve a completely clean finish by this means alone. The next stage is to use a stiff scrubbing brush. When all excess mortar is dry, brush the joints and soiled bricks with the dry brush.

This should give your bricklaying a neat finish, but if marks still remain because mortar has penetrated the surface of a few bricks, it can be removed with a dilute solution of hydrochloric acid, applied with an old brush. However, as this acid eats into mortar, it should be used only as a last resort and, when it has done its work, all traces should be washed away immediately by a thorough hosing down. Do not get it on your hands or in your eyes.

Garden seat
with a difference

PROJECT

14

This timber seat planter makes an attractive addition to any garden, either as a major feature in a small area, or as part of a large landscaped garden. The centre of the unit can be used to display flowers or shrubs, or you can build the seat round a tree trunk so that the branches will provide shade.

The construction of the unit is not difficult if you are experienced in woodworking techniques. In fact, the most important requirement for the job is patience because of the amount of repetitive work involved.

General construction details

The unit is a hexagonal or six-sided garden seat, the centre of which has a well that is filled with soil and planted out with a display of some sort.

The main framework consists of 2in. x 1in. or 50mm x 25mm softwood members, clad with 4in. x ¾in. or 100mm x 19mm cedarwood tongued-and-grooved (T & G) treated boarding; you will require 60 lengths of 1ft 8in. or 508mm boarding for the base, and

PAUL KEMBLE

99

80 lengths of 9in. or 229mm for the top. All other timber members, such as the seat boards, soil support and base corner plates, are of either 1in. or ½in. (25mm or 12.5mm) marine plywood.

All these timbers must be treated with a horticultural grade of wood preservative such as Cuprinol. In addition the internal top lining of the T&G boarding, and parts O, H and J, must be coated with a bitumen based preservative such as Aquaseal to prevent damp soil from rotting the wood.

The outside supports consists of six outer base frames D joined with *halving* joints as shown in Fig.12. These form the outer hexagon. Six inner base frames E provide the internal support, and these radiate from the middle and are joined to the outer frames as shown in Fig.13. The inner frames are constructed with *bridle* joints as in Fig.6 to provide greater strength vertically.

The inner hexagon, which houses the soil, is formed by six rectangular frames, clad both sides, and with an internal base H of ½in. (12.5mm) marine plywood.

If you prefer to build the seat round a tree, then you will have to omit the centre base plate, and replace it with six blocks of ½in. thick marine ply, one under each inner base frame, to keep the structure off the ground and to keep it level with the base corner plates. The soil container will obviously have to be left out of the design. These alterations will not weaken the unit, because the missing pieces are needed only as a support for the soil.

All joints must be screwed—use non-ferrous screws such as brass or galvanized ones to prevent unsightly rust stains—and glued with a waterproof woodworking adhesive such as Cascophen RS 216-M. Remember, though, that not all combinations of wood preservative/ wood adhesive will allow a secure join. The above adhesive for instance, will adhere well to wood that has been treated with Cuprinol clear, or light oak, but not to wood that has been treated with Cuprinol red cedar. Your local supplier will provide you with details from the data sheets that the manufacturers send out.

The ground underneath the unit must be level. Otherwise it will be set at an unsightly angle and you will be sitting on a sloping seat. You will usually be able to level the area with a shovel. But if the ground slopes too much you might have to raise the structure on a concrete foundation.

Outer base frames

First make up the six outer base frames as shown in Fig.12D. Each frame consists of four members, with halving joints at each corner. The edges of the two sides or vertical members are bevelled or mitred so that the frames will butt together and form the hexagonal shape shown in Fig.2.

The technique for making a square halving joint is quite straightforward. In this case, however, the joint has to be angled, because the corners are not square. This is done using the

same technique, except that the angles are marked out using a bevel guage (as shown in Fig. 7 on page 101).

The next step is to mitre or bevel the edges as shown in Fig.7. With the bevel gauge, mark out the angle on the end grain of each end, then draw with a marking gauge and pencil a line along the inside of the timber between each marked point. Cut the wood down to this line, preferably using a power bench saw and using one of the special attachments. If one is not available, the angle can be cut with a rip saw as shown in Fig.9. Place the timber vertically in a wood vice. To prevent the wood from vibrating while sawing, start with only about a 10in. or 250mm length of wood above the vice and gradually raise the member as the cut is made.

The last few inches can be cut by reversing the member in the vice and continuing along the opposite end. If you don't have a power saw or a rip saw, you could plane the wood away—but your arms will ache when you have finished.

Assemble the frame and check that the angles are correct. To do this, measure the side members and see that they really are identical in length, then measure the diagonals. Each measurement must be identical. Glue and screw the joints and leave for the adhesive to set.

When the glue has set, cut the notches to house the ends of the inner base frames. (The housing recesses on the top that will take the outside ends of the seat support members J can be cut later after marking out by direct marking.) Make up the other five frames in the same way.

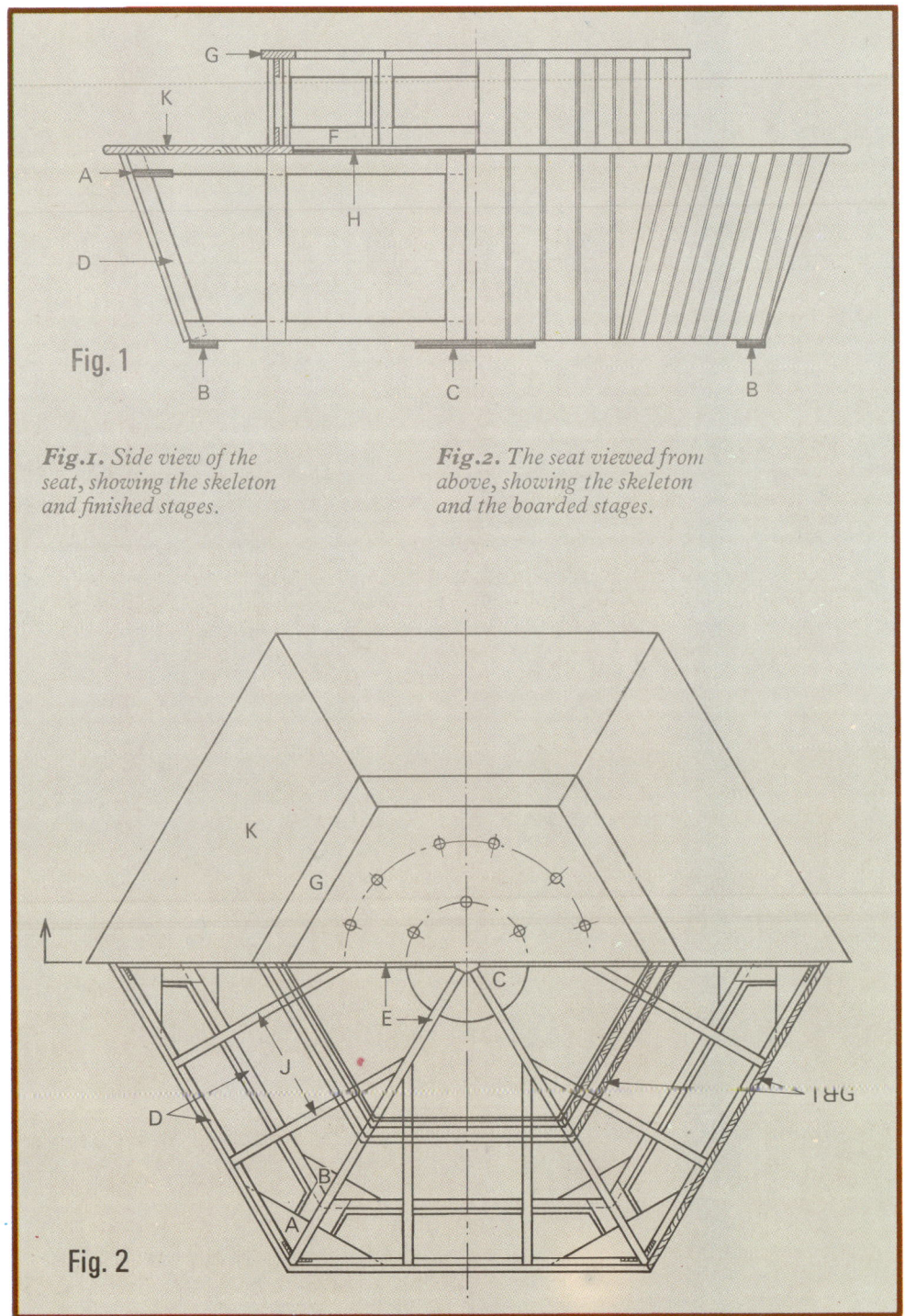

Fig.1. *Side view of the seat, showing the skeleton and finished stages.*

Fig.2. *The seat viewed from above, showing the skeleton and the boarded stages.*

Right. *A planter full of moist soil will weigh a considerable amount. Ensure that secure foundations are underneath points B & C (Fig. 1) to prevent twisting.*

Fig.3. Using a mortise gauge. Loosen the screw at the base and slide the stock back to adjust the width between the spurs.

Fig.4. The bridle joint is made by marking out a $\frac{5}{16}$ in. gap and chiselling out the recess with a wood chisel of the same width.

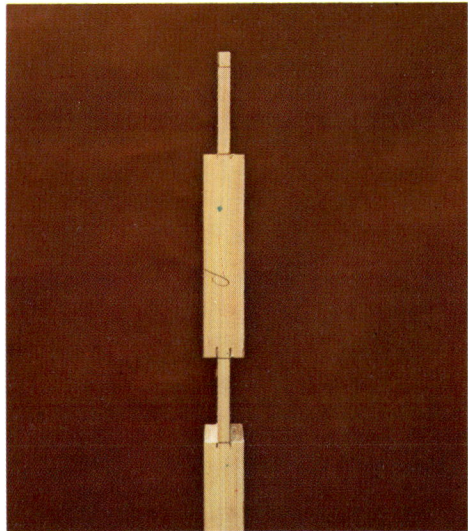

Fig.5. The opposite or mating part of the bridle joint. The recesses are cut with a tenon saw and then chiselled out.

Fig.6. Once the bridle joints have been glued and screwed, the projecting ends are sawn off and planed down.

Fig.7. Marking out the bevel angle on the end grain of the vertical timbers of the outer base frames.

Fig.8. When the angle has been drawn on the end grain, a line is scribed along the side of the member from end to end.

Fig.9. The bevel edge can be cut with a bench power saw, or it can be planed down by hand if you feel really energetic.

Fig.10. A close-up of the framework before the upper corner braces have been fitted on the outside frames.

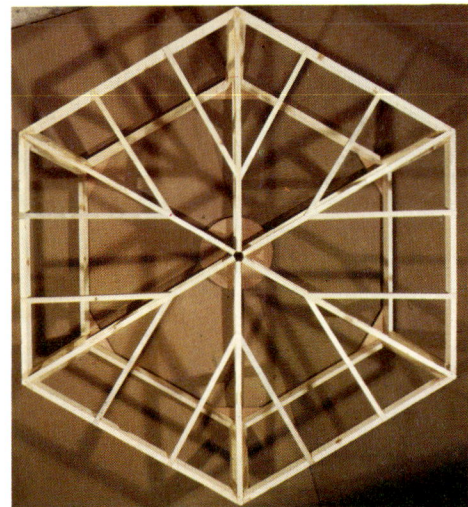

Fig.11. Aerial view of the framework. The inner base frames are joined in the centre only to the circular bottom plate.

Inner base frames

The construction outline of these is shown in Fig.13E.

Each frame consists of a top and bottom member, and two vertical ones—one centrally placed and one at the side, creating, in effect, one 'open' side and one closed. The open end of the frame is housed into notches cut into the corners of the outer base frames.

The frame is secured with bridle joints as shown in Fig.6. These are the best joints to use when vertical timbers are under compression—as these will be when supporting the amount of soil required.

The bridle joints should be marked with a mortise gauge, which is similar to an ordinary marking gauge except that it has two scribing points or spurs, one of which is adjustable to give varying widths of mortise or tenon. To set the gauge, first loosen the stock setting screw (Fig.3) and slide the stock back. Next adjust the width—in this case 5/16in. (8mm)—and set the gauge so that the distance between the points locates in the centre of the member. Check that it does, by measuring the distance from each scribed line to the edge of the timber. Each measurement must be identical.

After marking out, cut the joints. Cutting techniques are similar to those used for a mortise and tenon joint. Trial assemble the frame and check the diagonals for squareness, then glue and screw. Don't worry too much about the lengths of the top and bottom members at the open end. They can be finished off by direct marking at a later stage.

Top frames

These are simple rectangular frames with a halving joint at each corner. Full construction details are shown in Fig.14F. These frames form the walls of the soil container and are boarded over on the outside to provide the seat back. They can if necessary be built at a much later stage.

Other components

The *centre base plate* is just a disc of ½in. (12.5mm) marine plywood as shown in Fig.17C. It is not essential for this piece to be circular, and if you want to save some time you can just as effectively use a 12in. or 300mm square of plywood.

You may, however, prefer the neatness of the circle. In this case lay a piece of 12in. x 12in. ply on a table, lightly tap a nail about one third of the way into the centre of the board, and tie a 6in. (150mm) long piece of string to the nail. Tie the other end to a pencil, stretch the string out and draw a circle on the board. Then cut out the circle with a bow saw.

The *soil support* is the hexagonal base for the soil and is shown in Fig.18H.

It is cut from a 3ft 1in. x 2ft 8½in. (940 x 816mm) sheet of ½in. (25mm) ply. Lay the ply on a level surface and mark a line lengthways down the middle. Along each *long* side *only*, mark off a point 9³⁄₁₆ in. (234mm) away from each corner. This will give you two marks along each long edge. Mark a line from each of these marks to the nearest end of the middle line, and you have your hexagon ready for cutting out, in four cuts, with a panel saw.

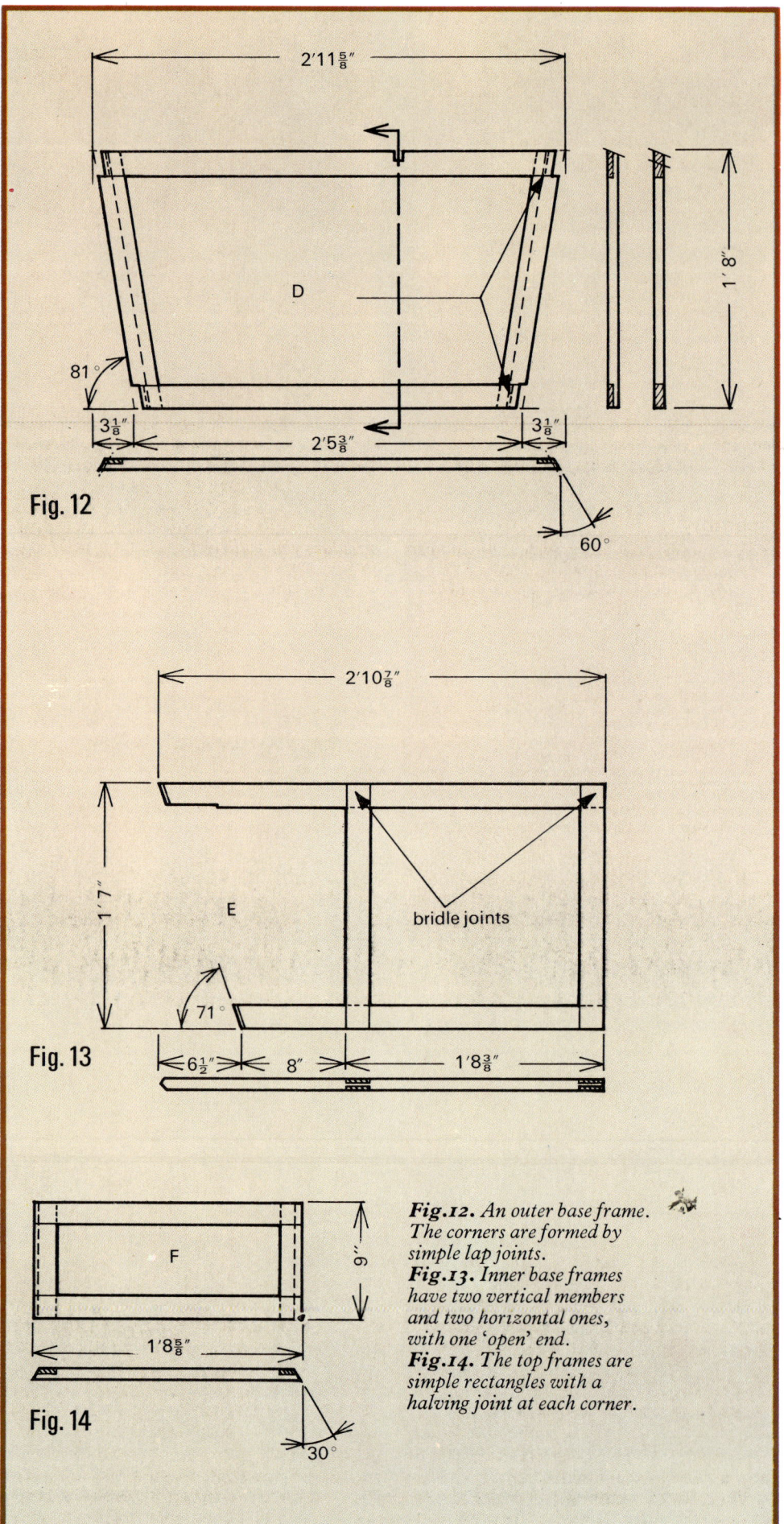

Fig. 12

Fig. 13

Fig. 14

Fig.12. An outer base frame. The corners are formed by simple lap joints.
Fig.13. Inner base frames have two vertical members and two horizontal ones, with one 'open' end.
Fig.14. The top frames are simple rectangles with a halving joint at each corner.

TRI·ART

Corner plates are triangles of wood that provide bracing for the outer frames. They are easily cut from sheets of ½in. (12.5mm) plywood by following the diagrams in Fig.16A and B.

Coping pieces are run around the rim of the top frame to protect the end grain of the boarding and conceal the boarding/framework join. Each one is cut from a 1ft 9¾in. (553mm) length of 3in. x ½in. (75mm x 12.5mm) ply as shown in Fig.20G.

Seat supports—the cutting details for these pieces are shown in Fig.15J—are housed at one end into the top of the outer frames, and butted, at the opposite end, at an angle, to one side of the top member of an inner frame and screwed in place.

Seats

These are cut from 1in. (25mm) ply as shown in Fig.19K. The top surface should be lightly planed and sanded down, and the front edge radiused slightly with a plane to provide comfortable seating.

Assembly

There are several ways in which the unit can be constructed, but the following method is one of the easiest. You commence by building part of the structure upside down.

Place the soil support on level ground. Mark out the frame positions on it, place two adjacent inner frames in position and skew nail them in position (leave the heads protruding slightly in case the positions need adjusting). This will allow one of the outer frames to be fitted in position. Repeat this procedure until the hexagon is complete, gluing and screwing each piece into place when you are sure of the fit. Each outer frame is joined to its adjacent outer frame by screws through the inside of the side members.

While the unit is still upside down, screw the centre base plate and all the base corner plates in position.

Carefully turn the structure right way up and, using direct marking, mark out, cut and fit the seat support members.

Trial assemble the top frames round the soil

Fig.15. The seat supports are housed at one end into the top of an outer frame, and butted at the outer end to an inner frame.

Fig.16. The corner plates provide bracing for the outer frames. They are easily cut from sheets of ½in. plywood.

Fig.17. The centre base plate is a disc of ½in. marine plywood. It does not need to be circular; you could leave it square.

Fig.18. Only four cuts are needed to form the hexagonal soil support.

Fig.19. Seats are cut from sturdy 1in. marine ply, and heavily varnished.

Fig.20. Coping pieces are run round the rim of the top frames to protect the end grain.

support and when you are sure that the fit is correct, screw the top frames to the tops of the inner frames, and to one another as for the outer frames.

Trial assemble the seats. When you have made sure they fit (by planing a few edges if necessary), secure them by screwing from underneath through the inner base frames or seat supports.

Mark out, cut and fit the boarding for the bottom section. Skew nail each T&G board through the tongue at each end so that the nail heads do not show. Repeat this for the top section.

Trial assemble the coping pieces round the top lip of the well and, when the fit is accurate, skew nail them in position using lost head nails and punching the heads down.

Filling the planter

The well of the seat planter can now be filled with soil. If you can afford to do so, use one of the peat-based composts. These are only a fraction of the weight of soil and, apart from easing the strain on your back, will lessen your watering problems because peat retains much more water than soil.

If you intend growing shrubs in the well, make sure that you do not plant ones that tend to deep-root. The depth of the growing medium is only about 9in. and so is unsuitable for some shrubs.

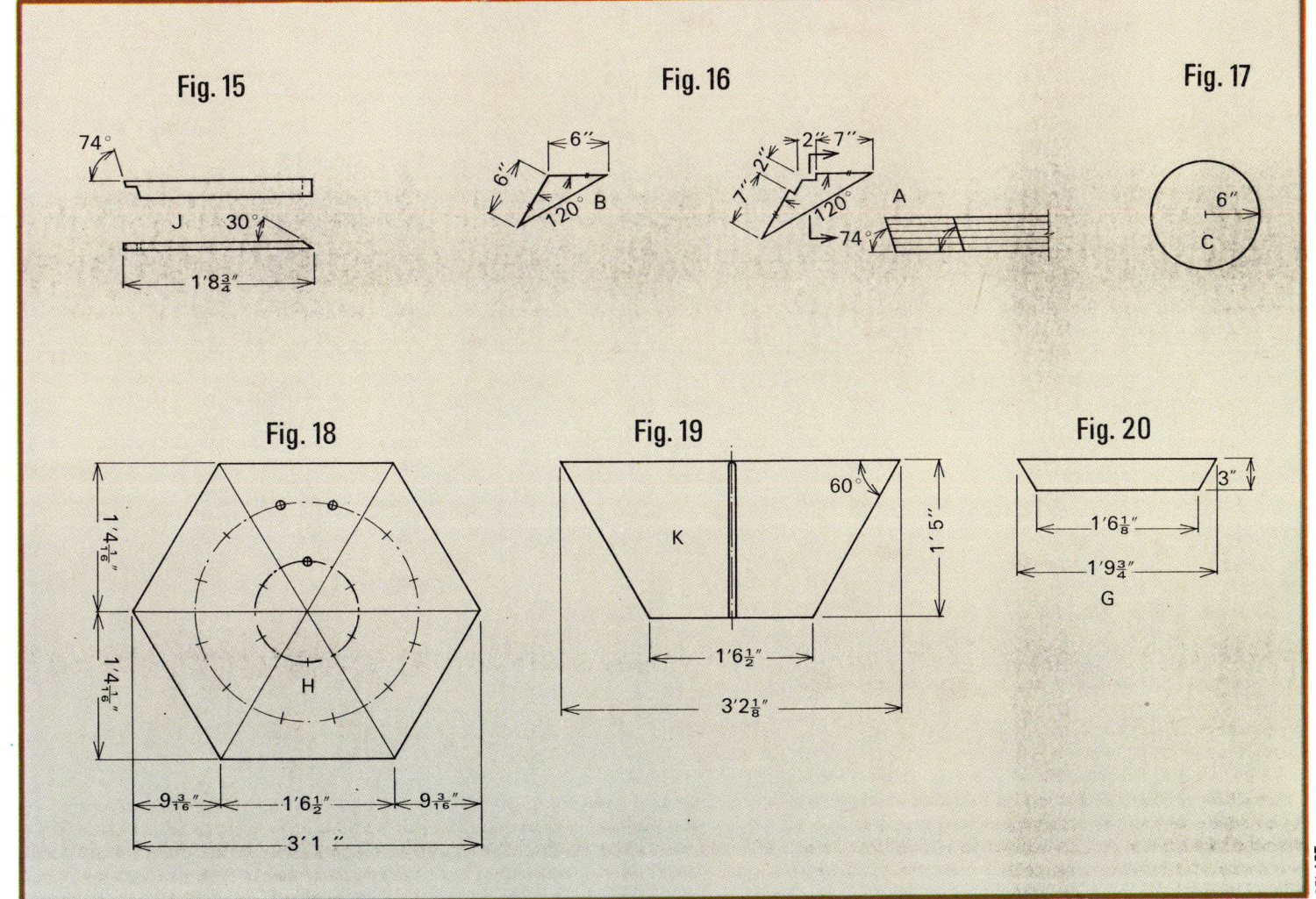

No adhesives, nails or screws are used to hold the box together. As shown in Fig.3, protruding portions are cut out of the panels, and these are fitted into slots cut in mating panels—a simplified form of mortise and tenon joint—and held in position with split dowelling tapped through holes cut in the 'tenons'. Use only marine or exterior grade plywood for the panels.

Cutting out

First cut the four sides, as detailed in Figs.1-2, with the panel saw. Carefully mark out the outlines of the tenon portions and slots, then cut these out.

The tenons can be cut out with a tenon saw for the right angled cuts from the outside edges, then the pad or coping saw for the parallel cuts. But if you have a powered jig saw, use this and the job can be done in a fraction of the time.

To cut the slots, first drill a $\frac{3}{4}$in. (18mm) diameter hole at each end of the marked slot. Then cut through from each hole to the other along the outside edges, with the coping or jig saw, to form the slot.

When the slots have been cut, briefly assemble the four sides to check that they mate properly. At the same time, take the opportunity of marking out the holes for the dowelling. Dismantle the sides and cut the dowel holes with the brace and bit. Note that only half of each dowel hole must be visible when the box is finally put together.

Mark out and cut the base panel. Using the procedure outlined above, cut and shape the tenon projections. When you have done this, trial assemble the unit again to check for fit.

Finishing off

Next, round or bevel the sharp edges of all protruding tenon pieces. This is done with the bevel edge chisel. Carefully pare off the corners with the chisel, taking very small strokes—if you take off too much at once, you will have to fill the indentation, wasting valuable time. When the edges are well rounded, sand down to a smooth finish with fine glasspaper. If you prefer, the rounding off can be done with a toothed plane or file such as a Surform, but you will still have to finish off with glasspaper.

Now drill a series of drainage holes in the base panel, as shown in Fig.4. Each hole is approximately $1\frac{1}{8}$in. (28mm) in diameter. The size of the holes is not critical, but they must be distributed evenly over the panel.

The dowelling pieces are now cut into wedge shaped halves, about $3\frac{1}{2}$in. (89mm) in length. This is done by placing each one in a wood vice, upright, and cutting downwards, at a slight angle, with the tenon saw. As each pair of 'plugs' are cut, trial assemble the appropriate panels and fit the plugs in place by hand. When

A slot-together planter

This planter is not only attractive, it also has a rather unique construction that provides many interesting and useful features. It is simple to make, and with a little imagination you could easily adapt it for other uses by altering the dimensions and using plywood of a different thickness. The main advantage of using this type of construction is that you can take the box apart for ease of storage when it is not in use.

Above, left. This attractive planter can be dismantled and packed away when not in use. This is because of its construction, which requires no glue, screws or nails—the panels are slotted together and secured with pegs fashioned from dowelling.

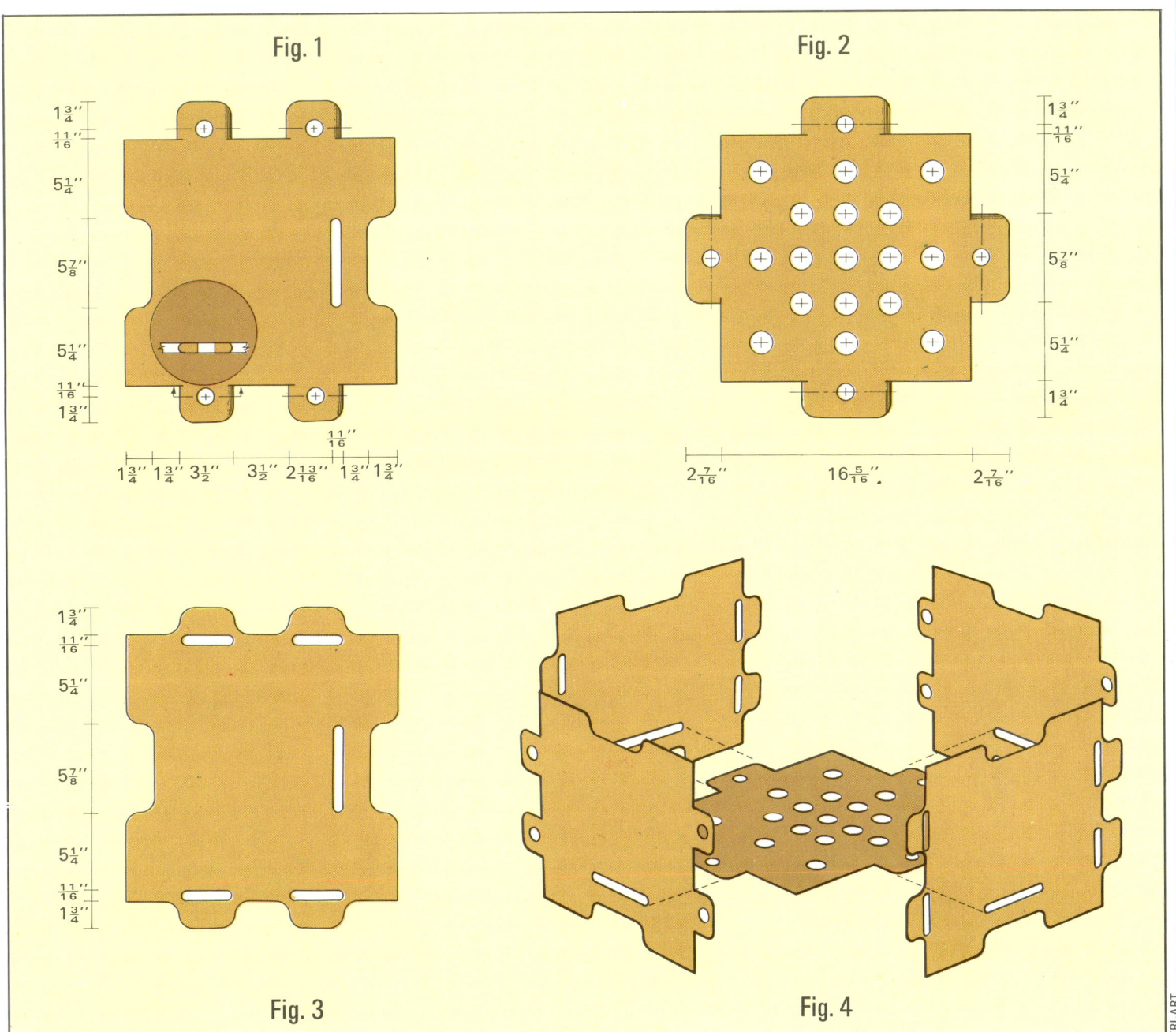

Fig. 1

Fig. 2

Fig. 3

Fig. 4

TRI-ART

Fig.1. *This is one of the side panels—the one that has the mortise holes cut along the 'corner' edges. The slot at the bottom takes the tenon of the base panel.*

Fig.2. *This is the 'mating' panel for Fig.1. It has tenon projections along the sides, and these slot into the mortises cut out of the adjacent panel.*

Fig.3. *An exploded view showing the construction of the planter. The whole unit slots together. When cutting the panels, it is important to mark out by direct measuring, and to constantly check the fit by trial assembly as each part is cut. This is particularly important for the dowel holes.*

Fig.4. *Plan of the base panel.*

Cutting list

Plywood	imperial	metric
4 sides	$21\frac{1}{2}$ x 18 x $\frac{3}{4}$	539 x 458 x 18
1 base	$21\frac{1}{2}$ x $21\frac{1}{2}$ x $\frac{3}{4}$	539 x 539 x 18
Dowelling (or broom handle)		
12 pieces	$1\frac{1}{4}$ diameter	32 diameter

You will also need ;
Fine toothed panel saw.
Brace and bit.
Tenon saw.
Pad, coping or powered jig saw.
$1\frac{1}{2}$in. bevel edge chisel, or toothed plane such as a Surform.
Small mallet.
All imperial measurements are in inches. All metric measurements are in millimetres.

all the plugs are in place, tap them securely into place with the mallet.

The final step is a coat of protective paint or varnish. Because *marine or exterior grade* plywood is used, it is not necessary to apply more than one coat to weatherproof the unit. Although the planter has been designed for use in the garden, this should not be an excuse to leave a poor finish on the visible surfaces of the side panels ; so glasspaper all visible surfaces down to a smooth finish before you apply a thick coat of paint or varnish.

This design will also make an excellent toy box for children. The only alteration from the design is to leave out the drainage holes, and use thinner plywood. With a little ingenuity, you could incorporate a lid and make an attractive chest.

PROJECT

16

From any angle, a greenhouse with a difference!

The garden gazebo, or octagonal greenhouse, was popular in Victorian times as a place to sit and enjoy the garden. In gardens on higher ground it had another name 'belvedere' and provided a lookout point over the surrounding land. This garden gazebo provides a pleasing alternative to the conventional greenhouse; it can be built to suit most gardens.

Designer Roy Day built the gazebo shown in the photograph to suit a tiny, walled-in rear garden. For a larger garden, a larger structure may suit you better—but either way, the construction details are the same.

ROY DAY

Left. *A 'plant's eye view' through the roof of the garden gazebo, showing the 'sunburst' convergence of its roof struts in the centre.* **Inset** *is a picture of the greenhouse, indicating its neat lines. Opening windows can be fitted to suit, to provide the necessary ventilation.*

(Fig. 1). Now mark at right angles with a spade, at the top and bottom and the side pegs of the cross, the width of the frames which form the greenhouse sides. Join up these marks diagonally. This gives an accurate octagonal profile.

Mark out with the spade the line of the footings. Do this by marking slightly in front of the octagonal outline, and also slightly deeper than the greenhouse side frames—giving a total width of about 6in. (152mm). The foundations need to be slightly wider overall than the structure to provide a firm bearing.

Excavate a trench to a depth of about 4in. (101mm) and place timber shuttering in this, proud of the ground by about 3in. (76mm). It is important to raise the foundations slightly above the surrounding earth, since this could rot the greenhouse timber.

The shuttering should be even throughout in height, since the top of this is the top level of the concrete. Use a straight edge and spirit level to check the shuttering levels.

Once the trenches are filled with concrete, this is well tamped down and allowed to set. Shuttering is then removed, leaving the 'footings' with an upstand.

Finally, lay $4\frac{1}{2}$in. (114mm) damp-proof bituminous felt on top of the footings, to prevent damp rising into the timber framework.

As an alternative to concrete footings, the greenhouse can stand on raised paving or brick. The main requirements are that these footings are both firm and level, otherwise it will not be possible to assemble the greenhouse accurately on site.

Timber preparation

Dependent on the type of timber you use, and the climate in which you are building, some pre-treatment of the timber may be necessary to prevent its rotting quickly. In some circumstances, every joint in the timber—particularly end-grain—must be given a thick coat of priming paint as the joints are assembled. When you buy your timber, ask your timber merchant for advice on this point.

Building the wall frames

The first stage is to make up the four opposed square frames (Fig. 2). Frames B and A are made up in the same way, except that the latter uses a doorstep section in place of the bottom rail (Fig 3.) Frames are made from 4in. x 2in. or 100mm x 50mm planed timber, joined together by 4in. nails inside the uprights of each frame. For all construction use non-rusting sheradized, galvanized or aluminium nails.

Half-lap joints are cut with a tenon saw at an angle of 45° in the top rail sections before assembly. Nails are then driven through these joints into the top ends of the side stiles (Fig. 4). Details of the joint are shown in Fig. 5.

Sections marked 'triangle X' on Fig. 4 are sawn from 3in. x 3in. or 75mm x 75mm soft-

The greenhouse can be built largely of softwood or entirely of hardwood. The lower 'cheeks' of the greenhouse sides are timber clad; but plastic cladding could be used here.

The greenhouse is largely prefabricated, then assembled on its foundations. The main structure consists of eight equal panels, forming the octagonal shape when assembled.

Site preparation

Select a position for the greenhouse which makes the best use of sunlight, yet gives ready access. Next, level the overall site area, using pegs, a straight edge and a spirit level (full details of site preparation are in PROJECT 2). It is a good idea to provide a slight fall in the level of the ground so that water does not collect around the base of the greenhouse.

The footings are then marked out. Find the overall depth of the structure, from front to back (in the case of the greenhouse illustrated it is 5ft or 1.524m), and mark this, using a measured string line. Place a marking peg at each end of the line. Find the centre position and then take the string across to form a cross; place pegs at each end. Measure between the four pegs to find the half-way points and put in four more pegs, the same distance as before from the centre position, but this time in the form of a letter X. This gives a roughly octagonal shape

wood to the desired height of the window sills. This is simply a matter of deciding how much window area above these you want.

Next cut the base rails (plates) C and place a piece of section X at the end and draw the angle. The V section is formed by returning the angle at 45°. (A piece of section X can be used to help scribe this). The wedge is then cut out as shown in Fig. 7. This procedure is followed at both ends of rail C.

The X and C sections are nailed together as shown in Fig. 6. In Fig. 8, B. C and X are seen butted together.

The completed framework is assembled on the damp-proof felt (Fig. 3) and joined together by nailing through the triangle X sections into adjacent uprights of frames A and B. Additional support can be given by fixing angle brackets to the internal edges of floor rails B and C and doorstep A.

The top rails C1 (Fig. 9) are angle cut to 45° and lapped. These are slotted into the lapped sections of frames A and B and nailed downwards into the side rails.

Angle brackets can be screwed to the internal side of the top rails to provide added strength.

Below. *Basic constructional details of the main assembly of the octagonal greenhouse are shown in the diagrams.*

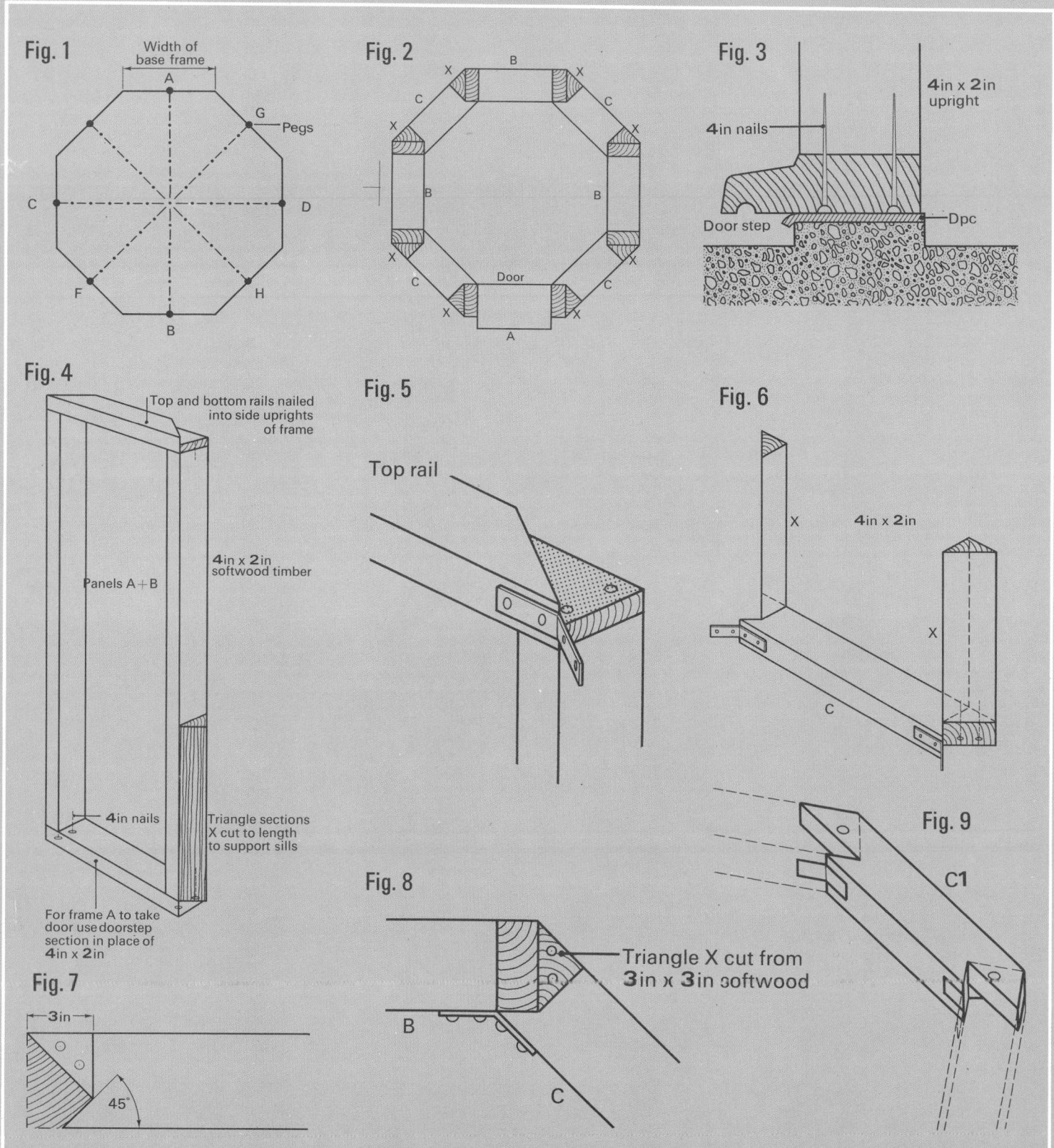

From any angle, a greenhouse with a difference: 2

The octagonal greenhouse can double as a summer house where a larger version is built. This concluding section shows how to complete the job from cladding the walls to finishing.

The exterior cladding can be either timber-shiplap, tongue-and-groove or feather-edged board—or plastic panelling.

If you are particularly handy, you could even construct the exterior in different materials to those used here. For example, some simple cross members would enable you to use hardboard cladding – provided it is an exterior grade.

Cladding and window sills

Horizontal boarding (Fig. 10.) Unless you have a fair amount of experience with this material, is tricky to work with. The boards must be mitred at $22\frac{1}{2}°$ at both ends, because cutting one board to $90°$ and the adjoining one to $45°$ would throw the vertical joints off the true line of the corner. Two things will help you get a snug fit: **1,** Cut the mitres just a fraction too 'sharp', so that no gaps show at the outside edges when they are joined; and **2,** As you fix each row of boards, butt them against a temporary vertical stop (mitred lengthwise at an angle of $22\frac{1}{2}°$) so that the ends of all the boards align accurately with one another.

Vertical boarding is much simpler, since only the boards at each end of any particular wall need to be mitred—that is, you make two mitre cuts per wall, instead of a dozen or more. Start by vertically mitring a pair of boards a 'whisker' sharper than $22\frac{1}{2}°$, and fix them around the angle farthest from the door. Then work progressively back towards the door.

Whichever type of board you use, fix it with non-rusting nails.

Once all the cladding is in place, the sills can be fixed. Try to buy the type, which has a flat base. Other patterns, whose base is angled, are more difficult to work with.

Each length of sill must be housed at the back (Fig. 11) to accept the vertical members of the greenhouse frame. At its outside edge, it must be cut accurately to $22\frac{1}{2}°$ to meet the adjoining length of sill. If, when fitting the sills, two adjoining pieces are found to be slightly over-length, this can be adjusted by running a saw cut through the joint—but be careful not to score the panelling beneath.

The roof struts W are cut from eight pieces of 4in. x 1in. or 100mm x 25mm softwood and pitched at an angle of $10°$ to converge at a centre point (Fig. 17). The convergent top ends

are mitred to $12\frac{1}{2}°$, and trimmed back to make a flat platform of about $5\frac{1}{2}$in. (107mm) square. At the lower end they are cut to a 'bird mouth' to fit over the top rails A, B and C1—a cardboard template will help get the angles right—and slightly oversail the sides to take rainwater clear. Detail of the roof structure is shown in Fig. 12.

Next, cut eight sections of triangular timber diagonally from 4in. x $1\frac{1}{2}$in. or 100mm x 35mm softwood (Z). These are cut 1in. shorter than the overall length of the octagonal sides and are nailed to the top rails of frames A, B and C1, fitting tightly between roof struts W. The ends of the sections are mitred to an angle of $22\frac{1}{2}°$, the angle at which the roof struts converge.

An octagonal capping piece is fixed to the roof struts at the point of convergence, with an octagonal patrice beneath them (Fig. 13). These are cut from hardwood and screwed into the struts with brass screws to form a water cover to carry away water from the open joint beneath the capping. They also add extra strength to the structure. The pieces are made from 6in. x 1in. blocks of hardwood—beech, oak or mahogany. A block plane is used to shape the sections to produce the eight upper faces; the corners are cut away to form an octagon (Fig. 14). The capping piece is bedded on mastic; this is not necessary for the patrice on the underside (Fig. 15).

Cut glazing strips S from 1in. x 2in. or 25mm x 50mm softwood and nail these to each side of roof struts W between the triangular sections Z and the centrepoint of the roof. The top surface edge of S should form a continuous line with the top surface of Z, to provide support for the glass roof (Fig. 16).

Eight pieces of glass, cut to the triangular shape of the roof, are required, each to overhang the outer edges of Z by about 1in. The panels are bedded down on to putty spread over the top edges of S and Z.

Eight sections of hardwood R, shaped like an inverted L, are cut to fit to the exact lengths between roof struts W. Hardwood angle section could be used here. The top edges should be rebated to receive, later, the end sections of the glass panels Y. Sections R are pinned and glued to the roof struts W and screwed through the centre of R to top rails B and C1. Bed putty between the glass and rebate after fixing.

Cut 16 hardwood fixing patterns T to the length of struts W and fix them together to form a flush top surface (Fig. 17). Putty should be bedded between the glass and under the edge of section T.

Outward-opening pivot windows can be

fitted if desired. It is a sensible provision to provide greenhouse ventilation; two or three windows would do.

The windows are made up to size using rebated timber. The choice of joint to make the frames is a matter of personal preference. The frames are hinged to swing open from the top and can be kept open by fitting conventional window stays at the bottom.

Figs. 18 and 19 show glazing details. The glass is fixed in position by pinning in place window glass-fixing heads H at the rear. The glass is lightly bedded in putty or mastic.

The fixed lights are similarly bedded and fixed in position by four fixing beads. The lower front one K is angled forward slightly to

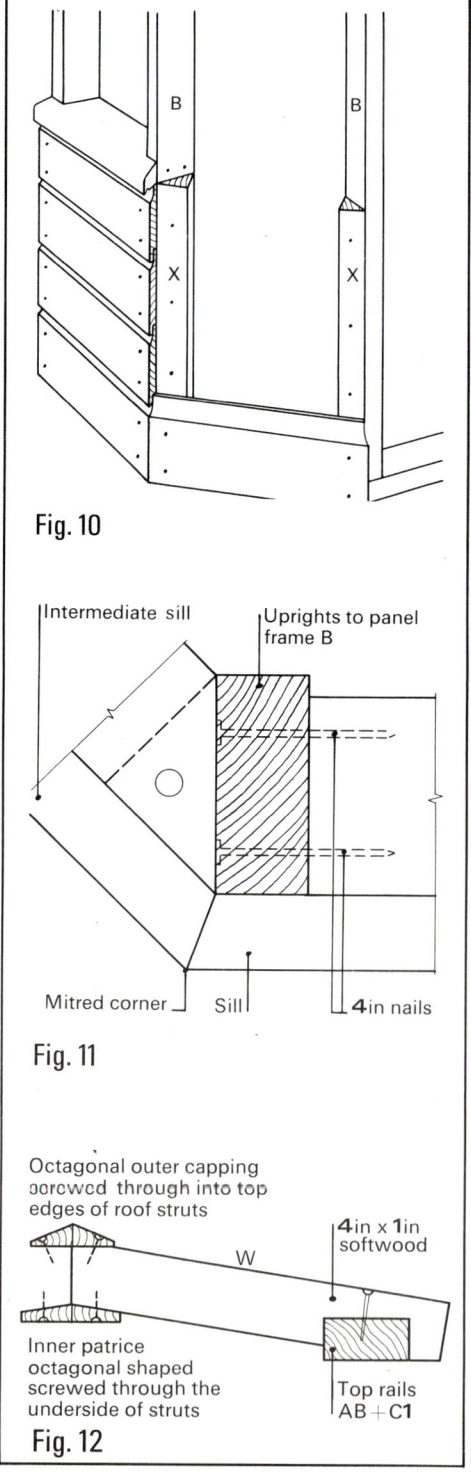

Fig. 10

Intermediate sill | Uprights to panel frame B

Mitred corner | Sill | 4in nails

Fig. 11

Octagonal outer capping screwed through into top edges of roof struts

W

4in x 1in softwood

Inner patrice octagonal shaped screwed through the underside of struts

Top rails AB + C1

Fig. 12

DGW

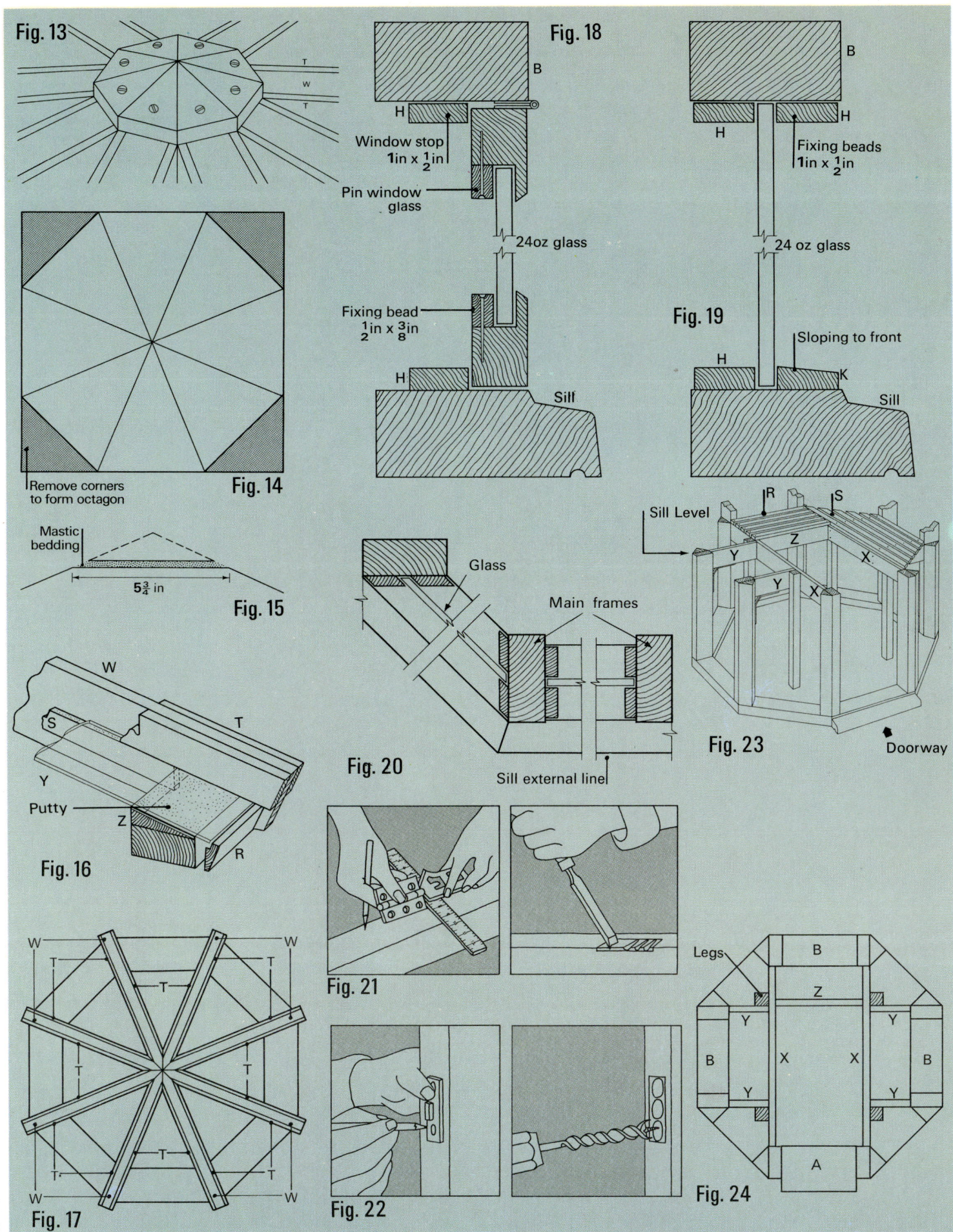

Fig. 13

Fig. 14

Remove corners to form octagon

Mastic bedding

$5\frac{3}{4}$ in

Fig. 15

W

S

T

Y

Putty

Z

R

Fig. 16

W W

T T

T

T T

T

T T

W W

Fig. 17

Fig. 18

B

H

Window stop
1in x $\frac{1}{2}$in

Pin window glass

24oz glass

Fixing bead
$\frac{1}{2}$in x $\frac{3}{8}$in

H

Sill

Fig. 19

B

H

H

Fixing beads
1in x $\frac{1}{2}$in

24 oz glass

Sloping to front

H

K

Sill

Glass

Main frames

Fig. 20

Sill external line

Fig. 21

Fig. 22

Sill Level

R

S

Z

Y

X

Y

X

Fig. 23

Doorway

Legs

B

Z

Y

Y

B

X

X

B

Y

Y

A

Fig. 24

allow water to run down.

The fixing beads in the angled windows between the main frames, are chamfered at an angle of 45° (Fig. 20).

It is possible to make the door, but a suitable whitewood one may be picked up 'off the shelf' from a timber supplier. The door should be suitable for full or partial glazing—again, a matter of personal choice. If the garden greenhouse is built to the small dimensions shown, a 2ft (610mm) door may have to be ordered. A standard 2ft 6in. (762mm) door, however, should be easy to obtain from stock.

Fixing the door

The door should be fixed to open outwards, to give the maximum space in the greenhouse and permit staging to be fitted inside.

The long rails, or stiles, have protruding ends, known as horns or joggles, which you have to saw off. These are to protect the door in transit and storage. The door may have to be planed to fit well, but first it should be tried against the opening.

Planing should start from the edge on which the hinges are to be fitted, known as the *hanging stile*. You should aim to make this stile as good a fit as possible to any curves or variations in the frame. A jack plane is best here, since this will give a truer edge. If the edge is planed to a slight bevel, this will give slight extra clearance without increase of the visible gap.

Once the hanging stile is fitted accurately to the jamb, plane the opposite stile. This must have a slight bevel, of about $\frac{1}{16}$in. (1.58mm) for a satisfactory fit. A top and edge clearance of about $\frac{3}{32}$in. (2.38mm) is necessary to allow for painting.

When trying the head of the door, allow a little less clearance above the lock stile, since doors tend to drop slightly as hinges wear. The bottom rail should have a clearance of about $\frac{3}{16}$in. (4.76mm). Allowance must be made for any weather board fixed across the bottom of the door, which must be 'throated' on the lower edge to throw water clear of the step. The board must, of course, project beyond the step to throw the water clear.

Hinges and latches

Cast-iron hinges or butts can be used to hang the door, though brass or plastic are suitable. Pressed-steel butts are not as strong as cast ones and may rust, unless you can buy galvanized. The door may be hung on two hinges, though three would spread the work load and prevent possible middle distortion.

The depth of each leaf is marked on both the door and the door frame. Each leaf is recessed to this depth. Using a chisel, make a series of cuts across the grain as deep as the gauge line, then pare with the grain to remove the waste (Fig. 21). The hinges can now be screwed to the door which is then fitted into the frame opening. Slide a wedge underneath and a piece of $\frac{3}{32}$in. (2.38mm) packing at the top to line up the door in position. The edge positions of the hinges can then be pencilled on to the frame, squared into this using a try-square and marking gauged to leaf depth. The recesses are chopped out in the same way as those of

the door.

Try the door by inserting one screw in each hinge. Provided no adjustments are needed, a second screw can be inserted and a further check made. Should any recess be too deep, use a piece of card to pack and adjust this. Before final hanging, it is advisable to remove the door and give the bottom edge one or two coats of paint.

Door stops, consisting of a frame of $\frac{1}{2}$in. x 1in. or 13mm x 25mm timber are nailed around the door frame $\frac{1}{16}$in. (1.58mm) from the inner face.

The door 'furniture' can now be fitted. The height for this is optional, around 3ft (4.828m), though this will look best if it lines up with any glazing bars in the doors or any other features such as the height of the sills.

The latch is fitted by squaring a line round the stile at the required height with try-square and marking knife, and measuring the distance from the stile edge for the latch spindle. Bore a $\frac{1}{2}$in. (13mm) hole for this. Now make a similar hole in the edge of the door, the size of which will depend on the size shape of the latch barrel. Gauge the face of the barrel on to the face of the stile and drill a hole or a series of holes in line (Fig. 22) ; chop these out to accommodate the barrel. Fit this to the depth of the front plate and mark this on the stile. The depth of the plate can then be chiselled out.

Use three 3in. (76mm) or two 3$\frac{1}{2}$in. (89mm) or 4in. (102mm) butts. Hinge positions should be marked in pencil across the door edge. Width and depth are marked, using a gauge.

Once the door is chopped out for the thickness of the leaf, it is hung with the knuckle on the outside, in the case of an outward-opening door.

Doors open better if hung with what is called a 'kick'. The top knuckle protrudes slightly forward of the frame ; and bottom slightly more so. Middle hinges are set in a halfway position between these distances, so that as the door opens, it is raised slightly out of vertical, increasing the bottom clearance.

The latch spindle and plate and handles can then be fitted.

To find the position of the striking plate, close the door and mark on the side the position of the latch tongue. Next, put the plate in position on the door edge and mark round this. Chop a small mortice in the centre to accommodate the tongue. Bend the lead-in part of the plate backwards slightly and recess it as this will make the action smoother.

Glazing

You may wish to cut your own glass, but usually a glass supplier or handyman's shop can do this for you. Three mm (24oz) glass should be used.

There is a special variety of glass suitable for greenhouses which admits plenty of light yet keeps down the temperature, but this you may have to order in advance.

To cut glass, a steel glass wheel is satisfactory for most work and works out cheaper than the traditional glass cutter's diamond. You need a large, flat surface to cut glass. A felt-tipped pen can be used to mark guide lines on the glass. A long straight edge or 'yardstick', or a home-made T-square is needed to guide your cutter

accurately along the line.

First, clean the glass. To cut, use a firm stroke, holding the cutter vertically. Never back track, since the glass is unlikely to break along the cut line. After the surface has been scratched, put a strip of wood, or the yardstick, beneath the glass under the score line. Place your fingertips as closely as possible to the line and on both sides and press down slowly and firmly. You should get a clean break. If you have to trim surplus from the glass, scratch a further line and gently break off the waste in small bites with a pair of pliers with emery cloth held in the jaws.

Before glazing, apply pink or white lead primer to all timber rebates to prevent oil in the putty from being sucked out. The putty should be rolled in the hand until malleable. Use linseed oil to soften it if necessary. Next line the rebate with bedding putty by 'rolling' this in a thin strip from a ball in the hand. Now press the pane into place at the edges. Never press at the centre. This will squeeze out surplus putty leaving a bed to a depth of $\frac{1}{16}$in. or $\frac{1}{8}$in. Cut off the surplus with a putty knife. Once glazing is completed the glazing beads can be tapped in to hold windows firmly in place.

Glazing presents little difficulty, although a few general points in glazing are :

All four beads shoud be inserted before any of them is finally fixed in place. Pins should not be inserted too near the corners.

When smoothing putty round newly glazed areas, it sometimes tends to stick to the putty knife. This can be avoided if the knife is kept moist with water, providing a smooth finish. In some putties, there is a tendency towards excess oiliness and over-softness of the material, particularly if it is bought in a polythene or plastic wrapper. To remove the excess, the putty should be wrapped in newspaper, which will absorb the oil.

Staging and finishing

Staging can be fitted to choice in the greenhouse. The following is a suggested arrangement to meet average needs. This provides shelving racks at all levels, consisting of a 4in. x 1in. framing with 2in. x 1in. decking (Figs. 23 and 24).

Framing is screwed by non-rusting metal brackets to the greenhouse frame uprights. Fixing of the cross members, staggered to facilitate this, is through the face of the cross bearers into the ends of those which butt to those at a right angle (Fig. 23). Non-rusting nails are used to make these fixings. Where heavy pots have to be carried on the staging, timber centre posts can be fitted.

The level of the shelf rail should be 1in. below that of the sill level, so that the decking is at this height. Paving slabs can be laid inside the greenhouse, leaving the earth at the sides free for planting.

Finally the finish, inside and out, is a matter of choice. Hardwoods and cedar will not rot, but a preservative or clear varnish will prevent discoloration from weather or atmosphere. The timber can be painted or finished with a polyurethane varnish. An attractive effect can be achieved by using a polyurethane wood-stain varnish.